CANADIAN LITERARY POWER

CANADIAN LITERARY POWER

by
Frank Davey

THE WRITER AS CRITIC SERIES: IV
General Editor, Smaro Kamboureli

© Copyright Frank Davey 1994

First Edition

All rights reserved. The use of any part of this publication reproduced, transmitted in any form or by any means, electronic, mechanical, recording or otherwise, or stored in a retrieval system, without the prior consent of the publisher is an infringement of the copyright law. In the case of photocopying or other reprographic copying of the material, a licence must be obtained from the Canadian Reprography Collective before proceeding.

Canadian Cataloguing in Publication Data

Davey, Frank, 1940-

  Canadian literary power
  (The Writer as critic series; 4)
  Includes bibliographical references and index.
  ISBN 0-920897-57-6

  1. Canadian literature (English)—20th century—History and criticism.* I. Title. II. Series.
PS8071.4.D38 1994   C810.9'0054   C94-910055-2
PR9189.6.D38 1994

CREDITS
Cover and interior design: Bob Young/BOOKENDS DESIGNWORKS
Editor for the Press: Smaro Kamboureli
Financial Assistance: NeWest Press gratefully acknowledges the financial assistance of The Canada Council; The Alberta Foundation for the Arts, a beneficiary of the Lottery Fund of the Government of Alberta; and The NeWest Institute for Western Canadian Studies.

Printed and bound in Canada by

NeWest Publishers Limited
#310, 10359-82 Avenue
Edmonton, Alberta
T6E 1Z9

Every effort has been made to obtain permission for quoted material. If there is an omission or error the author and publisher would be grateful to be so informed.

CONTENTS

Acknowledgements

Preface

1. The Power to Bend Spoons *1*

2. It's a Wonderful Life: Robert Lecker's Canadian Canon *45*

3. The Collapse of the Canadian Poetry Canon *79*

4. English-Canadian Literature Periodicals *103*

5. The Conflicting Signs of *As For Me and My House* *125*

6. Agony Envy: Atwood's "Notes Towards a Poem" *151*

7. Words and Stones in *How Hug a Stone* *167*

8. The Struggle for 'Phyllis Webb' *197*

9. Contesting 'Post(-)modernism' *245*

Bibliography *294*

Index *311*

ACKNOWLEDGEMENTS

Shorter versions of some of the chapters in this book have appeared in W.H. New, ed., *Inside the Poem* (Oxford, 1992), David Stouck, ed., *Sinclair Ross's As For Me and My House: Five Decades of Criticism* (U of Toronto P, 1991), and in the journals *Line*, *Open Letter*, and *Canadian Poetry*.

Preface

Many readers may find the emphases of this book on contemporary anglophone-Canadian literary power peculiar. It contains no chapters on commercially large publishers like McClelland and Stewart, Penguin Canada, Oxford University Press, or General Publishing, none on major public literary figures like Northrop Frye, Marshall McLuhan, Mordecai Richler, Michael Ondaatje, or Timothy Findley, and none on figures intermittently fashionable in Toronto book columns like Anna Porter, Douglas Gibson, Daniel Richler, or Barbara Gowdey. Instead there are chapters on academic periodicals, on a relatively obscure poem by Margaret Atwood, on academic quarrels over postmodernism and canonicity, and on the work of two west-coast lesbian writers, Phyllis Webb and Daphne Marlatt.

These emphases reflect both my sense of where to begin to distinguish 'literary' formations within those of the general culture in which literature participates, and my sense also of the small amount of effective 'power' that the more public literary figures actually exert outside of certain Toronto cultures. To a large extent, the prosperous, self-celebrating literary community of international prizes, Toronto media events, and photogenic faces that appears in journals like *Books in Canada* is a self-sustaining illusion, one that is increasingly disconnected from the disagreements Canadian writers have among each other, from the books that are chosen for academic reprint and study, and from the anthologies that are produced and reviewed in communities outside of downtown Toronto.

This book's emphases also reflect my own experiences of literary power in Canada from my work over the years as a poet, critic, cultural theorist, editor for two major literary presses, chair of a large urban university English department, member of numerous awards juries, and editor of a journal of criticism and theory. 'Power' is by and large a relative term. Materially, it exists only where one encounters it—when it enables or prevents. Psychologically, it exists only when one allows it to exist by allowing oneself to work within the terms that it proposes and by acknowledging the legitimacy of its constructs and evaluations. Of course material circumstances—the control of publishing resources, the glamour of media success, the promise of large royalties and of economic freedom—can often coerce or educe acknowledgement. But material circumstances in Canada over the past decades, including the strength of regional publishing, the independence of individual universities, the democratization of arts council grant procedures, have to a large extent limited such coercive power. In fact, I would argue that there is very little 'national' power left in Canadian literature, and that one symptom of this is the extent to which Toronto literary institutions, like the Harbourfront reading series, or Coach House Press in its recent publication of Marguerite Duras and Marco Denevi, or the media's excitement over Michael Ondaatje's Booker Prize, have increasingly turned to the international literary scene for values and recognition.

To those who would complain that there is too much of 'Frank Davey' in this book, I can only suggest that the inherent relativity of its subject—i.e. that power exists where one has experienced it—has led me repeatedly to places where I have already been. The fact that I encounter myself there, often as both participant and witness, and with at least peripheral stakes in the contests for power that I recount, has obliged me, I believe, to at least acknowledge my presence and interest. I am also present, of course, as author of this text—of a recounting that is also inevitably a construction. That in itself—the fact that I am able to assemble and publish this construction (albeit from a 'regional' press) is also an aspect of power. Other observers would simply have different viewpoints, and in these I might quite reasonably not appear.

Canadian Literary Power, and the power it may possess, is dedicated to the continuation of a national English-Canadian literary community. This is not a national community imagined in Toronto and constructed by authoritative national anthologists, or at another extreme a battlefield of mutually suspicious, self-aggrandizing cultural interests, but a polylogue of strong, locally produced institutions, discourses, and practices. Such a concept may be unwieldy, and vulnerable to competition from the hegemony-creating institutions and discourses of other, more glamourous cultures, but it is one which large numbers of Canadians, in the wake of the Meech Lake and Charlottetown Accord disagreements and the 1993 federal election, may well desire.

October 1993

The Power to Bend Spoons

"They think we have power—all we have is the power to bend spoons," bpNichol would often lament (in bitter reference to psychic Uri Geller's scandalous deceptions and to the social uselessness of the tasks Geller undertook with his alleged powers), when he encountered yet another comment about the 'influential' Coach House Press, the 'dangerous' *Tish* group, or was told by an unpublished writer that he should read his or her manuscript—'because you have power.' It was an ironic lament—bp was always aware that he had some Dickensian power to intervene 'for good' as a Coach House editor or Canada Council referee. But he was also aware of how complex literary 'power' is, of how closely tied it is to social and political power, and of the vast distance between the power to help one writer get a book published by a small literary press and the power many of us might imagine could alter the world 'for good.' It can be naive and self-limiting, even disempowering, to simplify or exaggerate concepts of power. One may lose a sense of what actual power is, of how it operates not merely to influence whether a particular manuscript is published but to shape which continents' peoples will thrive, how long we may live—as individuals or a species, how much education we may seek or have access to, how much choice we may have in work or personal relationships.

It is the discursive operation of power in culture, its constituting of itself and its working on and through us *in language*, that makes the issue of literary power so complex and elusive. Although some may have an illusion of possessing power individually, any of us can participate in power only socially, relationally, through language and its available codes and exchanges, and through the institutions, practices and conventions that have been constituted through and upon it. We exert power only through what others 'do' with the texts which we produce, and we can produce these texts only from pre-existing textuality. We bend the spoon, but the spoon must first have been there to be bent—and is anyone watching as we bend it, and after it is bent will anyone take it up, eat with it, or re-bend it to a new shape? The bending will remain a staged trick, its power confined to the theatre of its own happening, unless it becomes part of the network of signifying processes that, by means of an audience, can extend it from that theatre.

It is because of the social nature of discursive power that most literary struggles focus on dissemination, and on the institutions through which the dissemination of texts is accomplished—on control of publishing houses, access to magazines, anthologies, and classrooms, access to grants, availability and promptness of book reviews. A text that is read by only its writer has little power unless it contributes to that writer's production of texts that themselves reach other readers. The power of the latter will be in indeterminate proportion to the extent of their own dissemination, to the facility with which readers can find within them constructions of psychic use, and to the ability of those readers to effect changes in their lives and discourses. A text which reaches 5,000 readers who have low paying jobs, seldom vote, and are powerless themselves to write texts which can enter print circulation will have less power than a text which reaches 5,000 relatively affluent readers, who participate in political parties, and some of whom write book reviews and letters to editors, and a few of whom books and articles. In practice, however, such tidy contrasts are rare. Texts 'for' a group of readers such as the former, who as a class are more numerous, will tend to be produced and marketed in larger numbers, and to be read not only by that group but by others who seek power—like the producers of tabloid newspapers—by writing texts for it. The discourses of these texts will in addition be frequently reified in popular film and television. Texts 'by' and 'for' the latter group will have greater variety, more fissures and conflicts within and among them, fissures produced by the variety and interplay of professional, theological, regional, gender, economic, ethnic, and sexual-orientation interests made available by greater social participation. Moreover, our two hypothetical groups will not be discrete—individual subjects may not only move from one to another as their circumstances change, but will likely participate to a greater or lesser extent in both simultaneously; their discursive constructions themselves will often overlap—from the *Financial Times* for example to the *Edmonton Sun*—because subjects from the more powerful group will produce text for both publications.

There is an unfortunate tendency in our culture to construct power segmentally—as economic power, political power, literary power, etc—as if the structures of wealth production and distribution did not effect electoral processes, as if which governments we elect did not effect cultural institutions and funding and effect ultimately what gets published, by what publishers, in what regions, and with what amount of distributional force, as if the political issues that various interest groups construct in our culture as 'important' (and which often thereby, in effect, become important)—women's rights, environmental protection, aboriginal rights, northern development, economic nationalism, free trade—did not influence what literary texts get published, how they are received, and which first enter university course-lists and challenge for canonical recognition. Literary texts are inseparable from general textuality; they become 'literary' only by shifting convention. The designation points to no intrinsic quality but instead to a social process: a literary text is merely one that continues to reward re-reading—by individuals or by groups. Literariness is dependent on social factors—a text like Susanna Moodie's *Roughing It in the Bush* can acquire increased literary standing in a period of increased Canadian historical consciousness, or when the political aspirations of women construct a need for examples of textual construction by women, or when the expansion of the concept of 'Canadian Literature' into historically structured university curricula creates a need for period texts. The demise of Canada as an independent political unit would threaten the literariness of most of the various 'Can Lit' canons (just as the demise of the United States would threaten that of most of the American Literature canon). As individuals and as communities, we read and re-read a text because of the 'utility'—in the most general sense of the word—of its signs and constructions to satisfy our (socially-constructed) desires. That 'utility' varies according to a reader's relationship to circulating meaning systems—which is why a Canadian reader might in many situations find a text by Wiebe more 're-readable' than one by Steinbeck.

Sharing signs, semiotic systems, and discursive strategies with a myriad of competing varieties of textuality in our culture, literary texts become involved in the same competitions for power as characterize the culture at large. No more than an individual subject can get outside of textuality, literary texts cannot get outside of the politics of discourse. In periods of relative textual homogeneity, many texts may seem 'non-political' because, by adopting accepted discursive conventions, and by constructing images of harmony and plenitude and structures of resolution, they silently endorse an ostensibly non-controversial status quo. But in times as politically fractured as the last few decades in Canada, the politics of literature is foregrounded. Writers without visible political affiliations, who by the lack of such affiliations appear to endorse the status quo that controls most of the systems of text-dissemination, will seem disadvantaged, disempowered, as much of the readership for 'literary' texts becomes constructed on the sign systems and discursive strategies of communities held together by special interests and social desires. Writers whose texts participate in such sign systems will seem newly empowered, even though most will continue to have at best a marginal relationship to the state and commercial 'status quo' powers that dominate the funding of text production and distribution. This situation underlines the extent to which literary power is social and communal in the widest sense of those terms. An individual subject, no matter how 'talented,' is powerless to construct a reading community on his or her own, or to alter 'status quo' values—the texts of that subject must be published, distributed, and read—all this occuring within existing power relationships—and have their meanings newly produced by readers, who in turn must enter these into discursive circulation, reproduction and exchange. A flourishing 'ready-made' community, such as the emerging Canadian nationalist one which greeted Al Purdy and Dennis Lee in the 1960s and 70s, or the counter-culture with its discourse of mysticism, its bookstores, recording industry and alternative newspapers which greeted Leonard Cohen in the 1960s, or the feminist community with its newsletters, magazines and bookstores that was in place for Daphne Marlatt, Bronwen Wallace and Gail Scott in the 1980s, can on the other hand offer an ongoing process of discursive construction within which the writer can appropriate (*viz.* the 'bibliography' in Marlatt's *Ana Historic*), re-process, and contribute signs and structures.

This imbrication of literary 'power' within the texts of generalized social aspiration and conflict means that, while literary 'power' may seem limited and unspecifiable, it is also neither illusionary or trivial. While it may seem much less than adequate to accomplish changes which particular writers may imagine accomplishing within their culture—the power of Geller's momentary illusion, Yeats' poetry that 'makes nothing happen'—by being part of the general process through which experience is interpreted and given meaning through language, and through which individual subjects can be led to construct their own lives and the meanings of those lives, its power can be large. While it may seem that the dominant forms of power exercised by the state and by multinational capitalism, operating through their myriad and interlocking institutional array of rewards, punishments, and prizes, are monolithic and unchangeable, the very power trade-offs and appropriations that maintain these forms of power causes within them recurrent alteration. Some power does shift, reputations and incomes change, social configurations are reshaped or recast in standing, size, and complexity.

◆

> The 'little mags' [of the 1960s]...were an affront to the literary establishment. They did not, in fact, address themselves to the literary community, but to each other. Their young writers,

> editors, and publishers were intent upon developing not simply new writing but writing that would reflect a whole new vision of reality, cosmic in its reach, and profoundly challenging to existing values. [...] The writers who published in such magazines represented the first wave of Postmodernism; and their most influential poet-editors—Frank Davey, George Bowering, Victor Coleman, bill bissett, and bp Nichol—were to continue to be in the vanguard of that movement throughout the seventies.
>
> Wynne Francis (460)

How we map literary power is itself one of the discursive means by which power is constructed, disputed, contained, and allocated. For the first six decades of this century, literary power in Canada was usually mapped in terms of oversimplifying binary oppositions—the published and the unpublished, the establishment and the vanguard, the conservative and the radical (the Canadian Authors Association vs the McGill Group), the colonizing and the nationalist (*Preview* vs *First Statement*), the centre and the margin, mass-art and 'serious' art. In this map the 'published' was usually constituted as established, reasonable, adequately funded, reconciled with mass-taste, and located in central Canada, while the unpublished was constituted as idealistic, peripheral, limited in financial resources and eager to either become or join the establishment. (Within these construction one can detect elements of the discourse of avant-gardism, in which culture is a series of liberating armies which in turn become 'rear guards' or new despotisms.) Both the McGill Group poets and ex-Trotskyist Earle Birney sought publication by Macmillan, Louis Dudek and Raymond Souster by Ryerson Press, George Bowering by McClelland and Stewart. This dichotomy served both to glamorize dissent as high-minded, selfless and futile, and aggrandize the establishment as both the object of the dissent and the ultimate destination of most of the dissenters. Concealed within it were gender tensions (both the old fogies and young Turks were nearly always male), regional tensions (most publishing was done in Toronto), ethnic conflicts (Layton tellingly constructing his Jewishness as a force of liberation against an established culture that was monolithically moneyed, Christian, colonial and conservative), and class conflict (at some point Livesay, Finch, Ethel Wilson, Charles Israel, Wayman, Pratt, and MacEwen were all Macmillan authors).

Although youth versus age had been an occasional element in this dichotomy—young F.R. Scott, old "Carman, Lampman, Roberts, Campbell, Scott"; young Sutherland, old Smith—in the 1960s, as the large postwar 'baby-boom' generation reached the age of cultural activity, it became *the* major construction of literary power, as deployed by Wynne Francis above. As with the earlier dichotomies, this construction was a strategy of containment—specific agendas that might indeed have political effect could be grouped together first of all as "profoundly challenging to existing values" and second as the agendas of "young writers," who might in time become old writers, and themselves perhaps representative of "existing values." For the moment, however, they are pointedly excluded by Francis not only from the "literary establishment" and but also from "the literary community," which she curiously equates. This exclusion, however, their addressing themselves "to each other" rather than "to the literary community," would have unexpected consequences both for the dichotomy and for later constructions of Canadian literary power.

For their own strategic reasons, the "young" 1960s generation Francis examines also tended to accept her construction. One of these reasons was that the construction set the established literary community aside, bracketed its relevance, set it up in opposition without positing it either as a temptation or an active enemy. The construction, of course, was inconsistent with the facts. Seeking to maintain general prestige and power, the establishment of the 1960s and 70s courted the 'youth' generation, inviting many of its writers to read on the CBC, publish with Ryerson (Hood, Marlatt, Kearns, MacEwen), McClelland and Stewart (Bowering, Newlove, Wiebe, McFadden, Matt Cohen), and Macmillan (Kroetsch, MacEwen, Wayman), write for *Canadian Literature*, *Tamarack Review*, and *The Canadian Forum*. Another strategic reason the 'young' had for accepting a 'youth-age' dichotomy was that it implied among themselves a 'common front,' and papered over conflicts among them so that these would not divert attention from their overall challenge to Francis's "existing values." So the Marxist-Leninists who published *Alive* magazine welcomed contributions from literary nationalists; *The Georgia Straight*, with its main constituency of self-employed artists, activists for the legalization of marijuana and L.S.D., and advocates of communal lifestyles, published poems by home-owning university-employed writers like George Bowering and myself. bill bissett's untheoretically anarchist *Blew Ointment* published Margaret Atwood; Dave Godfrey, whose conservative nationalism invoked the Scottish crofters as a cultural model, published my technology-endorsing analysis of Canadian postmodernism *From There to Here*. Although most of the new writing and publishing was regionally based, discursive constructions like 'generation gap' and 'flower power,' with their implications that the 'young' shared common situations and ideals, led to cross-national publishing links and exchanges, particularly between Toronto and Vancouver.

> In those days [the 1960s], unless I am romanticizing it now, anyone who came into the room found community and common purpose even though we were very different from each other. Then, there were socialists, communists, conservatives and liberals, Jews, Christians and atheists, white and black and homosexual and heterosexual and even men and women in the same room. Because once you walked into the room, once you had answered the call to resist the war or fight discrimination, you were recognized as a brother or a sister. There were no questions asked and no voices raised against one another. We knew who the real enemy was in those days. And it was not us.
> Sharon Airhart (A16)

The failure of this youth-age construction, and with it the 'brother-sister' rhetorical strategies for containing difference, is one of the central features of power relations in the current period in Canadian culture and Canadian writing. The historical reasons for this failure are fairly clear. The 'youth' generation of the 60s and 70s was the first challenge to established Canadian culture to be too large to be assimilable. The tendency Wynne Francis detected within its writers not "to address themselves to the literary community but to each other" was a symptom of that fact. Without sufficient room for them within the existing institutions of Canadian publishing and literature, these writers would have to build their own institutions, their own "literary community." However, lacking the capital to create national institutions, and in many cases ideologically hostile to the kinds of institutional and financial accommodations that had helped establish earlier national ones (like Ryerson Press's connection with the Methodist Church, and Oxford's and Macmillan's sponsorship by offshore publishers), they would also tend to create institutions that were local to specific regions and constituencies, institutions which were asymmetric with earlier ones, which emphasized the disagreements among them, and which in both respects resisted dichotomous totalizations.

The sheer size of the 'youth' generation, which had made it impossible for it to be absorbed—one individual at a time—into existing institutional structures, and which pushed its writers to found their own magazines and presses long before Canada Council assistance was regularly available (the little magazines *Cataract, Moment, Tish, Mountain, Catapult* founded in 1961-62 alone), by the late 1960s moved the Canadian federal government to begin making funds available through a variety of programmes—Opportunities for Youth, The Company of Young Canadians, Local Initiatives—for youth assistance. In combination, however, with other concurrent factors—the miniaturizing of publication and communications technology, the globalization of mass-culture with its tendency to delegitimize national institutions, and the generation's own prior valorization of 'small' and 'local' because of the small and local nature of its material resources—this assistance resulted mostly in the generation's establishing of additional regional institutions—provincial arts councils, regional presses, 'parallel' galleries, regional literary magazines. Moreover, the relatively fewer national institutions that the generation founded or helped to found—institutions like the Association of Canadian Publishers (ACP), the Canadian Magazine Publishers Association (CMPA), the Writers Union of Canada, The Association of National Non-Profit Arts Centres (ANNPAC)—were mostly umbrella organizations designed to give national reach and lobbying power to its small or regional enterprises. The generation's new national public institutions served—like the new European Community promises to serve the interests of a more independent Scotland or Flanders—as a protective umbrella under which the much more specifically focused new local institutions could operate. (This is one of the reasons why in 1992 many regional Anglo-Canadian arts interests so strongly resisted Charlottetown Accord proposals to 'devolve' responsibility for arts funding from the federal government to the provinces.) As immigration to Canada in the 1980s shifted decisively from white to non-white countries, the umbrella organizations, particularly those like the ACP and CMPA, which offer distribution services to small book and magazine publishers, have enabled the establishment of increasingly specific kinds of publishing, like the African-Canadian publishing of Williams-Wallace and Sister Vision, or the culture-specific publishing of the *Toronto South Asian Review*.

The fissures and contradictions within this Canadian 'youth' generation relate directly both to the specificity of its own cultural activities and to contemporary contestations for power. To some extent this generation continued to accept the international discourse of avant-gardism, to view itself as the 'vanguard' of social changes that would end what Sharon Airhart remembers as "the war," liberate the oppressed from centralized controls, and 'expand' consciousness, at the same time as it viewed itself as the first wave of a new society of multiplicity and difference, a society whose very heterogeny contradicted the progressivist assumptions of 'vanguard' thought. Milton Acorn declared "I shout love." Marshall McLuhan announced "the global village." The generation foregrounded the 'youth' construction of itself in its acceptance of the international 'flower child' image, and slogans like 'don't trust anyone over thirty.' While among its writers there were regional conflicts and differences, and a few visible class and gender conflicts, these tended to be contained within this general paradigm of youth and age—a 'youth' which hoped, as in bissett, Godfrey, Persky, Atwood, Cohen, Symons, Gilbert, or MacEwen, to defeat instrumentalism and systematicity and expand diversity and eccentricity: to re-legitimize the marginalized (as in Marlatt's Japanese-Canadians or Acorn's factory workers), to assert the regional against central (as in Hodgins, Bowering and Nowlan), the national against the American (as in Lee, Atwood, and Acorn). As the coordinate syntax of Airhart's recollection suggests, few noticed or took seriously ideological differences among 'young' "socialists, communists, conservatives, and liberals,... white and black and homosexual and heterosexual." Few readers noticed the sharp ideological contrasts between MacEwen's belief in transcendence and Persky's in collective social action, or between these and Godfrey's village model of mutually helpful small entrepreneurs, or noticed the different gender emphases in Acorn's and Marlatt's constructions of the marginal. Members of visible minorities like Michael Ondaatje and Fred Wah, rather than foregrounding their racial difference, constructed themselves, and were constructed by readers, through the available discourses of youth, avant-gardism, and anti-instrumentalism. Gay writers like Symons, Persky, and Webb, were similarly constructed; Webb's *Naked Poems* was generally known to be about lesbian lovers but was read—by myself and others—as only formally audacious.

The most visible fissure in this generation of writers was class, repeatedly foregrounded in the 70s by Guelph's *Alive* magazine, by Jamie Reid's move from *Tish* to Marxist-Leninism, by the general contrast between those writers who went on to academic or other salaried positions and those who chose to subsist on grants, and by Milton Acorn's public refusals to adopt codes of dress and behaviour that would mark him as merely eccentric artist rather than as angry and poor. This fissure was particularly visible in the protests that greeted Bowering's winning of a 1969 Governor-General's Award for poetry over Acorn. Bowering received his award at Rideau Hall; Acorn received his 'people's medal' at Grossman's Tavern on Toronto's Spadina Avenue. The protests focused on the membership of Warren Tallman, an American academic who had taught Bowering, on the award's committee: Bowering was university-educated and 'Americanized,' Acorn was an ex-carpenter, who had learned poetry through toiling on authentically Canadian work sites. However, the fact that Acorn's ex-wife Gwendolyn MacEwen had also that year received a Governor-General's Award for poetry, an award that also could have been given to him, and that perhaps regional and gender issues had also influenced the committee, did not become part of the controversy.

◆

In Gail Scott's 1987 novel *Heroine*, set in late 1960s, the young woman protagonist, an anglophone and would-be writer who has joined a group of Québec marxist activists, experiences intense conflicts between utopian left-wing thought and the differences it attempts to suppress. Rhetorically addressing her lover and leader of 'F-group' and recalling the afternoon on which she was about to have an affair with N (in order to demonstrate her marxist contempt for bourgeois monogamy), she writes:

> You're sitting there with your hand on my knee. All titillated because tonight N and I...(though nobody's said a word). I notice it doesn't over-preoccupy you. You just keep writing your text defending F-group's decision to drop questions like feminism and anti-imperialism and intervene directly in the worker's movement. The anger buzzing in my mind gets stronger. Despite

the fatigue that's setting in. At 6 AM we were distributing pamphlets to hospital workers. Now I'm too tired to grasp the shaft of light which was the poem I was going to write. As an artist I need to be my own woman. Not handing out pamphlets, but writing. Writing.

I have to be careful about thoughts like that. The comrades are suspicious of any over-involvement in art. On that trip back from Vancouver, one of them said in a Regina living-room: 'You'll never be anything but a fellow traveller.'

'Why?' I asked in a small voice....

'Because you're an artist.' (97-98)

To some extent this passage is a miniature of the collapse of 1960s cultural idealism and its consequences. The general 1960s discourse of cultural homogeneity within generations (bissett's "LEGALIZE MARIJUANA NOW, let yr children out of jail") is here the F-group's credo of left-wing solidarity. The group's goal of helping workers ignores the latter's heterogeneity—that they are marked by different combinations of age, gender, colour, education, experience, etc.—just as it ignores the heterogeneity of its own members. Not all are male, and exclusively committed to marxist action; some may share the social goals of the group and also be women, and/or have ambitions as artists. F-group is in practice hostile to difference. Members who exhibit 'bourgeois' tendencies are shunned; women members who appear possessive of their male partners are to be re-educated; members who take time from group work for writing risk being dismissed as 'fellow travellers.'

Much as the protagonist of *Heroine* eventually deserts F-group to assist at a shelter for battered women, to work at her own writing, and to attempt to become her own "heroine," in the later 1970s numerous constituencies split from the eclectic, regional 'youth' culture to establish communities and publishing ventures of their 'own.' Feminists were the most visible in this regard, establishing magazines like *Room of One's Own*, *Canadian Women's Studies*, *Fireweed*, and *Tessera*, Women's Press, and taking over *CVII*, but other groups were nearly as active: the gay community in establish *Body Politic* and Pink Triangle Press, the First Nation community in establishing newspapers like *Ontario Indian* and *Windspeaker*, magazines like *Sweet Grass* and *Trickster*, and eventually presses like Theytus and Pemmican. In part this change was a product of the aging of the 'youth' generation, its learning the limitations of idealist ideologies and gathering a store of betrayals and disillusionments. But it was also configured, as in *Heroine*, as a response to a grand betrayal; in this narrative the 'youth' generation's discourses of freedom, peace, and brotherhood had been deployed to continue the privileges of white heterosexual men. While men led the political demonstrations and founded small magazines and presses, the women made coffee and typed the correspondence.[1] White writers celebrated First Nations culture in books that brought little to those nations while bringing royalties and acclaim to the white writer.[2] Heterosexual writers and editors welcomed their gay colleagues as long as the latter's sexuality was not constructed as the major element of their writing.[3]

◈

I first became aware of the shift from defining power as something differentially held by youth and age to defining it in terms of special constituencies in 1975, when I returned to teaching at York University after a year of sabbatical leave to find that the authority-questioning, 'relevance'-seeking students of 1973-74, who often 'opted out' of university to travel, and many of whom simply assumed that—whatever their education—they would eventually construct their own futures in concert with their peers, seemed to have been replaced overnight by obedient students anxious to qualify for employment by those older than themselves. The most noticeable sign of this change for me was the students' responses to Leonard Cohen's writing. The students of 1973 and earlier had demanded that Cohen be on the curriculum. They had identified with the self-transcending ideology of *Beautiful Losers*, aspired to the history-effacing world constructed in his lyrics, where "the mist" of human action "leaves no scar" of consequence, where differences between nations, ethnicities, religions, and races are erased by sacramental love and the mysteries of time. The students of 1975, however, regarded Cohen's writing as escapist and irrelevant to their career concerns. They had come to university to equip themselves to compete in a world which for them was not "the Magic Length of God" but a Darwinian realm of economic competition among individuals, corporations, ethnic communities, regions, and nations. At York's Calumet College, where my office was located, 1973's most influential male common-room student had been white, had lived in a commune, written poetry, helped manage the college's vegetarian cafe, had been bearded, pony-tailed, a dope-smoker, and had studied English and Film; within a very few years the new 'big man' at Calumet was part-Japanese, wore a Canadian militia uniform, a military haircut, talked about hating 'Commies,' helped organize beer-and-burger barbecues, and planned to study economics and law.

At York this sudden ideological shift among the students was being accompanied by less dramatic but equally significant change at the academic level: a "general arts" programme, established in the mid-1960s, in which all first-year students took an array of multidisciplinary humanities division courses, and in which disciplinary departments were prohibited from offering first-year courses (the humanities division motto was Terence's universalizing "nothing human is alien to me"), was being slowly but successfully challenged by those disciplines. Even more significant was a push to establish specific interdisciplinary studies programmes, each tied to communities with specific political interests (Caribbean Studies, East Asian Studies, Native Studies, Urban Studies, African Studies, Women's Studies), and the surging enrolment in professional faculties and programs such as law, business administration, film studies, and social work. While these two phenomena were often viewed as divergent, both were based on conflictual rather than utopian models of society. The future was to be not utopian but Bakhtinian. It would hold not social revolution, but endless political struggle in which both individuals and special 'interests'—women, blacks, gays, lesbians, Asians, small business people, doctors, truckers—would have to separately seek 'rights' that the general polity would be at best diffident about obtaining for them. A new discourse of 'rights' and 'equality' was rapidly being constructed by these groups, in which the 1960s understanding of equality as a kind of 'oneness' (Joe Rosenblatt's "Jesus Dwells in Every Tulip," bill bissett's "Prayrs for th One Habitation") was replaced by equality as a condition of being 'separate but equal.' Equals were no longer understood as coalescing into a whole but as receiving mathematically precise representation—'equal pay for work of equal value,' a share of jobs, grants, and subsidies proportional to representation in the population, 'fair' representation on arts juries and public commissions.

Closely related to these changes was the growing influence of figures of mistrust, cynicism, and disillusionment. The increasingly asserted doctrines of 'rights' and 'fairness,' whether deployed by individuals seeking the 'protection' of greater personal wealth, or by groups seeking strength through collectivity, were responses to an increasingly globalized culture, one in which the raw economic power wielded by government, business institutions, and wealthy individuals outweighed the power of most individual subjects even more decisively and 'undemocratically' than Thomas Jefferson had feared some two hundred years earlier when arguing for statutory limits on state power, individual wealth, and land ownership. The Watergate scandals, the Trudeau-government's invocation of the War Measures Act, the exposure of the CIA's 1950s experiments with LSD in Montreal, the Corvair scandal, the Karen Silkwood case, were appropriately perceived as symptoms of the relative powerlessness of individuals in a society in which enormous wealth and power were becoming more and more concentrated in fewer and fewer mutually interdependent institutions and individuals. Such perceptions have continued in Canada with the 'libel chill' engendered by the Reichmann brother's suit against *Saturday Night* and Heather Robertson, with the success of logging companies in obtaining licenses to cut trees in 'heritage' areas like the Temagami and the Queen Charlotte Islands, and with the success of U.S. businesses in obtaining 'dumping' rulings against Canadian industry. While mass art to a large extent responded to this climate of rising social suspicion by popularizing fantasies of successful underdog individualism—'Rocky,' 'Rambo,' 'Superman,' 'Spiderman,' 'Luke Skywalker'—and while numerous individuals responded by enrolling in the professional faculties of universities, other areas of society have responded by constructing more elaborate and powerful concepts of collective rights: the class action suit, environmental rights, women's rights, rights for the physically and mentally handicapped, non-smoker's rights, taxpayers' rights, the legal entrenchment of various anti-discrimination principles—all are readable as products of an enormous post-1970s fear of growing power disparity. In the Canada of 1994 the various and often conflicting signs of this construction are ubiquitous: the fresh concrete of sidewalk wheelchair ramps, 'affirmative' hiring programmes, seat-belt and bicycle helmet legislation, Toronto's Black Action Defence Committee, family law revisions, widening non-smoking regulations, 'father's rights' organizations, the 1992 and 1993 Ontario Human Rights Commission's rulings on gay 'spousal' benefits, Gwen Jacobs' campaign for 'equal' dress-codes for men and women, aboriginal groups' success in becoming constitutional negotiators.

◆

In the current decade in Canada literary power is fiercely contested, and in that very fierceness constructed as significant. The sites of conflict in recent years, however, have rarely involved institutions with large commercial scale—changes in government policy which might facilitate foreign takeovers of Canadian commercial publishers, or actual takeovers, have raised relatively little general concern. High-profile commercial publishers like Hurtig, Anansi, and Lester & Orpen Dennys have ceased independent operation with none of the furore that years before had greeted the demise of Ryerson Press. At dispute, instead, has been influence within the umbrella

organizations which the 1960s generation helped establish—
the Writers Union, the Canadian chapter of PEN, control of
institutions of dissemination like *CVII* and Women's Press,
and influence on the policies of government arts councils.
The contestants have for the most part been those new
constituencies of the 1970s—women's groups, First Nations
writers, visible minorities—which have been successful in
constructing literary discourse as a power instrument. The
grounds of their contestations have not been that their
writers are more 'talented,' deserve more money, or more
publication; rather they have been that only increased
writing and publication of their authors can put into social
circulation the discursive constructions necessary to the
'equitable' treatment of their group. Literary policy, cultural
policy, and social policy are closely linked in their arguments
as interrelated aspects of the linguistic mediation of culture.

One major example of this discursive linking of
literature, culture and social policy has been the general
deployment in Canada by regions, visible minorities,
feminists, gays, lesbians, and First Nations of the discourse
of equality, to displace older bilingual, bicultural and
binational conceptions of the Canadian nation. One of the
primary sites of this discourse has been multiculturalism,
with its argument of the equality of Canadian cultural
groups, and its opposition to special standing for
francophone culture. Another has been quarrels over the
1982 Charter of Rights, particularly attempts to construe its
anti-discrimination provisions as guaranteeing the same
kinds of 'equality' by gender, colour, ethnicity, and sexual
orientation as other sections explicitly guarantee to
individuals. A third has been the constitutional debates over
the Canadian Senate, in which supporters of a 'triple-E'
senate—"elected, equal, and effective"—have opposed the

concept of Canada as a binational joining of francophone and anglophone peoples, and favoured a construction of Canada of which Québec would be one of ten 'equal' parts, not the smaller of two halves, and would have Senate representation 'equal' to that of each of the other provinces.[4] At the Canada Council, the discourse of equality led by the late 1970s to a policy under which each region of the country was unofficially entitled to a portion of arts funding and to representation on juries, regardless of the nature or amount of artistic activity in those regions; this policy has often been carefully coded by Council chairs: "we must continue to talk the language of excellence and quality, but always within the context of where the artist lives," Joyce Zemans, chair in the early 1990s, explained (quoted in Drainie,C3). With the growing strength of ethnic communities in the 1980s, the discourse of equality and equity became an implicit argument that each ethnic, racial, gender or sexual-orientation community within Canada was entitled to share of arts funding at least equal to and perhaps larger than its per capita representation in the population. Sheilagh Day of the National Action Committee on the Status of Women expressed this understanding even more strongly: "equality is not a question of same treatment, or different treatment, but a question of whatever treatment is necessary to put a group which has historically been disadvantaged on an equivalent footing with the dominant group in society" (quoted in Simpson A16). In the fractious debates involving June Callwood and the claims of 'writers of colour,' led by spokesperson Marlene Nourbese Philip and the 'Vision 21' group, for larger representation in the 1989 PEN 54th International Congress panels than they had been given, both PEN and its defender Margaret Atwood offered arguments that percentage representation similar to representation in the Canadian population at large (6%) should satisfy Philip's constituency, arguments which Philip refused on the grounds that any percentage should represent a redressing of old injustices rather than a precise representation of current demographics.[5] By the spring of 1992, a Canada Council advisory committee was recommending that various ethnic and cultural groups have "equitable access to the council's programs," and chair Joyce Zemans was announcing "expanded juries to achieve a better regional and cultural balance, and reviewed programs to ensure that they are accessible to professional artists from all cultural and racial backgrounds" (Letter by Zemans to the *Globe and Mail*, June 29, 1992: A14). Literary power here clearly involved money, access to textual circulation, and increased opportunity for influential discursive construction and cultural legitimation. The involvement of well-funded wide-circulation publications like the *Globe and Mail* and *Books in Canada* in the debate suggested that the stakes were substantial, that the power and money to be gained by the new writers were likely to be lost by writers and institutions well-known to those media.

The concepts of 'equity' and 'equality' deployed in these debates imply conflict between rival constituencies and between individuals and constituencies; they argue the incomparability of the artistic productions of these constituencies, and move the perceived grounds of the rivalry away from aesthetics (and its masking of power-relations) and toward power itself. Aesthetic judgments are perceived as relative to regional and cultural representation on the juries that make these judgments. 'Access' becomes a code-word for the construction of aesthetic values as socially produced by communities that may or may not have knowledge of the values of other communities.[6] The concepts also illuminate the extent to which individuals are not 'equal' even in a nominally 'equitable' society: institutions, whether multinational corporations or relatively small associations and editorial boards, not only have more power than individuals, but individuals who are affiliated with such institutions can often have more power than those who do not. The struggle for power in a culture is often not a struggle for individual legitimation but for institutional affiliation—to be hired by a corporation, to be named to an editorial board, or to be perceived as a 'Chinese-Canadian,' 'Japanese-Canadian,' 'African-Canadian' or 'lesbian'; or it is a struggle to found and legitimate new institutions, groups, or identities, or to disaffiliate oneself from institutions or groups whose legitimacy and power are waning.

The discourse of equality, with its major term culturally enshrined in such concepts as 'equality before the law,' 'equality of opportunity,' and its tendency to mask conflicts between competing grounds for equality, has been a difficult one to oppose. Opposition has frequently disguised itself as a defence of equality,[7] as conflicting constituencies attempt to affiliate their interests with 'equality' and disaffiliate the interests of their rivals. The 'equal' rights of individual artists, regardless of where they live in Canada, or what ethnicity they claim, to receive Canada Council grants or serve on juries, has in recent years been constructed as a lesser equality than the right of regions, the genders, and visible minorities to 'equal' access and representation. The 'equalities' of the latter can themselves come into conflict, as Gillian Steward has noted in a related context:

> under the Canadian Charter of Rights and Freedoms, women and men have the same rights before the law. But in many Asian, African, eastern European and South American cultures, women traditionally have few rights. The man is master, and, if he so chooses, can beat his wife and children, without interference from authorities.

Steward goes on to cite a criminal case in which cultural tradition was introduced as a defence against murder, and to quote feminist law professor Kathleen Mahoney, "Do we have fundamental law in Canada that applies to everyone or not? If cultural relativism is to be used as a defence it means we are willing to ignore the provisions for gender equality and individual rights in the charter" (B9). Here the claim for equality of cultures is rhetorically delegitimated by Mahoney's translation of it into "cultural relativism," while the claim of women for equal rights is legitimated by being termed "fundamental law." Similar conflicts between collective 'equalities' claimed by ethnic, racial or language groups and group rights claimed by women have arisen in connection with Québec's claims to a special relationship to the Charter, and with the claims of many aboriginal leaders that the Charter's provisions regarding women offend tribal custom and should not apply to aboriginal communities.

In these conflicts a specific Québec anglophone community has rarely been able to construct itself as a force within the national community. Québec anglophone writers—fractured themselves by ethnic origin, age, gender, sexual orientation, and by differing relationships to francophone culture, and unified mainly by binary conflict with francophone culture, a conflict that the rest of anglophone Canada associates with a discredited bicultural ideology—now tend to enter anglophone-Canadian conflict, if at all, under other signs, such as ethnicity, feminism, or genre. Many appear to unconsciously distance themselves from anglophones outside Québec when they define themselves in terms of a Québec politics—in terms of a struggle for visibility and institutional support within Québec—that is not perceived outside of Québec as an anglophone-Canadian issue. It can be argued that the 1971

White Paper of Multiculturalism and the ensuing Multiculturalism Act of 1988 represented a crucial turn in anglophone-Canadian culture, a turn in which western Canada successfully challenged bilingual and bicultural constructions of the country, substituting a multiply-centred model in which binary conflict, such as that between anglophones and francophones in contemporary Québec, can not easily find a place.[8] This model has, in a sense, by excluding bicultural constructions from much of English-Canadian consciousness, also excluded Québec from that consciousness. "English-Canada," in the usage of both Québec francophones and non-Québec anglophones, most often does not include Québec.

In a 1990 article on the marginality of Québec fiction in English within anglophone-Canadian literature, Linda Leith noted how few representations of Québec occur within anglophone fiction written outside the province. She might have noted also how rarely Québec has appeared within recent anglophone-Canadian literary controversy. The only recent one in which it has even indirectly figured has been that concerning the Charlottetown Accord proposal to 'devolve' arts funding from federal to provincial jurisdictions. The arguments over this issue also focused on possession of the discourse of equality.

> Show me a politician enthusiastic about devolution and I will show you a parochial backbencher, one whose idea of Canadian culture is a one-night stand at *Les Miz* or *Phantom* (on comps), or the anguished choice between *Jake and the Fatman* and a hockey game.
>
> Marian Botsford Fraser (C1)

The case for devolution rested, with some irony, on both the Québec claim for equality as a nation and on the insistence of many other Canadian provinces on 'equal' constitutional treatment of provinces. The case made by arts groups against it rested similarly on 'equality,' as they argued that only federal cultural programmes could guarantee Canadian artists equal funding opportunities regardless of province of residence, and avoid a "patch-work" of programmes. The opponents were principally national umbrella organizations like the Writers Union, The Association of Canadian Publishers, and The Ontario Association of Art Galleries, which joined together in the Common Agenda Alliance for the Arts, and federally-funded regional institutions skeptical of provincial governments commitments to the arts. 'Equality' for these groups was very close to 'unity.' Although the Common Agenda Alliance for the Arts occasionally employed the politically expedient code words of "accessible" and "diversity," its language in endorsing national institutions emphasized monological constructions of Canadian diversity—"our shared experience of being Canadian," "cross-country consistency"—and hierarchical notions of aesthetic quality—"national standards of excellence." Its characterizations of a culturally 'devolved' Canada were openly pejorative: "chaos...country wide," "a patchwork of regulations and policies," "watertight compartments of jurisdiction" (untitled pamphlet, January 1992). At visible conflict with 'devolution' here were not only the 'rights' of humanists who, since the founding of the Canada Council in 1955 have had privileged access to grants awarded on 'standards of excellence,' but also relatively new, non-regional and equality-claiming special interest groups—feminists, gays, lesbians, and numerous geographically dispersed ethnicities.

The Common Agenda Alliance position was not only anti-Québec position, in the sense that it effectively opposed nationalist desires in that province for more control over cultural policy in that province, but also an anti-multiculturalism position. Paradoxically, however, many multicultural groups, often constituent parts of the national institutions that had formed the Alliance, also opposed devolution because of fear that provinces would be less supportive of multicultural difference than would be the "national standards" of a federal state.

❧

> Keeshig-Tobias said one starting point was the definition of appropriation itself as 'taking something without permission and using it for profit.'
> Stephen Godfrey (May 23, 1992, C9)

A major site of contestation for contemporary Canadian literary power has been the issue of appropriation of voice. The quotation above is taken from a *Globe and Mail* story about a "planning session" organized by the Racial Minority Writers' Committee of the Writers Union of Canada "to allow racial minority writers to discuss issues such as racism in publishing, appropriation of voice, review standards and language recognition." The sly pun on 'raise' in the headline signalled the newspaper's skepticism about the event, associating it with discourses of evangelism and self-interest; it signalled also the paper's political distance from it, and resistance to whatever power the event was claiming.

Appropriation of voice has been closely linked in recent debate with the notion of cultural appropriation, and with the idea that it may be immoral for a writer from a financially prosperous and politically comfortable ethnicity or racial group within Canada to profit by writing and selling to publishers literary representations of a less prosperous, and presumably less literate, ethnicity or racial group. The notion emerged in the late 1980s with growing resentment among First Nations writers at white lesbian author Anne Cameron's various children's books *Daughters of Copper Woman, Raven Returns from the Water, Orca's Song, Dzelarhons: Myths of the Northwest Coast*, and *Dreamspeaker* in which she appeared to package and re-tell native stories so that—in one commentator's words—Cameron's "radical lesbian feminist" ideologies were promoted and the stories themselves were "turned white" (Halpin 315, 316).[9] The second major 'voice-appropriation' controversy erupted in 1990 from Rudy Wiebe's objections to W.P. Kinsella's representations of First Nations life on the Ermineskin reservation near Hobbema, Alberta, to how Kinsella, "with a wilful ignorance," made up stories that "defaced," "exploited," and stereotyped "a distinct racial minority" in order to achieve commercial success (C3). The concept of cultural appropriation has strong political appeal, being founded on analogies of theft and invoking the exploitation of the weak by the strong. At least as it has been argued to date, however, it has weak epistemological grounds. Cultures are not essences to be stolen, but complexes of activity continually constructed in language and action. All that writers external to a community can assemble are simulacra of that culture, their own constructions of it, which point not to that culture but to the writer him or herself, with her or his own culture, politics, and needs. The 'crime' committed is one of fraud rather than theft; a white construction of native culture is passed off as if it were a native construction. The fraudulent object brings profit to the counterfeiter, and obstructs the circulation of native-authored constructions. This obstruction in turn causes the counterfeiter's political and cultural constructions to enjoy social force and credibility, and subverts the force and credibility of the natives' own self-presentations.

Keeshig-Tobias's terse definition makes a similar metaphysical error—"takes something"—but then quickly reveals the substance of what is at issue: "profit." It is not that voices are being appropriated, it is that racial minority constructions of their own cultures lack the power to compete in cultural marketplaces with majority constructions of those cultures. Kinsella's Indians sell better, both commercially and ideologically, than do Jeannette Armstrong's Indians or perhaps even Wiebe's Indians. Keeshig-Tobias is back with Barrie Nichol's accusatory interlocutor. "You have power." It is a substantial power, which can eventually determine how much money goes into the pocket of the interlocutor and, in Keeshig-Tobias's case, perhaps, into the economy of the First Nations community. The difficulties around this power extend far from the simple notion of 'cultural appropriation' to the literal production and sale of signs as commodities within a capitalist economy—Keeshig-Tobias's cry against "profit." They involve also a sharp contrast in concepts of cultural production, based on individual 'talent,' 'rights' and profit in white culture, and on collective creativity and benefit in the native culture. How can a First Nations community sell its own signs 'profitably' within capitalism, when nearly all the available means of production and dissemination are controlled by white culture? Are these signs commodifiable? How can this community assert its collective ownership of these signs and claim the discursive and ideological power available to those who use them, when, in the majority culture, such signs are configured as 'individual' property? Are we perhaps witnessing here in such speakers as Keeshig-Tobias not only the First Nations rise to awareness and articulation of its own abjection, but also its first fumbling moves to be a full participant in the commodity-exchanges of mass-market verbal constructions?

◆◇

> Women writers have been ostracized for not toeing the party line at feminist-theory-based workshops operating more like Maoist re-education camps than inspiring environments for writing. Some women writers have agreed to stop writing as a gesture of good faith toward issues of "appropriation." Uncomfortable silences and an almost palpable anxiety befall social gatherings lest someone utter a forbidden word or idea.
> Sharon Thesen (1991, 16)

In any power struggle there are winners and losers, those who manage to bend the spoon and those whose spoons get bent. Sharon Thesen's angry attack on "feminism," workshops for "unlearning racism," and theories of appropriation is a sign both of the power being gained by those she attacks and of Thesen's own discomfort at seeing the humanist assumptions with which she identifies— "common sense," "objective truth," "good writing" (1991, 16)—disbelieved and threatened. Thesen's strategy in this essay is to return to the binary forms of analysis which have traditionally supported the universalist, individualist values of humanism. Grounding her essay in the cultural analyses of George Orwell in *1984* and "Inside the Whale," she posits a world of truth vs. untruth, common sense vs. theory, freedom vs. totalitarianism. Those who challenge the power distributions of social practice, by constructing some of these practices as racist, sexist, homophobic or classist, Thesen joins together and condemns as 'theory'; the efforts of such theorists to change social practice she names as "totalitarian." Ignoring the often conflicting goals of feminist, First Nations, black, and gay cultural theory, Thesen not only conflates these with each other, but also—in a receding series of equations—with deconstructionist theory, then with a specific deconstructionist, Paul de Man, and then with the pro-Nazi writing of de Man during his youth in occupied Belgium. The logic of this series is that de Man's pro-Nazi texts are to reveal the "totalitarian outlook" of "theory" in general—i.e. of those who threaten Thesen's transcendent humanism by arguing on behalf of women, native peoples, blacks, the poor, the marginalized for more social power. At some points in her essay, Thesen is amazingly open about her opposition to such empowerment and, by implication, of her own power agenda:

> The name of this game is, as usual, power. And as long as one ideological position has the institutional power or assigns itself the moral authority to imprison others in "little cages of lies" or to require "self-consciousness in the production of meaning" (i.e. voluntary self-censorship), a totalitarian outlook is with us, no matter how desirable the envisioned outcome. (16)

Few of those threatened by the growing power of special constituencies in Canadian literature have been as frank as Thesen in their dismay at that growth, although many have adopted similar rhetorical strategies and, as in her reference to *1984*, attempted to demonize social activism by associating it with dystopian, fascist and totalitarian ideology. The individualism-supporting vocabulary of *1984*—*newspeak, thoughtcrime, thoughtpolice*, also deployed by Thesen—has become a familiar element of rear guard discourse. In the recent anthology of essays on "the relationship of feminism to writing," *Language in Her Eye*, that vocabulary is adopted numerous times, and often by high-profile writers who enjoy relatively open access to the publishing institutions of established cultural power.

> I view with some alarm the attempts being made to dictate to women writers, on ideological grounds, various 'acceptable' modes of approach, style, form, language, subject, or voice.

....

> An accusation of Thoughtcrime...can have damaging practical consequences.
> (Margaret Atwood 22-24)

> When we say the artist (writer, musician, painter and so on) has to be *free*, we do not necessarily mean free of family or free of other work and all those boring lifeless suggestions about retreating from the world in order to write. We mean she or he has to be *free of dogma*. It is most difficult to write under an umbrella of some kind of doxology.... The writer need not worry about what she or he *should* say....
> (Kristjana Gunnars 129)

> I will write in any voice that occurs to me. Girls, use any language you want. Don't go around saying 'girl' to each other in private and 'woman' in front of politically correct Feminists. Trust yourself. It's possible that all sorts of voices may pass through you, and be spoken, full of electricity! I now declare all women free of Thought Police....
> (Paulette Jiles 161)

> ...while I value the tremendous energy and extraordinary vision that emerge from radical feminist engagements with language, I recoil from any attempt to assert the primacy of one ideology over another.... At the risk of reducing and slurring the issues, I could call it Fem-speak vs. male-speak, and say 'a plague on both your houses.'
> (Janice Kulyk Keefer 167)

Ironically, Keefer is herself asserting the primacy of one ideology over another, the ideology—both romantic and Thatcherite—of 'freedom' and the 'free individual' over ideologies of social obligations and group 'equalities.'[10] Similarly, Gunnars and Jiles are not "free of dogma," particularly at the moment that the former asserts this favoured doctrine of market economists and government deregulators.

Another face of this power struggle has been evident in

protests that followed Joyce Zemans' March 1992 announcement, reported in the *Globe and Mail*, that Canada Council's juries were likely to be "sensitive" to issues of cultural appropriation and to look for "collaboration with minority groups" should the groups' cultures be a focus of the proposed artwork (Godfrey, March 21, 1992: C1). The *Globe* received so many letters in protest that it published them as a featured block the following weekend. Again some of the protestors were writers who have had long and fruitful relationships with powerful publishing institutions; again several attempted to demonize the cultural appropriation issue by affiliating it with fascism. Timothy Findley violently misrepresented the Canada Council's declared desire to help create a wider range of art as being a crude wish to destroy books and homogenize culture—and in the process managed to bizarrely portray the hopes of relatively powerless, oppressed Canadian minorities to be free to circulate their own representations of their cultures as being similar to the zeal of an all-powerful, murderous Nazi majority to preserve the 'purity' and dominance of its constructions: "In 1933 they burned 10,000 books at the gates of a German university because those books were written in unacceptable voices. German Jews, among others, had dared to speak for Germany in other than Aryan voices." This equation of weak minorities with a brutal state apparatus was so emphatically illogical as to be itself an act of social brutality. Joy Anne Jacoby was similarly obliged to reverse the relationship between minority and majority cultures in her attempt to associate Zemans' announcement both with fascism ("In Germany during the 1930s there was much discussion about forbidding German Jews to write about life in Germany") and Stalinism ("[A]nti-semitic critics [in Russia] are denouncing Russian writers of Jewish descent for daring to write about Russia"). Other protestors raised the related concept of censorship, Richard Outram proclaiming that "[n]o spurious concepts of 'intellectual property' or 'intellectual copyright' can be allowed to constrain the human imagination," Alberto Manguel arguing that "discussions on 'cultural appropriation' are incipient censorship," and Robert Cishecki accusing the Council of wishing "to sanitize artistic output...to a censored, politically correct form of expression" ("Letters to the Editor," March 28, 1992: D7). Hidden behind all of the protests was a general ideological construction of creativity as individual rather than social, and of art distribution as a form of free enterprise.

Lost in the rhetoric of 'freedom' were both Zemans' observation that the Council was "merely reflecting a significant change in society at large," and the central issue for First Nations protestors of 'voice appropriation,' that the individual appropriators were more likely to profit, materially and culturally, from their use of native culture than were native artists or communities. A jury system such as that of the Council always reflects the values of the artistic community from which it is drawn. The humanist beliefs of the protestors—that the artist is free, idiosyncratic, possessed of an unconstrained imagination—have been powerful ones in recent years not because they are 'true' but because they have had wide political support in the Canadian arts community. Such beliefs are blind to the fact that 'constraints' are constructed by all societies in attempts to negotiate among competing 'rights' and claims to 'equality.' The structure of these constraints is a political structure, a product of lobbying, financial power, electoral politics, and various other contestations among interested parties. These constraints can be legal (and there are a myriad of these, from laws concerning libel, slander, obscenity, and child labor to ones concerning conflict of interest, the formation of cartels, and the hiring of strikebreakers) or they can concern custom or fashion, as whether a visual arts jury prefers abstract expressionism, hard edge, or super-realism, painted canvas or room-size installation. The preference of publishers for a plotted, realistic fiction may be experienced as a kind of 'censorship' by those who would write fiction that illuminates the impossibility of representation, but indeed this preference has often reflected the preferences of Zemans' "society at large." The conception that the artist has untrammelled freedom is itself a constraint on those who perceive the artist as discursively produced by society, and contained by its general prejudices and desires.

The desire by minority cultures to have the opportunity to be participants and creators in their own culture, and to have their self-constructions circulate in Canadian culture as easily as do the constructions mainstream white writers devise about them, was mentioned by none of the protestors. Keeshig-Tobias's contribution to *Language in Her Eye* is tellingly apt:

> But who determines whether a story will sell, if there is a market for it, whether it is 'Indian,' 'too Indian,' or 'not Indian enough' (comments Native writers have received on our writing at different times from various publishers)? Who determines how best to tell the Native story, present the Native perspective?
> ....
>
> The loss of Native sensibility in a story is of little concern to these liberal elitists, who stand firm on ideas of 'universality' and 'global society'definitions, no doubt, reflecting their own small worlds and a certain degree of self-hate. They'd rather masquerade as Native than understand Native. They'd rather not confront and deal with issues of appropriation, rather not recognize the fact that we can tell our own stories and that there

is protocol for the acquisition of stories, and rather not accept responsibility to and for the stories they tell. Instead, white Canadians cry censorship and decry self-censorship. (174)

◆◇

Literary power struggles tend to break out mostly in institutional space, particularly in that of public institutions like arts councils or publicly subsidized institutions which have become directly or implicitly associated with doctrines of 'fairness' or 'equality.' Publicly subsidized associations, presses or magazines can somewhat insulate themselves from power challenges by narrowly defining their mandates: a press can define itself as operating for constituencies like women writers, First Nations writers, gay writers, or 'women of colour'—although, as in the 1988 Women's Press case,[11] they can still be vulnerable to internal power conflict. Because of the present Canadian arts council policies and their jury systems, it is very difficult for less well-defined institutions to receive subsidy and resist political pressure. While a magazine or press that sets out to represent a group of writers united by their sharing a disadvantaged ethnicity, gender, region, or sexual-orientation can usually receive subsidy and retain this specificity (and in many cases receive subsidy *because of* this specificity), one that sets out to represent what it conceives as an 'aesthetic' or as an aesthetic ideology, without openly identifying the politics of this position, will be vulnerable to power challenges. Contemporary juries will be likely to characterize the group as 'a clique' interested only in the career aggrandizement of its individual members, and to suggest that it represent other constituencies on its editorial board, and become more eclectic in its publishing. One of the effects of the development of this kind of power in Canada during the

1980s has been the gradual political fading of once sharply-defined publishers like Coach House, Talonbooks, Press Porcepic, House of Anansi, and their transformation into almost indistinguishable general literary publishers, together with the simultaneously increasing strength of newer sharply-defined presses under the banner of political constituencies—Theytus, Women's Press, NeWest, Turnstone, Press Gang, Ragweed, Sister Vision. Publishers like *The Vancouver Review*, *Ruebsaat's Magazine*, and *The Idler*, that would avoid the generalizing effects of this power, have often had to forego or jeopardize public funding.

Publishing institutions that had tended to construct themselves as general and open—newspapers, general-circulation magazines like *Maclean's* or *Books in Canada*—have paradoxically had the most success in fending off power challenges. In part this is because a policy of generalism or eclecticism tends to enforce the status quo, and to enable a publisher to frame or restrict the effect of whatever dissident texts it publishes by accompanying them with conservative ones, as well as to employ the discourses of equality and freedom to disqualify dissent as unfair special-pleading.[12] Behind many such publishers is the power of commercial business, with its ability to avoid the political pressures of public subsidy, and to finance and focus its activities through the interests of its advertisers. Nevertheless, even if framed and restricted, because of these publishers' policy of *appearing* equitable and inclusive, and the apparent profitability of that policy in terms of circulation and advertising revenue, dissenting interests do often manage to get their texts to circulate in these media.

Nowhere is the socially contingent nature of literary power and value more visible than in such publications, nor the fact that any set of literary values can be displaced by another set should the latter prove more socially and economically useful. The struggle for literary power in Canada has always been a struggle for social and political power, but in many periods disguised as 'aesthetic' or 'moral,' as Keefer, Thesen and Findley attempt above. This disguise has often featured appeals to allegedly 'transcendent' or 'fundamental' norms—'beauty,' 'humanity,' 'freedom,' 'creativity.' Such appeals are political strategies; the terms of the appeals are themselves socially contingent: what is 'beautiful' to middle-income, lesbian Nisei need not be what is beautiful to a male, white welfare-recipient or to the publisher of *Saturday Night*.

What is perhaps most important here is that this process of struggle be recognized, that groups and individuals with stakes in the outcome enter into it. For many this will mean defining, or re-defining, both their values and their interests. A small publishing house, for example, that flourished twenty years ago under the ideologies of youthfulness, rebellion, and creative freedom, will have to self-consciously struggle either to re-establish those values in the 1990s as competitive with the current values of rights and equality, or to define a new and narrow set of values based on the interests of its current owners, editors, and authors. Only very large, commercial, general market publishers can succeed today merely by attempting to 'open up' their activities to new 'equality' claimants. Smaller publishers that attempt this will risk rendering themselves valueless and powerless by contrast to those newer publishers that narrowly self-define themselves as representing vigorously 'special' constituencies. For these newer publishers themselves, the primary requisite for participation in these power struggles will be not self-definition but money. For them it will be crucial that federal financing for the arts and multiculturalism continue. For wealthier constituencies, and for those like Thesen, Findley, Manguel, Jiles, Gunnars, and Keefer ideologically closer to the wealthy supporters of the status quo, it may be even in their direct interest that such funding diminish.

General discursive power in Canada, as elsewhere in North America and Europe, is largely held by the wealthy—by the mass media, multinational advertising, and by the big businesses that in many countries can circumvent election financing laws to purchase the election of business-friendly candidates—and by those who write texts that circulate easily within this general discourse. Through public subsidy of the arts, however, and the jury systems and principles of 'equity' that govern such subsidy, much of the power of literary discourse has in recent years been seized by other interests. This seizure would not have been possible without the public funding of the arts which followed the 1951 Massey Commission Report, nor without the continuing scramble for regional and national political power alliances within English-Canada that has been a consequence since the 1960s of the threat of Québec separation.[13] Ironically, the seizure of discursive power by regional and minority interests has diminished the power of both the national mass media and the traditional literary community that since the early nineteenth century had defined itself in opposition to mass values. Power is, after all, measurable in its effects, and this seizure has had effect. While the world-wide consequences of this seizure may seem small—famine, disease, economic oppression, and desperation continue in most of the non-industrialized world, the global environment continues to deteriorate—a lot of local and individual Canadian spoons have been severely twisted. As I will argue in many of the chapters that follow, these effects include not only the re-shaping of Canadian literary publishers and their mandates, as above, but also the fragmentation of literary audiences, the destruction of a national Canadian literary canon, the demolishing of any progressive concept of 'avant garde,' the ending of Romantic notions of resistance on which so much male-authored literature has been written, and the construction of regional and other 'special' literatures. The small power many male poets could access 20 years ago by attaching themselves to oppositional positions—like Layton's against Puritanism, Lee's against Americanizing technologies, or Cohen's against cultural pragmatism—has been rendered irrelevant by the more specific and socially contextualized protests of the newly constituted constituencies. Audiences have been split and re-split by region, gender, colour, and class. The literary anthologies of the 1980s suggest an imminent fragmentation of English-Canadian literature itself on a similar pattern. No wonder writers like Sharon Thesen and Alberto Manguel, hopeful of national audience, cry "totalitarianism" and "censorship," while even one as 'safely' established as Margaret Atwood "view[s] with alarm." However, the current situation will itself evolve: exactly how will depend to a large part on the determination and rhetorical skill of those crying 'freedom,' 'equality,' 'misogyny,' 'totalitarianism,' 'systemic discrimination,' 'censorship,' and 'racism' in service of their various conflicting causes, and on their strategic skill in responding to and influencing institutional change.

NOTES

[1] Pauline Butling, in "'Hall of Fame Blocks Women': Re/Righting Literary History," argues that women's contributions to Canadian little magazines of the 1960s and 1970s were generally erased, both by the "informal" and "peripheral" nature of the work they were permitted to do on magazines generally "edited and produced by men" and by subsequent historiography. She points in particular to poet Sharon Thesen's role in doing "nearly all the work of putting out" *Iron* magazine, edited by her husband Brian Fawcett, and contributing "informally to editorial discussions," and to Fawcett's subsequent failure to mention her in a discussion of the magazine's history (63). Thesen herself, in an interview by Constance Rooke, says that her marriage to Fawcett "was the end of my poetry writing and the beginning of my typing his poems." "I never wrote another thing until four years after we had split up. So for close to ten years I didn't write" (36). Butling concludes that the issue is not so much "who did the typing as who occupied the centre. Not until the seventies...do women begin to move into the traditionally male-dominated position of editors."

[2] See Lenore Keeshig-Tobias, "The Magic of Others."

[3] See Pauline Butling's preface to the Webb issue of *West Coast Line* in which she argues that Webb criticism before 1990, written mainly by male critics, "has not noted" the "lesbian context" of *Naked Poems* (15).

[4] The use of the discourse of equality in attempts to redesign the Canadian Senate shows how the discourse can be used to deny or conceal inequality, as in journalist John Defoe's phrase "a fair and equal Canada—in which the smallest and poorest partner would be equal to the biggest and richest." The provinces here are to be given 'equal' representation not because they are equal but because they are unequal in size and economic power. Conflicting possible claims to 'equality' by region, founding people, or gender are denied in such a construction. The arbitrariness of an 'equality' claim can be demonstrated by the imagining of other equalities: for example, a Senate of equal Western, Central, and Eastern representations, of equal francophone, allophone, and aboriginal representations, of equal female and male representations (which Judy Rebick of the National Action Committee on the Status of Women began calling for in August, 1992), or a Senate of 15 equal provincial representations achieved through Québec, for strategic reasons, dividing itself into 5 new francophone provinces.

⁵ See Atwood's letter in the January-February 1990 *Books in Canada*, Philip's article in the Winter 1990 *Fuse*, "Expletive Deleted," and Philip's three essays, "Disturbing the Peace," "Am I a Nigger? Incident at Congress," and "The 6% Solution," in her collection *Frontiers*.

⁶ In discussing the Ontario government's 1992 refusal to continue funding the Art Gallery of Ontario at the preceding years' levels, culture minister Karen Haslam commented that the AGO would become a gallery "that will look at issues of access and cultural equity" (quoted in Stephen Godfrey, "Big arts groups lose out under NDP policy," the *Globe and Mail*, July 11, 1992: C9).

⁷ In the May 1992 *Books in Canada* (27) Wayne Jones attacks the language of 'political correctness' for being "a partial solution to the very real problem of discrimination" and for attempting inequitably "to impose political correctness." Jones presents himself as being against both "real" discrimination and "forcible" attempts to end it.

⁸ See Evelyn Kallen's "Multiculturalism: Ideology, Policy, and Reality" for a discussion of this change in cultural models. E.D. Blodgett in "Ethnic Writing in Canadian Literature as Paratext" interestingly assumes this view of Canadian multiculturalism policy in considering ethnic writing from a western-Canadian perspective.

⁹ Marjorie M. Halpin summarizes this controversy in her review essay "First Words." Cameron's own version and commentary appears in Scheier, et al. ed., *Language in Her Eye*, 61-71.

¹⁰ The conflict between group concepts of equality such as those of the National Action Committee on the Status of Women and those of the Thatcherite 'Orwell' individualism espoused by Thesen, Jiles, Gunnars, Atwood, and Keefer can be seen elsewhere in the ongoing conflict between the Committee and other women's groups with the Canadian Civil Liberties Association over the latter's refusal to support feminist-proposed legislation on rape, pornography, and employment equity. See "Women Take Aim at Civil Liberties Groups," *The Toronto Star* (August 30, 1992), A1, A6.

¹¹ After a conflict over whether an anthology entitled *Imagining Women* should contain texts in which white authors wrote in the voices of 'people of colour,' the Policy and Publishing Group of Women's Press judged the pieces "structurally racist.' In protest, a number of white women resigned

from the press to found the feminist Second Story Press, and the Writers Union denounced the decision as contrary to freedom of expression and imagination. See *Globe and Mail* story August 9, 1988.

12 Jennifer Henderson argues that the editors of *Language in Her Eye* framed and restricted the dissident texts of non-white contributors Lenore Keeshig-Tobias, Marlene Nourbese Philip and Dionne Brand in this way. See her "Gender in the Discourse of English-Canadian Literary Criticism," *Open Letter* VIII, 3 (Spring 1992): 47-57.

13 Politically, the threat of Québec separation has severely weakened the power of 'Central Canada'—Ontario and Québec—to jointly dominate the rest of the country. Separation has placed the political and economic interests of Ontario and Québec in conflict, as in 1988 federal election when the two provinces supported opposing sides of the free trade issue. Apart from periods of strong federalist leadership from Québec, as the Liberals enjoyed under Trudeau, the major federal parties cannot presently hope to get a majority in Parliament by sweeping the federal seats in both central provinces. They are left attempting to forge regional electoral alliances—Ontario and Atlantic Canada, Québec and the Prairies—or appealing to special constituencies like women, New Canadians, or pensioners, that cut across regional or linguistic divisions. Power, mostly in the form of bargaining power, has correspondingly shifted in this period from the center to the regions and to special interest lobbies. The perception during the Meech Lake and Charlottetown Accord debates that the Mulroney government encouraged national decentralization was to a large extent a misreading of how the lack of a central consensus was obliging any governing party to play brokerage politics. Culturally, Québec separatism has prevented the continuance in English-Canada of pre-1960s binary centre/margin cultural politics, and opened culture to the participation of many of the previously marginalized. This phenomenon implies that the regions and special interest lobbies (including those represented by the Reform Party) need the presence of the separation-threatening Québec within Confederation in order to retain their current level of political participation. Even Ontario has begun constructing itself more as a region and less as as part of an hegemonous Central Canada—as the 1993 federal election, in which Ontario voters successfully asserted their provincial interests by blocking regional attempts in both the west and Québec to gain a balance of power in Parliament, demonstrated.

It's a Wonderful Life:
Robert Lecker's Canadian Canon

The canon of Canadian literature has been for more than a hundred years a major site of contestation for both literary and social power. In the nineteenth century the establishment of a Canadian literature was viewed by such literary-political figures as Thomas D'Arcy McGee and Edward Hartley Dewart as a crucial element in establishing the legitimacy of Canada as a society and a nation. In the first three decades of this century, the fact that there was a history of writing in Canada, and thus possible canons of texts and writers to be listed and discussed, led critics like Archibald MacMurchy, J.D. Logan and D.G. French, Archibald McMechan, Lorne Pierce, and V.B. Rhodenizer to use this literature as a grounds on which to announce Canada's having taken its place among the English-speaking nations of the world. As MacMurchy wrote,

> Canadians ... are not one whit behind in the gifts of imagination and fancy which adorn the communities of the English race to be found in other parts of the world. The truth appears to be that the literary production of the people of the Dominion is proportionately equal, in quantity and quality, to that of any like part of the English-speaking race. (iv)

In the 1950s and 60s the Canadian canon became the site of several new nationalist projects: to give international legitimacy to Canadian culture through the writing of scholarly histories and companions; to popularize things Canadian within Canada by re-publishing Canadian texts for secondary and post-secondary school study; and to increase English-Canada's knowledge of Québec by the regular publishing of English translations of 'classic' francophone texts. These projects were stimulated by the 1955 founding of The Canada Council with its dual mandate to assist scholarship (a mandate presently held by the Social Sciences and Humanities Research Council of Canada) and artistic production. In the 1980s struggles for entry to the canon, or possession of one or more of its constituent parts— particularly regional writing, women's writing, and ethnically marked writing—became, as I have just argued, one of the defining characteristics of Canadian canon-activity.

Precisely what might comprise the 'Canadian canon' was in none of these periods established beyond dispute. The place of francophone writing within Canadian literature has varied from complete absence, to constituting a supplementary final chapter in some histories, to constituting in several early poetry anthologies one-half of the whole. In some English-Canadian universities today francophone-Canadian literature, in both French and in English translation, is taught in French departments as a branch of French literature; in others, this literature is taught both in French departments in English translation and with English-Canadian texts in English departments; in yet others it is hardly taught at all. The place of Atlantic-Canadian writers has steadily diminished since their predominance early in the 19th century to their virtual exclusion in many contemporary expressions of 'the canon.' The location until recently of most of the major printing facilities in either Toronto or Montreal, and of most English-language trade and educational publishers in Toronto, has helped create the illusion of the pre-eminence of Ontario-resident writers. Many writers from elsewhere—like E.J.

Pratt, Eli Mandel, or Margaret Laurence—have been lured to Ontario by its institutional strengths. Resistance to constructions of Ontario pre-eminence has been able to circulate freely within the country only after the founding of numerous regional presses and journals in the 1970s and 80s. Nationalist conceptions of the canon, usually based in Ontario, have met resistance or indifference whenever they have gathered strength—from A.J.M. Smith and his "cosmopolitan" standards in the 1920s, and in recent times from intermittently expatriate writers like Norman Levine, Mavis Gallant, and Mordecai Richler, from immigrant writers like Kristjana Gunnars, Stan Persky, Alberto Manguel, and M.G. Vassangi, from regionally-based writers like George Bowering, Dennis Cooley, Aritha van Herk, and Alistair MacLeod, and from internationally focused writers like Janet Turner Hospital, W.P. Kinsella, Susan Swan, and Robertson Davies. Possession of nationalism itself has been contested, mostly in Ontario, on ideological and class lines by (on the left) Robin Mathews, Rick Salutin, and James Lorimer, (at the near right) George Grant, Margaret Atwood, Dennis Lee, and Jack McClelland, and (from the further right) John Metcalf, Hugh Hood, W.J. Keith, and Mel Hurtig. Writers of English, Irish, or Scottish origin dominated the canon until the emergence of anglophone-Jewish writers in Montreal in the 1920s and 30s. Non-'British' names nevertheless remained a rarity in the 'canon' until the arrival of names like Ondaatje, Wah, Kroetsch, Wiebe, and Blaise in the 1960s and 70s. Women—Crawford, Wilson, Livesay, Webb, Thomas, among them—have often had to wait many years to become canonical, and to accept minor places within canonical hierarchies when they become so.

Although the Canadian canon, if one can even use that term, has been as fractured and contentious a construction as any element in Canadian culture, little direct attention had been paid to the word itself until 1989, when Robert Lecker, co-editor of *Essays on Canadian Writing* and co-owner of ECW Press, delivered a paper on the subject to the annual meeting of the Association of Canadian University Teachers of English (ACUTE). Within four years he had published this paper in the University of Chicago's widely read journal *Critical Inquiry*, edited and introduced an anthology of essays entitled *Canadian Canons* for the University of Toronto Press, and published an essay in *Mosaic* that repudiated much of the argument he had presented in his first essay and introduction. This lack of attention, however, did not mean that conceptions of a Canadian canon had been undiscussed or uncontested before Lecker's interventions. Nor did Lecker's new and concentrated focus on such a canon or canons mean that his essays were any less political interventions in struggles for canonicity.

Lecker's 1989-90 essay, entitled "The Canonization of Canadian Literature: an Inquiry into Value," argued that since the publication of Carl F. Klinck's *The Literary History of Canada* in 1965, a "conservative, historically oriented" Canadian Literature canon had been established, one that emphasized realistic fiction, and was "aligned with nationalism and mimesis" (666). Unlike contemporary critics in the United States, Canadian literary critics "continued to enshrine the literary models they had invented," and to turn "a blind eye" to issues of legitimacy and the contingency of literary value (657).

This essay, with its two incarnations and audiences, presented readers with a number of interpretive problems. The first-person plural pronouns of its conclusion ("There are voices everywhere. But we've shut them out. We inhabit a silent museum. We protect the permanent display. Our position is secure and unexciting" [671]) were hortatory in the context of the ACUTE audience which they addressed and included, but became confessional and self-deprecating—a 'colonial cringe'—when written to *Critical Inquiry*'s subscribers. Its claim to 'inquire into value' was readable in Canada as a *Canadian* effort to interrogate the role of nationalism in Canadian critical constructions; in the United States context it seemed merely a false claim: the paper was now not about value at all but about the hegemony of conservative literary values in the writer's home country. Its virtual erasure of the history of Canadian writing before 1965, and its distorting representation of Canadian criticism as being defined by the work of Frye, John Moss, D.G. Jones, D.J. Dooley, Wilfred Cude, W.J. Keith and David Stouck, would have been supplemented and contextualized by the Canadian audience; to the U.S. audience these could indeed be reasonable representations. The two versions of the essay presented Lecker himself in two different relationships to power; at ACUTE he was a contestant, seeking allies, attempting to discredit or eclipse rivals; in *Critical Inquiry* he was the authoritative insider, affiliated with the U.S. audience by numerous citations of U.S. literary theory, disassociated from the Canadian criticism he described as "blind" and naive by his 'un-blind' and penetrating analysis.

Moreover, both versions offered no position for someone like myself and numerous others who had worked, since the early 1970s, to open Canadian criticism to regional, ethnic, and gender difference, raised questions about value and legitimacy, pointed to the Ontario-centrism of most nationalist canons, and argued for theoretical understandings of language as constructive rather than mimetic.

In Lecker's bleak vision of a triumphant realistic and nationalistic Canadian canon, such theorists were left like the James Stewart character in Frank Capra's *It's a Wonderful Life*—nowhere a sign that they had lived, written, edited, taught, lectured, or published. However, while not offering someone like myself a position, the paper was in a sense forcing various positions upon me: disbelief, non-recognition, refusal. In Canada, where the numerous 'excludeds' of Lecker's essay were widely known, this refusal could take the form of laughter, or astonishment. But my first opportunity to respond to Lecker came from outside Canada: an invitation from *Critical Inquiry* to write a reply that would accompany the publication of his essay. Thus my response was to be marked, even more than was his essay, by the United States context. Unlike him, I was writing specifically and exclusively for *Critical Inquiry*: providing numerous details with which I could not assume its readership to be familiar, and employing a restrained rhetoric through which I hoped to avoid provoking him into embarrassing both of us in international view.

⁕

In the recent history of Canadian Literature there have been a number of direct and indirect attacks on the particular 'canon'—nationalist, central Canadian, mimetic, realistic—which Lecker assumed to be hegemonous in "The Canonization of Canadian Literature." These attacks have been a part of the ongoing cultural politics of Canada, particularly its regional and ethnic politics. Many of these have come from Western Canada: George Bowering's "A Great Northward Darkness: The Attack on History in Recent Canadian Fiction" (1986) and polemic introduction to his *The Fiction of Contemporary Canada* (1980); Dennis Cooley's *The*

Vernacular Muse (1987); my own "Surviving the Paraphrase" (1976) and hostile and alarmed review of Atwood's *Survival*, "Atwood Walking Backwards" (1973). Many have come from anglophiles hopeful of increasing their own legitimacy: Bruce Powe's attacks on Grove and Callaghan in *A Climate Charged* (1984); John Metcalf's proposal that the Canadian short story begins with his arrival in Canada in *What is A Canadian Literature?* (1988); Mordecai Richler's periodic grumbling about the inferiority of the national literature to which he has contributed. Some have been made on ideological grounds, like the arguments for literary and cultural diversity on which both my *From There To Here* (1974) and Linda Hutcheon's *The Canadian Postmodern* (1988) were founded. Most recently, challenges have come from minority ethnicities, eager to displace 'canonical' texts to make room for their own productions: Arun Mukherjee's *Towards an Aesthetic of Opposition* (1988), Francesco Loriggio's "The Question of the Corpus: Ethnicity and Canadian Literature" (1987). Presumably for his own political reasons, Lecker chose to 'forget' most such challenges to Canadian nationalism and realism, and to present himself as the first discoverer of this canon's potential power. At ACUTE this strategy constituted a claim to be a Moses who could lead Canadian criticism out of Harold Bloom's "dungeon of facticity" (2) and institutional conservatism. In *Critical Inquiry* it became an assertion that he belonged to a community of authoritative international critics.

The most notable difference between these challenges and Lecker's first essay is the extraordinary coherence and dominance the latter accorded to the literature of Canadian nationalist mimesis. Lecker constructed a Canadian realistic canon that was a canon "run rampant" (657). It was "hegemonic" (658). Its supporters were "impervious" and "blind" (657) to criticism. Its government support was "massive." Its "classics were taught at virtually every high school, college, and university in the nation" (658). Its values were "conservative" and narcissistically representative of the canonizers: "an image of themselves and of their values":

> These values are easy to identify: a preoccupation with history and historical placement; an interest in topicality, mimesis, verisimilitude, and documentary presentation; a bias in favor of the native over the cosmopolitan; a concern with traditional over innovative forms; a pursuit of the created before the uncreated, the named before the unnamed; an expression of national self-consciousness; a valorization of the cautious, democratic, moral imagination before the liberal, inventive one; a hegemonic identification with texts that are ordered, orderable, safe....
> (657-58)

This extraordinary canon and its attributes were his own inventions, buttressed with totalized generalizations about Canadian critics ("Canadian critics and literary historians have turned a blind eye" [657]; "the refusal by Canadian academic critics to acknowledge that the canon they support is also the currency used by the institution they inhabit" [661]), with a truncated schema of Canadian history, and with an idiosyncratic list of exemplary critics. In a move similar to Metcalf's assertion that the Canadian short story began when he arrived from Britain, Lecker (born 1951) proposed that canonical Canadian literature begins during the years he himself began serious reading of it: in 1965, with the publication of Klinck's *Literary History of Canada* and Frye's influential "Conclusion." The canon was solely academic, was produced only by "academic critics," educational publishers, and the curricula of "high school, college, and university" teachers. It was elaborated and entrenched with "startling" speed, a virtual coup d'etat, "in fewer than twenty years" (656). It was established in the early 1970s by the thematic critics—Frye, Atwood, Moss, and Jones—, entrenched by the 1978 University of Calgary conference on the Canadian novel, which attempted to establish by ballot "the most 'important' one hundred works of [Canadian] fiction" (Steele, 150), and consolidated by the criticism of D.J. Dooley, Wilfred Cude, W.J. Keith, and David Stouck.

As I suggested in my comments on the essay in *Critical Inquiry*, this was a highly edited and selective argument. Canadian literature had had a long history before its academic popularity in the 1970s, and before Klinck's *Literary History*; as Tracy Ware would later argue in his own critique of Lecker's paper, Klinck's history could not have been assembled if a Canadian literary institution had not been "already in place" (484). Lecker gave unsupportable weight to the decade of influence of the thematic critics, and ignored the cumulative discrediting of these critics from 1973 onward, a discrediting that had led Heather Murray—with some ironic hyperbole, I admit—to remark in 1986 that "thematic criticism is of course now universally despised" and to suggest that "it deserves a retrospective" (75). While Murray's epitaph for the thematicists had been perhaps as exaggerated as Lecker's construction of its continuing hegemony, it is apparent that his 'Canadian criticism' did not contain her any more than hers anticipated him. Instead, it read the refusals which thematic criticism had received as indicative of its continuing power, and attempted to appropriate these—particularly my "Surviving the Paraphrase" and Barbara Godard's 1986 essay "Structuralism/Poststructuralism"—as endorsements of its own thesis.

Lecker's arguments for the existence in the 1980s of a

powerful, conservative 'post-thematic' criticism—Dooley, Cude, Keith, and Stouck—were similarly weak. A more persuasive argument could have been constructed that these four critics had been relatively marginal to Canadian critical debates. I noted in *Critical Inquiry* that the texts cited by Lecker for three of these had been written for non-Canadian academic audiences: Keith's for a British publisher, Cude's and Stouck's for U.S. publishers. British-born Keith had often situated himself as an observer of rather than participant in Canadian literature; Canadian had only recently become his primary research and teaching field. Dooley and Cude had published one book each, and none since 1980. Although Keith had published at least four books since 1982 and nine articles on aspects of Canadian literature, the periodical indexes indicated that Dooley and Cude had done no publishing on Canadian literature in the last ten years and that Stouck, apart from his editing of the annual *Journal of Canadian Poetry* and the book cited by Lecker, had edited two collections and published one review.

The question therefore arises—a question I did not consider for *Critical Inquiry* readers—of why Lecker would have so exaggerated the power of these critics. And a larger question arises as well of why he would have attempted to construct such a monolithic and difficult-to-defend schema of Canadian literature and criticism. One clue to both seems to lie in the account he offered of the proliferation of his 'canon':

> Massive government support through numerous funding agencies, along with the institutional support of academics, accounts for the proliferation of canon objects associated with the Canadian literature industry: reference guides, critical studies, specialized journals, bibliographies, articles, anthologies, films, research grants, awards, medals, and even teacher-oriented 'crash courses' in what has become its own

thriving discipline. A card game entitled Canadian Writers ("suitable for ages 7 and up") is now available. (658)

This description closely resembles the activities of ECW Press which Lecker co-owns with Jack David: support from the Canada Council, the Social Sciences and Humanities Research Council, the Ontario Arts Council, the Canadian Federation for the Humanities, the institutional support given the various academics whom ECW employs to compile its "reference guides, critical studies,...bibliographies, articles, anthologies." The author-names addressed in these bibliographies and reference guides include nearly all the 'top-rated' canonical Canadian authors of the University of Calgary conference which Lecker constructed in the essay as critically influential. ECW catalogues foreground the prize and medal-winning record of the press's books; the back cover of the 1989 catalogue announcing 12 prizes since 1982. Overall, the canon he attacked in *Critical Inquiry* as all powerful appears to be the one his own activities as a prolific academic publisher have attempted to put into place. In a sense, Lecker may have stood to gain no matter whether his argument against the canon succeeded or failed. If it had succeeded, he may have indeed become the critic-prophet who defeated the Goliath he and his press have made out of the residue of thematic criticism. If it had failed, as it possibly has, its construction of the realist thematic canon as all-powerful might still hold the field and guarantee the relevance of ECW's publications. Were it to have both succeeded and failed—the most likely outcome—he had still constructed himself as a perceptive and controversial critic, and his publishing house a powerful publisher of arguably 'canonical' Canadian materials.

Lecker's construction of a monolithic, "conservative, historically-oriented" canon defended by a self-interested Canadian literature establishment was accompanied in his essay by an idealizing construction of U.S. and international criticism as open to self-criticism and difference while Canadian criticism is not. For Lecker, while interrogations of the canon had caused a legitimation crisis for the "American counterparts" (657) of Canadian critics, while "other canons and literary institutions were being named, explained, torn apart" (659), a monolithic Canadian canon had been unquestioningly invented. The critics and theorists who constituted for Lecker the new demystifying criticism were Frank Kermode, John Guillory, Annette Kolodny, Harold Bloom, Louis Montrose, Stephen Greenblatt, and Barbara Herrnstein Smith. Lecker repeatedly affiliated himself with their criticism, not merely by citing its example, but by allowing their words to make his arguments for him.

> Canadian critics continue to accept what Louis Montrose calls the "unproblematized distinctions between 'literature' and 'history,' between 'text' and 'context.'
>
> (659, quoting Montrose)
>
> Canadian critics show little interest in exploring "the range of aesthetic possibilities within a given representational mode" or in examining how that mode is tied to "the complex network of institutions, practices, and beliefs that constitute the culture as a whole."
>
> (660, quoting Greenblatt)
>
> An awareness of delegitimation and defamiliarization "empowers us to understand that the critic's nagging obsession to locate any and every text within a graded, evaluative hierarchy, irrespective of history, is no more (and no less) than one facet of an ongoing process by which competing interest groups vie for cultural hegemony...."
>
> (660, quoting Kolodny)

> The power of this [Canadian] institution, as of all canonical institutions, lay in its ability "to impose fictions upon the world and...to enforce the acceptance of fictions that are known to be fictions."
>
> (664, quoting Greenblatt)

These constructions blurred the distinction between Lecker and the United States theorists, and created a kind of syntactic transubstantiation whereby Lecker could become 'one' with them. In the oral presentation of the paper to ACUTE, the rhetorical effect of this had been to allow Lecker to speak in the voice and authority of the more widely-circulated and internationally prestigious United States criticism. In *Critical Inquiry* the effect was to give Lecker two voices, one that confessed Canadian shortcomings and a second that appeared to speak with the power of the American reader's canonical theorists.

This power strategy in Lecker's text was achieved, however, by considerable reduction. The binary construction of United States and Canadian criticisms, as revolutionary and conservative respectively, repeated the republican constructions of both societies, and ignored the diversity and conflict within both literatures. Contemporary American criticism and theory contains powerful rear-guard writers— Alvin Kernan, Philip Goldstein, Charles Altieri, Gerald Graff among others; its canonical revisions, as in the various Norton anthology revisions, appear designed as much to preserve the traditional canon against new claims as to open it to new claimants. Canadian criticism is much more heterogenous and conflicted than Lecker represented (he hierarchically suppressed much of this heterogeneity by relegating it to footnotes): the publications of several 'foursomes' we might assemble—W.H. New, Robert Kroetsch, Barbara Godard, and Sherrill Grace; Elspeth Cameron,

Shirley Neuman, Dennis Cooley, and Linda Hutcheon; Janice Kulyk Keefer, George Woodcock, Philip Stratford, and E.D. Blodgett—have arguably been at least as influential as Lecker's quartet of Dooley, Cude, Stouck and Keith.

Moreover, Lecker's borrowings of theory from American theorists had been neither absorbed nor understood. He could quote their skepticism about unitary concepts without altering his own unitary construction of either them or Canadian criticism; he could quote Kolodny's description of "competing interest groups vying for cultural hegemony" without noticing similar competition ongoing in his own country. As Tracy Ware has pointed out, both in his "Response" to my commentary and in the essay itself Lecker misunderstood or misrepresented the explicit arguments of the United States critics he implied would endorse his analysis. He claimed Kermode's support in lamenting the conservative force of the literary institution when "Kermode finds his liberty in recognizing the collective role played by institutions" (Ware 481); he implied that Bloom wishes criticism to escape "the historicized dungeon of facticity" while overlooking Bloom's conclusion that "criticism at the present time...cannot...liberate us from the brute factuality of our dependent relation to culture" (Bloom 20, quoted Ware 482). Ware comments: "It is one thing to disagree with Kermode and Bloom, but my objection is to Lecker's pretence that his argument follows from theirs" (482).

Lecker's employment of the term "institution" was particularly narrow and misleading. Ignoring its use in his quotation from Greenblatt, "'complex network of institutions, practices, and beliefs that constitute the culture as a whole'" (660), Lecker spoke of only one institution, "the institution called Canadian literature" (664), as if that 'institution' were not itself the product of complex conflict and interaction among numerous institutions—academic and textbook publishers, writers organizations, various levels of government and their purchasing and subsidy policies and agencies, the partly integrated North American 'free trade' marketplace, universities, academic 'learned societies,' various provincial secondary education systems, the trade bookselling industry, newspapers, little magazines, arts councils, and special interest organizations. Lecker's use of the word 'institution' may have been consistent with his general rhetorical strategy—to suspend in binary opposition two monologically constructed literary institutions, the radical American and the conservative Canadian—but it obscured the diversity of power interests in Canada and the way in which these interests interweave and collide to create a literary institution that is much more open and dynamic than the 'institution' required by his argument. It was not Klinck's *Literary History* that had made widespread teaching of Canadian literature possible as much as it was the launching in the late 1950s by McClelland and Stewart of the New Canadian Library series of reprinted texts. In the 1970s, while in Toronto it may have appeared that 'Canadian literature' courses were springing up across the country in response to nationalist sentiments, in the regions such courses were often responses as well to expanded regional publishing and to the increased power of provincial governments. Today it may not be contentment with a national literary canon that has caused "no generalized histories of English-Canadian literature [to] have appeared after Keith's" (670) but a new focus on specialized 'canons'— women's writing, First Nations writing, lesbian writing, Italo-Canadian writing, Manitoba writing, Atlantic-Canadian writing—that may itself be related to a general lack of interest in national constructions across the country.

Even the centralist impulses in Canadian literature, which Lecker attempted to view here as 'the canon,' have been produced by more complex institutional causations than his understanding of 'institution' can explain. As I wrote in my first comment on his essay (678), it has been the tendency of Canadian academic publishers in recent decades to restrict their publications to author-emphasizing monographs designed for high school and university students that has encouraged the production of biographical, interpretative, and thematic criticism. It has been the small size of the Canadian academic book market that has encouraged many publishers to seek readers among the largest part of it, high school and college students and teachers, rather than among the much smaller one of practising scholars (which, as the *PMLA* advertisements testify, provides a viable bookmarket segment in the United States). Meanwhile, the historical concentration of population, economic power, and political power in Ontario, particularly Toronto, has made Toronto publishers the only consistently 'national' publishers and has given their trade and textbook productions a near monopoly on national English-language distribution. The peculiar structure of Canadian bookselling, in which seventy-five percent or more of the retail stock routinely consists of books written in other countries,[1] has caused many booksellers, particularly the large chains, to prefer a small Canadian canon of highly valorized texts and authors. And the economic mismatch between these free-market booksellers and a Canadian publishing industry in which nearly every literary title receives government subsidy has made it difficult for new or generically dissenting texts to get out of publishers' warehouses and into Canadian bookstores, let alone into a canon.

There are at least two possible reasons for why Robert Lecker raised the issue of 'institution' without going on to look into actual institutions. The first is that the theory of institutional agency in literary history is a materialist one, founded on the belief that the material circumstances of human culture shape its institutional, ideological, and discursive formations, and that these in turn act as both facilitators and restraints on all cultural activity. Lecker's own announced position, as Ware pointed out, is quite different: it is humanist, liberationist; it "ignores the inescapable constraints set forth by the theorists he cites, whether those constraints be institutional (Kermode), historical (Bloom), or post-axiological (Smith)" (484). It envisions individual heroic action (including his own) that can "liberate [us] from the worn-out methodologies and antimethodologies we believe we should believe in" (Lecker 671).

A second possible reason for Lecker's reluctance to look too closely at the literary effects of institutional process in Canada would appear to be his own deep involvement in that process. An analysis of it would have involved not merely a confession on behalf of Canadian criticism but a confession of his own complicity in bringing about many of the features of Canadian literature which he claimed to deplore—including ECW's publication of the proceedings of the 1978 University of Calgary conference and dissemination of the canon of realist fiction to which he was claiming to object. While it was Lecker's pretence that his arguments were congruent with those of Kermode, Bloom, and Smith that Ware found most objectionable, it was his pretence that he stood aside from "the Canadian literature industry," that it had developed without his own efforts to direct and profit from its development, that I personally found offensive.

For Lecker was anything but unqualified to speak to ACUTE and *Critical Inquiry* authoritatively, if not theoretically, of various institutional forces in Canadian literature. Through ECW Press he had contracted for work with numerous institutionally employed scholars, applied for and received funding from the Canada Council, The Social Sciences and Humanities Research Council, the Canadian Federation for the Humanities, and the Ontario Arts Council, dealt with the Association of Canadian Publishers, the Canadian Booksellers Association, the Writers Union, and the Canadian Magazine Publishers Association, encountered the review practices of newspapers, and regional and academic journals, sold books to public and university libraries, independent and chain booksellers, school boards and ministries of education. Many of the publications of ECW Press have been explicitly designed and promoted to take advantage of the stability and conservativeness of the kind of canon he argues that the new 'Canadian literary institution' and the 1978 Calgary conference have promoted. The terms employed by ECW catalogues have often been ones of exclusion and hierarchy: the 1987-88 catalogue announced *Canadian Literature Index* as "the definitive current index to periodicals publishing Canadian literature." It described the series *Canadian Writers and Their Works*, edited by Lecker, co-owner Jack David and Ellen Quigley, as a series in which "100 Canadian literary specialists...write individual essays on 100 authors according to our guidelines...the best possible criticism by an authority on the subject." The "100 authors" recalls "the most 'important' one hundred works of fiction" sought by the Calgary conference. The 1989 catalogue announced *Canadian Fiction Studies*, "a series of books about *major* Canadian novels: each book...contains nothing but clear readable information on only one book." Throughout, these catalogues have relied on a discourse of canonical certainty and domination—*major* authors, *major* works, *authoritative* critics, *definitive* indexes—together with a discourse of simplicity—"clear readable information," "easy-to-use volumes," "a clearly written essay," "easy access." The two discourses appear closely related, both being reductive discourses that, like the rhetoric of Lecker's essay, classify and simplify literary history into highly organized, unproblematical, monolithic constructions. A single dominant canon is desired here because it will be "clear" to educators and bookbuyers, and "easy" for prospective readers.

The ECW catalogue copy has often demonstrated also one of the persistent structural problems in Canadian scholarly publishing—its construction of audience as undergraduate and able to understand the world only one item, clause, or book at a time:

> Do you get the idea? A single book, about 60 pages long, devoted to a single novel. Written by Canada's foremost literary critic. Aimed at the typical Canadian high school student or first-year undergraduate.
> (copy for *Canadian Fiction Series*, 1987-88, 3)

Moreover, in the case of this entry, the "foremost" critic whom ECW has chosen to write the series is George Woodcock, a writer whose numerous critical publications have been founded on precisely the sort of generalizing Leavisite conceptions Lecker in his essay argued that he opposes—"the human condition," "the essence of narrative poetry," "poetic excellence" (Woodcock 1987, 310, 305, 284), "the writer of genius," "bad books," "the test of time" (1975, vii-ix).

When I reminded Lecker of the ECW aspect of his life in

our *Critical Inquiry* encounter, he replied that my comments on this aspect of his life were "picky, personal, off target, and of little interest to readers of *Critical Inquiry*" (688)— evidently he had not read the journal's coverage of the publication of Paul de Man's World War II journalism. He went on to note that ECW is a partnership and therefore "expresses multiple viewpoints," that some of its books "affirm the canon; some don't" (a point I had made in suggesting that the conflict between the back and front pages of ECW catalogues should have persuaded him that "'Canadian criticism' is nowhere as monolithic as he depicts it" [680]), and that "the way we promote books is influenced...by our desire to stay in business" (688). Indeed, "business practice"—as I had noted (681) is one of the institutional determinants of Canadian literature; it is not surprising that it should 'influence' ECW's book promotion— nor one of the owners' analyses of canonicity in Canada. One could hardly expect a co-owner of an academic press to declare that he had cynically helped construct and totalize a small, easy-to-service, easy-to-read canon of Canadian writing together with a 'tradition' of easy-to-consume criticism, when such a declaration might make it awkward for him "to stay in business."

Lecker's first essay, my commentary on it, his response to my commentary, and Ware's further response imply a fair amount about academic literary power in Canada in the 1980s and 90s. Various sources of power come together here—the professional society, the publishing industry, the academy, the prestigious internationally circulating American theory and criticism appropriated by Lecker. The powerful academic term of the moment is *difference*—this is the term Lecker attempts to associate himself with and for possession of which I dispute his argument. The powerful commercial term—at least to the extent that ECW continues to stay "in business"—is *legitimacy*: major authors, definitive bibliographies, the best critics, award-winning books. Presumably, since government subsidies continue to come to ECW, this term has some continuing power with granting agencies and their juries as well. A problematical third term is *liberty*: Lecker presumed it to have power, either as a humanistic cry (the individual vs. the constraining institution) or as a republican or revolutionary call. However, the term is in conflict with the assumptions of the (powerful) United States critics he invoked, and led him to misapply or misunderstand their theories.

Lecker's paper at its 1989 ACUTE presentation was not well-received. Some listeners complained that Canadian literature began as a form of opposition to the Great Canon. Others disliked the way in which Lecker—a long-standing skeptic toward theory—appears to be re-packaging himself as theory's defender; "What is he up to?" one well-known Canadian feminist theorist asked. They suspected something self-serving in the way in which the paper discounted earlier critiques of centralization in Canadian literature and constructed its own writer as first discoverer of a potential monolith. Lecker then got the paper accepted by *Critical Inquiry* (whose Autumn 1983 issue had focused on canonicity and included the essays he cites by Herrnstein Smith and Guillory) and thus further affiliated it with the power of the U.S. critics he had rhetorically appropriated. This affiliation appears to have been more important for him than communication with the new U.S. audience; he made few revisions to the paper and retained in particular the hortatory rhetoric with which it addressed ACUTE. Behind this strategy are a century or more of similarly legitimizing but much less visibly opportunistic affiliations by Canadian writers—Carman and Roberts's associations with New England writing, the career-launching prizes won by Ostenso and de la Roche, Dudek's affiliations with Trilling and Pound, Richler's long association with publisher Andre Deutsch, Richler, Munro and Gallant's numerous publications in *The New Yorker*.

Critical Inquiry's practice of commissioning comments on polemic essays—a practice rare in Canada—led to my being invited to respond. Possibly I was invited because I am sympathetically cited in the article, or because I have never been published by ECW Press, or because I have been suggested by Lecker (who at the end of his response to my commentary would declare that he shares "with" me a desire to "liberate ourselves from...worn-out methodologies" [689]); quite possibly my being at the time chair of a large Canadian English department helped make me acceptable.

⁌

Lecker's subsequent interventions in the canonicity debate—his introduction to the anthology *Canadian Canons* (1991) and the essay in the Summer 1993 issue of *Mosaic* —have been, although substantial, much less dramatic and unequivocal than the first essay. Although neither has taken up the question of institutional determinants in canon formation, both have represented radical re-writings and re-thinkings of his initial arguments.

Much like many of the individual books published by ECW Press, the essays collected by Lecker for *Canadian Canons* (by Surette, McCarthy, Gerson, Scobie, Salter, Knowles, Robert, Bayard, Bennett, Mathews, Simon, and Weir), despite the scant attention they give to race and ethnicity, belied his own thesis that Canadian academic criticism is conservative, nationalist, and committed to realism. Perhaps finding his views altered by the essays he collected, Lecker in his introduction transformed his earlier views of Canadian canonicity. He gave up his idealization of United States theory, his polarization of American and Canadian critical practice, his simple understanding of 'institution,' his call for liberation, and his narrow argument that an entrenched, mimetic nationalist canon dominates the Canadian curriculum and controls its critics. He added material about recent French and British inquiries into canonicity, and in the opening sentence of his introduction offered a "deliberately plural emphasis on canons" and on "the multiple and shifting forms of recent canonical debate" (3). Many of his remarks echoed those of my *Critical Inquiry* comment. He offered an apology for a lack of materialist analysis in the collection, commenting that "the ideal examination of any canon would include an analysis of market forces, of the publishing and bookselling industry; of curriculum development in schools and universities; of government attempts to patronize a national literature and its supporters; of the dissemination of literary value in newspapers, magazines, scholarly journals, and books." The framing first and last sentences of the introduction, however, still displayed a penchant for totalities. The pluralism of his opening "deliberately plural emphasis" (1991, 3) remained a civility that at best dealt condescendingly with conflict as if it were some quaint custom; his concluding remark that his collection is "a rewarding start" (16) re-instated in a minor key the discourse of excitement and liberation he had emphasized in "The Canonization of Canadian Literature." The politics of canonicity, I would tell him, is not merely "plural"; it has winners, partial winners, local winners, and losers; it is exciting only for voyeurs and non-losers.

The third Lecker essay, in *Mosaic*, and entitled "A Country without a Canon?: Canadian Literature and the Esthetics of Idealism," appeared based on a paper Lecker is reported to have given to a conference of the Australia and New Zealand Canadian Studies Association in Wellington, N.Z., in December of 1992. In this essay Lecker responded to the critics of the *Critical Inquiry* essay, principally myself and Tracy Ware, by perplexingly characterizing them as having argued that Canada is "a country without a canon" (4) and that "interest in canonicity is... irrelevant to Canadians" (2), and by setting out to explore the implications and consequences of such arguments. Also perplexingly, he did an about-face in his choice of American theoretical authorities, grounding his new reflections on two essays by Charles Altieri which offer the humanist argument that canons constitute "a permanent theater helping us shape and judge personal and social values, [and] that our self-interest in the present consists primarily in establishing ways of employing that theater to gain distance from our ideological commitments..." (Altieri 44). Implying that he had been persuaded by both Altieri's arguments and the very different ones of myself and Ware, he abandoned his attempts to affiliate himself with the historicist theories of Kermode, Kolodny, and Herrnstein Smith, retracted his charges that Canada has been dominated by a conservative, realist, and nationalist canon, and argued instead that in the virtual absence of a canon, the establishment of a new nationalist canon is culturally imperative to enable Canadians to avoid "anarchy" and develop a "shared social and cultural narrative" (17).

Lecker's surprising new views rested as much as did his earlier ones on misrepresentations of Canadian and

American theorists. Neither Ware nor I had argued that Canada has "no canon": Ware had proposed that "[t]he Canadian canon has always been fluid" (487), while I had suggested that Canada has a network of competing canons rather than a single canon. Neither of us had suggested that interest in questions of canonicity was "irrelevant" to Canada; our arguments had been that Lecker had idealized United States literary theories about canonicity not by importing them but by pretending that their concerns had not already had Canadian counterparts. Altieri's essays had contained no endorsement whatsoever for the kind of nationalist canon Lecker now desired. Altieri's canonic ideal had been "the Western canon" (45)—a transnational, humanist conception that he founded on references to Longinus, Dante, Shakespeare, Samuel Johnson, Flaubert, Eliot, Habermas, Lacan, Edward Said, and the Canadians Northrop Frye and Charles Taylor.

Although Lecker's third essay contained generous references to my own criticism (3-4, 8, 12, 16), its overall effect in refusing to acknowledge the argument that Canada is a field of competing canons was again to deny significance to anything but nationalist constructions. The two extreme alternatives Lecker proposed—a country without a canon or a canon that "imagines our community anew"—constructed a binary that subsumed difference within both the appropriating force of its second-person plural pronoun and the singular forms the essay persistently gave to "canon" and "community." Between the poles of this binary, theorists like myself were placed under a "sign" of unhealth:

> the absence of a Canadian canon, or even the assertion that there is not one canon, but many of them, begins to seem like an unhealthy sign. It means we have not identified literary ideals that are worth defending, ... (10)

In addition, the new essay diverted attention from the contradictions in Lecker's first essay between his critique of nationalist canon-construction and his own involvement in ECW Press's commercial efforts to construct a Canadian canon. As in his *Critical Inquiry* "Response" and his *Canadian Canons* introduction, Lecker deflected my suggestion that he might reflect upon that activity and its relationship to various institutional forces within Canadian literary and scholarly publishing. Here Lecker's announced values—"I want to find a Canadian community, I believe there are Canadian ideals, I do not want to consider the canon only as an instrument of power and I do feel, with Altieri, that it can function as an agency of shared values" (8)—were much closer to the implicit one of his publishing house. The essay even suggested that some of the federalist ideology of anglophone Montreal (Lecker has taught for more than a decade at McGill), and the desperate interest of that community in national unity, may have been at work in both the earlier essay and the explicitly "Canadian" publishing initiatives of ECW. This suggestion in a sense reconfigures Lecker's own relationship to power in Canada. Rather than the contestant for national power he was four years before at ACUTE, he is now an anglophone-Québec outsider, excluded from the "anarchy" of cultural debate within English Canada, and eager for a return to the Canadian nationalist conceptions that sustained anglophone Québec during the F.R. Scott and Hugh MacLennan period.

◆

The network of institutions familarly known as 'Canadian Literature' is today both a very small and yet widely dispersed and fragmented thing. It is difficult to find a practising Canadianist who has not written a book for ECW

Press, applied for a subvention from the Canadian Federation for the Humanities' Aid to Scholarly Publications Programme, given a paper at the ACCUTE or ACQL annual meetings, or published a review in *Canadian Literature*. Senior scholars routinely act as referees for each other's grant, appointment, and promotion applications. But on the other hand the fissures and conflicts are often profound. Academics closely linked with commercial publishing, like Lecker or Gary Geddes, are often suspected of opportunism when they name themselves editors of one of their press's series or include their writing within an anthology they edit. Scholars who are repeatedly asked by prominent 'Can Lit' journals to prune their essays of the theoretical passages on which they are grounded grumble darkly about the unenlightened humanist editors and copy editors who don't understand theory. Lorraine Weir's dislike for George Woodcock's humanism, for *Canadian Literature*'s cheerful eclecticism, and for Linda Hutcheon's overviews of postmodernism have been openly displayed on several occasions.[2] Also in public view have been Robin Mathews' distaste for both my criticism and that of Margaret Atwood as too 'American' in one case and too individualist in the other,[3] Margaret Atwood's reservations about radical feminism,[4] Janice Kulyk Keefer's disapproval of Daphne Marlatt for asserting "the primacy of one ideology over another,"[5] Jean Mallinson and Janice Williamson's accusations that 1974 readings of Phyllis Webb's poetry, by John Bentley Mays and myself, as enacting modernist angst were "malicious" and "misogynist."[6] Recent disagreements among feminists have focused on Lola Lemire Tostevin's article "Daphne Marlatt: Writing the Space that is Her Mother's Face," and Smaro Kamboureli's "Theory: Beauty or Beast: Resistance to Theory in the Feminine," and on what some commentators have seen as implicit racism in the editing of Scheier, Sheard and Wachtel's *Language in Her Eye*.[7] Regional disputes have seen Frye, Atwood and Jones held in low repute in the West as Ontario-centrists, and vastly different curricula constructed in different parts of the country as 'Canadian literature.'

A good deal of the contention and conflict is kept hidden by scholars of all ages and ranks in fear of jeopardizing publication, grant, or appointment opportunities or useful editorial collaborations. A feminist editorial board may have fierce ideological disagreements in private but present an image of dialogue and consensus in their magazines. A pluralist may offer 'happy family' images of Canadian writing or criticism in public but in the privacy of an awards jury make condescending comments or distorted evaluations that effectively thwart applications by individuals or periodicals with marked ideological positions.[8] Young scholars may bridle at the formulaic structure demanded by ECW's 'Canadian Writers and Their Works' series but, because of understandable appointment or tenure anxieties, produce the requested monograph nevertheless. This concealment means neither that the conflicts are not significant, nor that a hegemony such as that constructed or desired by Lecker is allowed to reign. It more likely means that most participants in this relatively small field prefer the minimum of civility necessary to allow its network of institutions to continue to operate to the alternative of crippling open conflict. As Lorraine Weir warns, however, this 'civility' can be itself crippling if taken as an overriding value rather than as merely a strategy for institutional survival.

The current decentralized structure of the Canadian literature and literary studies discourages the kind of hegemonous power Lecker in both the *Critical Inquiry* and

Mosaic essay attempts, in different ways, to theorize. Canadian English departments are politically disconnected from one another, respond to internal priorities and practices, and are located within autonomous provincial ministries. Canadian literature curricula are constructed in isolation, from a variety of paperbacks and anthologies, and often based on in-department anthologies. As Ware points out in his comment on Lecker, there is no Canadian equivalent to the Norton anthology, nor prospect of there being one. On occasions of tenure and promotion, or the examination of doctoral theses, two of the few times when departments have opportunities to directly influence one another, current practices give candidates considerable power to contribute to the selection of external referees and examiners. Few scholars are ever invited to appraise candidates to whose work they are likely to be unsympathetic. The proliferation of conferences, particularly those organized by special interest groups within the academy, encourages the development of specific sub-fields and methodologies. So too does the current large number of journals and presses that publish scholarly writing, and the regional and ideological dispersion of these publishers. The publisher of this book offers opportunities for significantly different kinds of critical writing than does Women's Press, University of Waterloo Press, Oxford University Press, the Twayne World Author Series, Borealis, McGill-Queen's, Coach House, or Douglas and McIntyre. This situation, of course, could change, were reductions of government arts subsidies to undermine the viability of small-scale publishing, or were provincial governments to attempt to force 'higher' standards of legitimacy on their universities by instituting undergraduate programme reviews or general regulations for promotion and tenure.

The current condition of diverse and separate 'power'

centres, accompanied by a few nationally powerful funding institutions and publishers, encourages specialized 'powers' and occasional 'power grabs.' It is difficult to compare the power of W.J. Keith at Toronto among Leavisite scholars, Linda Hutcheon in contemporary Canadian studies, D.M.R. Bentley in nineteenth-century Canadian, Barbara Godard in feminist theory, Robert Kroetsch in 'prairie' literature, Shirley Neuman in Lacanian theory and autobiography, Aruna Srivastava, W.H. New, and Terry Goldie in Canadian/postcolonial studies, let alone construct in this sentence comparable fields of influence. As for attempted power grabs, Lecker appears correct in identifying the 1978 Calgary conference and Keith's *Canadian Literature in English* as two of these. These 'grabs' appear not so much because the participants consciously seek domination but because they lose sight of the relative position of their own power and perspective within the overall network of specialized powers—or simply lose sight of that network altogether. Something similar seems to happen in Lecker's first essay, where almost the only literature and criticism he can see are the conservative, nationalistic, documentary, and canon-building publications of his own publishing house. Even as he announces his misgivings about the canon such texts imply, his own rhetoric accumulatively aggrandizes this canon that is twice his own creation. Later, in the course of defending the essay, Lecker discovers that, far from having misgivings about this canon, it is indeed not only the one that as publisher he has been building but also the one that he has all along yearned to create—"a shared social and cultural narrative." Although his ending returns to the rhetoric of liberation which marked the end of his first essay, with a call to Canadians to risk "dreams [that] might redeem us," Lecker's own position has changed from being a self-declared authority to being only one more contestant for Canadian canonicity.

⁌

Terry Goldie has commented about the debate Robert Lecker and I had in the pages of *Critical Inquiry* that it focused only on the interior space of Canadian literature and not on "Canadian literature's position in the larger canons of 'English literature'…or of 'world literature'," that neither critic was interested in "mainstreaming" Canadian literature into an English or world canon (373). Of the explicit level of the debate Goldie is largely correct: Lecker and I devoted most of our arguments to the current power relationships evident within Canadian canonicity and to the history of these relationships within Canada. But related elements in the debate, both explicit and implicit, appear to have evaded Goldie's notice. Lecker's major argument rested on a comparison between American and Canadian criticism, and on the premise that the canon concerns of an alert and self-aware American criticism were not evident within a self-absorbed and complacent Canadian one. It was his argument that Canadian criticism occupied an inferior position to both American and British criticism that had attracted my comment that he had idealized American criticism, Ware's that he had misunderstood this criticism, and Godard's that his arguments, in the context of *Critical Inquiry*, constituted a "colonial cringe" (12). Lecker's project to locate his Canadian canon and Canadian criticism in an inferior relationship to Goldie's "larger canons" was symbolically repeated in his locating his own essay in *Critical Inquiry* and in his attempts to affiliate his criticism with what he argued was the more sophisticated American criticism. Ware's reading of his essay attempted to deny

Lecker a position in American criticism, and return him to "separate" Canadian space, by pointing out how institutionally 'Canadian' his arguments had been: that liberationist essays such as Lecker's were a recurrent part of the history of Canadian criticism, and that Lecker's conflation of postmodernism and poststructuralism (in his assumption that a poststructuralist criticism would not canonize realist texts) was alien to the United States but an instrinsic feature of the development of recent Canadian theory.

As well, the focus of Lecker and myself on the relative strengths of nationalist and other canons implicitly pointed to Canada's position as a site in various transnational canon-forming forces. The Canadian literatures which evaded Lecker's notice, and which most threatened his conservative-realist-nationalist construction by their presence, were for the most part literatures founded on conceptions that traverse the spaces among and within the "larger canons": women's writing, regional writing, gay and lesbian writing, aboriginal writing. This transnational textuality is not altogether separate or mainstream. It crosses the boundaries of earlier canons, and shares institutional resources with them, while also finding separate spaces and building new institutional structures. It creates substructures within the Modern Languages Association, the Learned Societies, and within the modular curricula of English departments; it publishes through long-standing university and commercial presses. Yet it also founds its own popular and academic journals and presses, organizes conferences outside of institutional venues, and establishes political lobbies.

It is this combination of independence and complicitous intertwining with older institutions across national boundaries that makes the theorizing of contemporary Canadian canonity so difficult. Rivals to national constructions of canonicity are not necessarily contained within Canadian national borders, nor can nationalisms such as Lecker's be viewed as not themselves expressions of transnational romantic forces that informed the establishment of nation-states throughout Europe and the Americas in the eighteenth and nineteenth centuries. The regionalisms of Atlantic, prairie, and western Canada echo not only with W.C. Williams's "local pride" but with the localist ideologies that have in various and not always attractive ways informed cultures from Texas and Western Australia to Puerto Rico, Singapore, and the Punjab. Feminist, aboriginal, and gay literatures develop both within the histories and institutional structures particular to their national and regional situations and within transnationally evolving theoretical discourses. There is a lot of separate space within Canadian canonicity—many productive writers and institutions focused on specific, and often at least partly transnational, politics and aesthetics, but indifferent to the triumphant or clarion nationalisms Robert Lecker proclaims. But these writers and institutions also help constitute, collectively, along with those nationalisms, the particular nation and canon Canadians live with, regardless of their wishes or desperations.

"Not a bad end," Daphne Marlatt writes of the turn to lesbianism her novel *Ana Historic* takes in its concluding pages—not necessarily implying that this is a 'good' end but that moral evaluation has little relevance to it. So too, I suggest, with the unstable and heterogenous Canadian 'canon.' It may not be the canon that each of us as individuals might prefer, or that accords us the power of our dreams or fantasies. But it is not a bad canon.

NOTES

[1] Ontario Royal Commission on Book Publishing, *Canadian Publishers and Canadian Publishing* (Toronto, 1973): 137.

[2] See Laurence Ricou and Lorraine Weir, "Editorial: Dialogue," *Canadian Literature* 110 (1986): 2-6, and Weir's essays "The Discourse of 'Civility': Strategies of Containment in Literary Histories of English Canadian Literature" and "'Maps and Tales': the Progress of *Canadian Literature* 1959-1987."

[3] See his essays "The Wacousta Factor" and "Survival and Struggle in Canadian Literature."

[4] "If You Can't Say Something Nice, Don't Say Anything at All," in Scheier et al., ed., *Language in Her Eye*: 15-25.

[5] "Gender, Language, Genre," Scheier et al., ed., *Language in Her Eye*: 167.

[6] Mallinson, "Ideology and Poetry: an Examination of Some Recent Trends in Canadian Criticism;" Williamson, "The Feminist Suicide Narratives of Phyllis Webb."

[7] See Margaret Christakos's reading of the editing of this collection, "Axioms to Grind," *Room of One's Own* XIV: 4 (December 1991), 57-81, and Julia Emberley's comment in the same issue, 82-96. See also Jennifer Henderson's "Gender in English-Canadian Literary Criticism," *Open Letter* VIII, 3 (Spring 1992), 47-57.

[8] A few years ago, for example, I served on a national jury whose three members were asked to evaluate independently approximately 50 poems by assigning them each a percentage rating. The ratings were then averaged to determine the prizewinner. I discovered afterward that one other juror and myself had both given 100% to a poem by Robert Kroetsch, and awarded values of 95%, 90%, 85% etc to the others. The third juror, however, the editor of a well-known literary quarterly, had given 100% to a different poem, and given extremely low percentages—perhaps as low as 0—to every other poem, ensuring that on average his first-place poem would be the overall winner. His action had, in effect, transformed the jury into a single judge.

The Collapse of the Canadian Poetry Canon

In the past few years articles expressing fear of an incipient crisis within Canadian poetry have almost become a subgenre of Canadian literary journalism. Poets have variously envied the legendary importance of poetry in politically oppressed Central and South American countries, lamented a diminishing readership within Canada, or deplored the directions their fellow writers have taken. David Solway has announced in *Canadian Literature* the "end of poetry," arguing that contemporary poets have chosen to abandon imitation of form for imitation of nature, and have thereby entered into a direct and suicidal competition with prose fiction: the poet now "goes on multiplying narrative upon description in odd linguistic constructs called poems that scarcely anyone bothers to read except other poets and an entrenched minority of academic critics" (132). Judith Fitzgerald, in an article printed in both *The Toronto Star* and *The Canadian Author and Bookman*, has told us that "poetry in the late 20th century has ended up in the cultural morgue" (14), and Susan Ioannou, writing in *Cross-Canada Writers' Quarterly*, has forecast that if poetry is to survive it will have to abandon the written word for the oral (32). Patrick Lane, also in *Cross-Canada Writers' Quarterly*, has commented that "people rarely, if ever, read...poems," but urged poets nevertheless to continue writing in search of the extra-social rewards of "Yeats' Bysantium [sic]" (4).

In 1990-91 similar concerns about the lack of a

significant audience for contemporary poetry were expressed in the general media. One of the most sustained discussions of this kind took place in a chain of four articles that appeared in the *Globe and Mail* and *Books in Canada*. The discussion was begun in the *Globe* by Kristjana Gunnars who, despite noting that poetry presently faced an "uninterested community," romantically proclaimed that there was an irreducible "human craving" for poetry "as strong as hunger, thirst and relief from pain," a craving that would lead to poetry being called upon to heal Canada's recurrent constitutional wounds (C15). Cary Fagan's prompt response to Gunnars, in the October 1990 *Books in Canada*, attracted notice in the daily "best home entertainment" endorsements of the *Globe*. Ignoring the implications of Gunnars' move to biologize poetry, Fagan focused on the success of recent specialized poetries—his examples were poetries "of feminism" and "of anticolonialism"—in finding "discerning if small audiences." He argued that the recent experiences of publishers indicated that no poet "was able to speak to the whole country" but that many could find readers in "political interest groups" (10). Fagan's article was in its turn taken to task in the *Globe* on December 12 by playwright Richard Sanger, who pointed to the example of popular music in suggesting that a metrical poetry that avoided political issues, and was "escapist, frivolous, pleasurable or even untrue" could find a large audience, and that politically engaged poems "catering to specialized groups" were precisely what was making poetry "socially insignificant" (C1). An escapist, frivolous poetry, he implied, could return poetry to social significance. On January 2nd, 1991, Sanger was himself taken on by *Globe* columnist John Cruickshank. Writing that "Sanger claims no one reads poetry in this country because our poets are humourless ideologues and their poems are prosy political screeds," Cruickshank argued that it is 'clumsy' writing rather than political commitment that creates "bad verse," and suggested that the readers who shun contemporary poetry shun equally the escapist rhymes of "high school yearbooks" and the metrical texts of "Wordsworth, Chaucer, Dante, Virgil, Homer and King David" (C1).

Although some readers might dismiss this second group of articles as 'mere' journalism, removed from actual changes in poetic discourse, its close resemblance to the laments appearing in literary magazines, together with the presence of practicing poets among the authors of both groups, suggests that it is at very least also a sign of discursive change and struggle. Throughout the conflicting representations of the articles and their various struggles with 'badness' and readership, a common element persisted: a yearning for a transcendent poetry. Solway wrote nostalgically of a poetry that once honoured "degree and precedence." Lane described poetry as a "rare gift" and invoked Yeats' golden bough (4). Ioannou called for "intense melodies" that could "dare to interpret the future" (32). Gunnars presented a poetry that "sees life" and transcends ethnic barriers by showing "what kind of blood flows in our neighbour's veins" (C15). Fagan's nationalist note of calling for a poetry "spacious enough to embrace us all" (10) invoked the related notion of a transcendent humanity.

●◆

Statistical evidence that might confirm whether or not there has been a decline in Canada in the number of volumes of poetry sold, or a decline in average sales per title, is difficult to obtain. Neither the Applebaum-Hebert Commission or the Ontario Royal Commission on Book Publishing distinguished poetry titles; the recent Canada Council studies of sales patterns among publishers supported by the Council's 'Block Grant' programme distinguish poetry but are not able to include the numerous 'desktop' publishers that may not qualify for the programme but nevertheless appear (on such evidence as book reviews and the offerings of Toronto's biannual Small Press Book Fair), to publish more than half of Canadian poetry titles.[1] The Council studies indicate that the seventy English-language presses supported by the programme during 1983-86 published a total of approximately sixty-five poetry titles annually, and that the roughly 80 English-language publishers supported during 1986-91 published a total of approximately 117 poetry titles annually. In 1985 the average press run was 935 copies, the average first-year sales 365 copies, and the average sales after two years 459 copies (49% of the press run). In 1986 the average press run was 880 copies, the average first-year sales 397 copies, and the average sales after two years 468 copies (or 53% of the press run). In 1989, the last for which there are full statistics, the average press run was also 880 copies, the average first-year sales 317 copies, and the average sales after two years 347 copies (or 42 % of the print run). The Block Grant regulation that requires participating presses to print a minimum of 500 copies suggests that the range between the smallest and largest print runs was likely narrow. The publishers I have spoken with[2] indicate that library sales per poetry title are now as low as 50 copies, and that by far the majority of their sales occur through trade bookstores. Gordon Platt, the Canada Council officer who administers the Block Grant programme, estimates that most of the participating publishers make the majority of their sales in their home region.[3] His statistics indicate that the highest average sales of poetry over the

1985-89 period were achieved by publishers located on the prairies: 529 copies. Other regional averages over these years were Ontario 435, British Columbia 410, and the Atlantic provinces 391. Québec's average, which included both English- and French-language publishers, was the lowest overall at 383. The highest average sales for a year was achieved by the prairies in 1987 with 639 copies; the lowest was by Québec in 1989 with 295 copies.

There are no comparable figures available for the 1970s. However, the minimum press run of 500 copies has been a part of the Block Grant programme since its founding in 1973. In an article published that year, Dave Godfrey estimated that there were then 217 Canadian publishers of all kinds in both languages; the Canada Council currently supports 113 French and English-language literary publishers. Printing records for most of the poetry-publishing presses of the period are not publicly available, and few publishers, except for Coach House Press, noted the press run in their colophon statements. The few such statements, however, are probably representative (two writers who published poetry in this period with both Coach House and McClelland and Stewart, George Bowering and David McFadden, have told me that their sales with the two presses have been usually similar, and sometimes slightly greater with Coach House), and suggest that print runs were at least no less than they are presently. The first edition of Michael Ondaatje's first book, *The Dainty Monsters*, from Coach House Press in 1967, notes a print run of 500 copies; its 1973 "third edition," printed when he was still not a canonical poet, indicates a printing of 1000. M. Lakshmi Gill's *Mind Walls* (Fiddlehead, 1970) records a printing of 500 copies; Daphne Marlatt's *Vancouver Poems* (Coach House, 1972) a printing of 1000; Christopher Dewdney's *A*

Palaeozoic Geology of London, Ontario (Coach House, 1973) a printing of 750; Patrick Friesen's *Bluebottle* (Turnstone, 1977) a printing of 750; Judith Fitzgerald's *Lacerating Heartwood* (Coach House, 1977) a printing of 1000; Robert Kroetsch's *Seed Catalogue* (Turnstone, 1977) a printing of 1000; bpNichol and Steve McCaffery's *In England Now That Spring* (Aya, 1979) a printing of 733; and Phyllis Webb's *Wilson's Bowl* (Coach House, 1980) a printing of 1500. The colophons and printer's records of bpNichol's *The Martyrology*, a continuing poem published by Coach House in six volumes throughout the two decades, and which received increasing critical attention in the 1980s, suggests that its overall readership has diminished. Book 1 and Book 2 were both published in 1972 in editions of 1000, and were reprinted in a combined edition of 1000 in 1977, and of 500 in 1992. Books 3 & 4 were printed in an edition of 1500 in 1976, and reprinted in an edition of 500 copies in 1993. The printer's records indicate that Book 5 (1982) and Book 6 (1987) were printed in editions of 750 copies; Book 6 went out of print in 1990, and approximately 150 of Book 5 remain unsold. Book '7&', published as *Gifts* in an edition of 1000 copies in fall 1990, had by the end of that year sold 390. While one could argue that *The Martyrology* is a difficult and unrepresentative text, with a highly specialized audience, one could also view it as potentially a median text in terms of readership, with neither the small audience that the writing of non-canonic poets unattached to any constituency finds, nor the larger audience that the writing of canonic poets like Purdy or Atwood has often found.

•◊

What is much easier to confirm about the past decade is that major ownership and policy changes occurred within

Canadian publishing—changes that affected editorial selection and distribution in all genres, and particularly poetry. What occurred was the defeat of early 1970s dreams of expanding Canadian-owned capitalist book production, and the retreat of many of the most ambitious new would-be 'national' publishers either back into petty-commodity publishing or, in a very few cases, into mergers with large corporations. One of the major causes of this defeat was a distribution system glutted with the low-priced books of American-based multinational publishers. At the beginning of the 1970s most significant Canadian publishers of poetry were located in Ontario, and either enjoyed or aspired to a national profile. McClelland and Stewart, Macmillan of Canada, and Oxford University Press had regular seasonal poetry lists, as did smaller Ontario presses like Oberon, House of Anansi, Press Porcepic, Coach House Press, NC Press. The national aspirations of the latter were marked by their frequent publishing of nationally framed titles— Oberon's *New Canadian Stories*, Coach House's *The Story so Far* and *The Long Poem Anthology*, Anansi's *Survival* and *Lament for a Nation*, Porcepic's *Our Nature, Our Voices*, NC Press's *The Trade Union Movement of Canada*.

By the end of the 1980s, among the large publishers only McClelland and Stewart regularly published poetry; among the smaller nationalist presses House of Anansi had become a literary division of General Publishing, and Press Porcepic had discontinued poetry publication. Although the largest concentration of publishers was still in Ontario (the Canada Council reports its 1986 English-language Block Grant recipients to be almost half in Ontario, a fifth each in the Atlantic and Prairie provinces, and 14 per cent in British Columbia), these had more and more become regional presses that made most of their sales in their home provinces. Some of the most active presses in poetry publication were now ones whose regional focuses were often evident in their names—Newfoundland's Breakwater Books, Winnipeg's Turnstone Press, Edmonton's NeWest Press, Vancouver's Harbour Press and Pulp Press, Saskatoon's Thistledown Press. Of sixty-five English-language poetry titles published by Canada Council publishers in 1986-87, thirty-seven were published in British Columbia or in the Atlantic or Prairie regions. Other presses focused much of their programmes on ethnic or gender constituencies: Women's Press, Press Gang, and Ragweed Press on women's writing; Sister Vision Press on writing by 'women of colour'; Pemmican Publishers and Theytus Books on native Indian writing; Williams-Wallace on black writing. Perhaps an even more significant change has been the way in which many of these presses have undertaken the legitimating tasks of criticism and canon formation previously the nearly exclusive functions of Ontario presses. The conception of canonicity they have employed has not been the national one of the 1970s; it has been plural, and linked directly to the presses' special constituencies. In the last few years Turnstone Press has published anthologies of prairie long poems and of Manitoba short stories, a collection of critical studies, *Contemporary Manitoba Writers*, and Dennis Cooley's *The Vernacular Muse*; Pulp Press anthologies of Vancouver poetry, East Vancouver poetry and of 'work' writing; Women's Press the anthologies *Baker's Dozen: Stories by Women*, *Dykeversions: Lesbian Short Fiction*, and *Dykewords: Lesbian Writing*; NeWest Press the fiction anthologies *Alberta Bound* and *Alberta ReBound*, the anthology of writing by Western Canadian native women *Writing the Circle*, and collections of critical essays on western writers; Press Gang the anthologies

Telling It: Women and Language Across Cultures and *InVersions: Writing by Dykes, Queers & Lesbians*; Regina's Coteau Books anthologies of new Saskatchewan poets and of stories from Saskatchewan. The success of these special-audience presses has complicated any attempt to understand poetry's readership; if 2000 copies of a nationally distributed book are sold in 1975, and a decade later 500 copies each of four 'regional' titles are sold in four different constituencies, has the circulation and 'power' of poetry increased or decreased?

•◊

Precisely why so many special constituencies became active in Canada during the 1980s, and why their power to interpellate individual subjects often eclipsed that of national and transnational ideologies, is much too complex a question to consider at any length here (beyond the suggestions made in the opening chapter), although it is a question that will ultimately be necessary to any large understanding of the recent history of Canadian publishing. Certainly the growth of new, special-constituency focused, small publishers was both enabled by the growth of these constituencies and enabling of such growth; the publishers often worked to record, define, reify and construct these constituencies' beliefs about themselves. This regional and/or special interest activity occurred in the context of a Central Canada electorally and culturally weakened by the recurrent strength of Québec separatism. It occurred also against a backdrop of enormous growth of the multinational economy, visible in the malls and storefronts even of small-town Canada, and of this economy's defeat of national economic planning, visible in evolution of the European Economic Community or in Canada-US Free Trade Agreement. The triumph of multinational capitalism appears both to have discredited national restraints on regional and other special-interest values (including the ethnically-founded sovereigntist aspirations of Québec), and to have created what one might call a 'resistance-vacuum' in the space in which nationalist ideologies had previously resisted external hegemonies—a vacuum which, if we follow Richard Terdiman's theorizing of resistance, the multinational may have indirectly 'called forth' resisting minority ideologies to fill. The clearly visible economic nature of the new multinationalism, uncloaked by the kinds of 'rationalizing' mythologies and ideologies that had concealed the economic and instrumental emphases of a nation-state, may also have operated to the general discredit of what Jean-François Lyotard calls metanarrative, and have opened the way for cultural assertions of difference even as the new multinational economic order burgeoned. In Canadian publishing what one finds in the 1980s is the national configuration being squeezed from two sides—from the multinational, where the Canadian publisher is bought out by international-scale diversified companies like Brascan or Torstar, or increasingly allied through agency agreements with international publishers, and from the regional, where the Canadian publisher's national market is re-made into a collage of special interest markets each dominated by two or three petty-commodity publishers.

⚬

One dramatic effect of regionalization on Canadian poetry, and further symptom of how suddenly the power relationships within Canadian literature have changed, has been the extraordinary disarray of the contemporary poetry canon as constructed by the 1980s' nationally-conceived anthologies. In the 1970s there were three academic anthologies of contemporary Canadian poetry available for classroom use—Gary Geddes and Phyllis Bruce's *15 Canadian Poets* (1970), Eli Mandel's *Poets of Contemporary Canada* (1972), and John Newlove's *Canadian Poetry: The Modern Era* (1977). All were edited by writers who had some association with Canadian nationalism: Geddes was editor of Copp Clark's monograph series Studies in Canadian Literature; Mandel was concurrently editing two other collections of Canadian poetry and the anthology *Contexts of Canadian Criticism*; Newlove was senior literary editor for his anthology's publisher, McClelland and Stewart. Although these anthologies covered slightly different periods (the Newlove collecting thirty poets who mostly began publishing after 1940, the Geddes and Bruce fifteen from a similar period, and the Mandel focusing on ten who began publishing after 1955), they showed considerable agreement about which poets should be represented. Of the fifteen poets in the Geddes and Bruce, all but two appeared in Newlove; of the ten in Mandel all but two appeared in Newlove, and all but three in the Geddes and Bruce. Although the disagreements concerned, as one might expect, mostly poets who were relatively young in the 1970s (Rosenblatt, b. 1933, Bissett, b. 1939, Coleman and Nichol, b. 1944), the editors were unanimous about Ondaatje (b. 1943), MacEwen (b. 1941), Atwood (b. 1939), and Newlove (b. 1938). The dimensions of this consensus were underlined by a prefatory note in the Newlove that its selection was "based on a survey...of Canadian literature instructors in universities across the country" (13). The consensus was also confirmed by the twentieth-century poetry included in the most widely used general academic anthology of Canadian prose and poetry of the period: Klinck and

Watters' *Canadian Anthology* (1966). Fourteen of Geddes and Bruce's fifteen, eight of Mandel's ten, and twenty-six of Newlove's thirty were included within its 1974 third edition.

The late 1970s and early 80s brought three further academic anthologies of contemporary poetry: Geddes and Bruce's *15 Canadian Poets Plus Five* (a 1978 revision of their 1970 collection), volume 2 of David and Lecker's two-volume historical anthology *Canadian Poetry* (1982), offering twenty-two poets born 1918 and after, and Bowering's *The Contemporary Canadian Poem Anthology* (1983) also with twenty poets, most of whom began publishing after 1960. The editors of the new collections again had nationalist affiliations. Bowering was the author of the satirical *At War with the U.S.* and of two novels, *A Short Sad Book* and *Burning Water*, that interrogated various national myths. David and Lecker were the owners of ECW Press, whose principal publications have been series of bibliographies and critical guides for Canadian literature teaching. However, the 1970 consensus began to vanish. Of the 'Plus 5' poets added by Geddes and Bruce, none had appeared in the Mandel anthology, and only those more than fifty years old (Livesay, Page and Webb) in the Newlove. Only six poets appeared in all three of the new anthologies: Ondaatje, Bowering, MacEwen, and Atwood, who had also been unanimous selections in the 1970s, plus the somewhat older Webb and D.G. Jones. Of Bowering's twenty writers, only ten appeared in David and Lecker, and seven in Geddes and Bruce. Although the Geddes/Bruce and David/Lecker agreed on almost all of their older poets, they disagreed on most of the younger—on Nichol and Coleman (b. 1944), Marlatt (b. 1943), Lee and Bissett (b. 1939). More interestingly, even though a decade had gone by, the youngest writer either included was still Coleman (b. 1944). Even Bowering, who offered the largest proportion of writers born after 1940, could offer only one writer born later than 1944, Christopher Dewdney (b. 1951).

Near the end of the 1980s Geddes presented a third revision of *15 Canadian Poets*, now titled *15 Canadian Poets x 2*. Coleman was dropped from the anthology and eleven new poets added. Most of these, however, were born before 1930, as Geddes acted to transform what had been in 1970 a contemporary anthology into a historical one. The new 'younger poets' included Geddes himself (b. 1940), Robert Bringhurst (b. 1946), and Bronwen Wallace (b. 1949). In eighteen years, despite a doubling of the number of poets, the age of the youngest poet in the anthology had risen from twenty-six to thirty-nine years.

The three historical multi-genre academic anthologies of the 1980s also had editors with strong links to Ontario and to the institutional structures of Canadian literature. These, Daymond and Monkman's *Literature in Canada* (1978), Bennett and Brown's *An Anthology of Canadian Literature in English* (1983), and David and Lecker's *The New Canadian Anthology* (1988), showed both a similar lack of consensus and a similar aversion to selecting younger poets. Of thirty poets born since 1926, the anthologies agreed on ten. Of twenty-one born since 1935, they agreed on five. Out of seven poets born after 1944, they agreed on none. Combining these with the 1980s poetry anthologies, one finds that of the forty-two poets they collected with birth dates in 1926 or later, they showed fifty per cent agreement on fifteen, and full agreement on only five.

There were also four major trade[4] anthologies of Canadian poetry published in the 1980s, two of these edited by prominent nationalists. Margaret Atwood's *The New Oxford Book of Canadian Verse in English*, Ralph Gustafson's fourth edition of *The Penguin Book of Canadian Verse* (1984), Ken Norris's *Canadian Poetry Now: 20 Poets of the 80s,* and Dennis Lee's *The New Canadian Poets, 1970-1985* (1986) together collected ninety-one poets born 1926 or later. Lee collected twenty-seven poets born 1944 or later, out of forty-three poets overall. Atwood concurred with fourteen of these, perhaps not surprisingly given her acknowledgement of having herself enjoyed Lee's "advice...about the most recent poetry" (xl). Gustafson, however, concurred with only three—the only three of his poets born later than 1944. Norris, whose twenty poets were *all* born in 1945 or after, agreed with thirteen of Lee's selections, with nine of Atwood's, and with none of Gustafson's. The four anthologies suggest no shortage of poets or poetry, and again considerable lack of editorial agreement. A comparison of Lee's *The New Canadian Poets* and Geddes and Bruce's *15 Canadian Poets* of 1970 suggests that a large gap was opening in the canon-forming process. A choice of fifteen poets largely confirmed by rival academic anthologies had become by 1986 a choice of forty-four of whom only thirteen were agreed upon by at least one academic anthologist and only three by more than one.

One general implication of these anthologies is that the national canon of Canadian poetry has been very little changed since the late 1970s. Nearly all of the editors of academic anthologies have been timid about representing writers born after the second world war. Most of the changes that have occurred have involved older writers, and usually women writers. The three Geddes anthologies illustrate this change fairly clearly. To the original twelve men and three women of *15 Canadian Poets*, whose birthdates ran from 1904-1944, the 1978 edition added one man, Patrick Lane (b. 1939), and four women, Dorothy Livesay (b. 1909), P.K.

Page (b. 1917), Phyllis Webb (b. 1927), and Pat Lowther (b. 1935). The addition of Livesay, Page, and Webb, writers already acknowledged as canonical in 1970s multi-genre anthologies such as the Klinck and Watters, helped Geddes and Bruce redress a gender imbalance that had the potential to reduce the anthology's course adoptions as the strength of feminism increased in universities. At the same time this addition appears to have helped them avoid dealing with active younger women writers. The one younger woman they added, Pat Lowther, had died three years earlier. The five additions were also all from western Canada, and radically altered the 1970 edition's regional representation of three poets from the west, eleven from Ontario and Québec, and one from the maritimes.

Geddes' 1988 edition continued this tendency to turn to the past in order to respond to the power shifts and political contentions of the present. It dropped one male poet (Coleman, the youngest of the 1970 edition's writers, and associated with the waning power of 1970s counter-culture), and added seven men and four women. Two of the men, Pratt (b. 1883) and Scott (b. 1899), moved the period of the anthology back into the 1920s and buttressed its national authority. Two others, Gustafson (b. 1909) and Klein (b. 1909), along with Waddington (b. 1917), revised, diversified, and expanded its representations of modernism. The youngest of the additions, Kroetsch (b. 1926), Szumigalski (b. 1926), Geddes (b. 1940), Wallace (b. 1945), Bringhurst (b. 1946) and Sarah (b. 1949), were, apart from Kroetsch, conservative choices of poets yet undistinguished by critical attention. Klein and Waddington expanded the collection's ethnic representation without acknowledgement of any of the younger writers who mark their work with ethnicity or race. Szumigalski was from the prairies, but did not represent the radical prairie poetics of Gunnars, Suknaski, Friesen or Cooley. Wallace and Sarah offered feminist themes but not the unsettling epistemological challenges of Marlatt, Tostevin, Fitzgerald, or di Michele, or the overt lesbianism of Marlatt or Mouré. Among male poets, Geddes shied noticeably away from many of those whose work most threatens the liberal humanist assumptions of the lyric: bissett, Nichol, Dewdney, McCaffery, Scobie, or Lush. In general, his revisions worked to save the canon while responding only minimally to potentially disruptive social change. This minimal response was mostly to how such change has altered the way poetries in circulation before 1970 are read; his response to new writing radically marked by ethnicity, feminism, regionalism or by other challenges to totality, was to represent it through its less extreme manifestations.

⚓

In introducing *The New Canadian Poets, 1970-1985*, Dennis Lee expressed astonishment that "[m]any of the best new poets were unfamiliar with one another's work. Not only that: often they were unaware of each other's *names*" (xvii). Lee attributed this situation in part to the expansion of poetry publishing in the 1970s and to the "rise of regional presses" many of whose "titles were never seen outside their home province" (xvii-xviii). He did not consider the possibility that his writers might not have wished to know each other's names, or experienced themselves as living in 'home' communities defined in other than 'provincial' terms.[5] Despite various 'poetry wars'—the McGill Group and the Maple Leaf poets, *Preview* and *First Statement*, Sutherland's attack on Robert Finch, Birney's resignation from editorship of *Canadian Poetry Magazine*, Robin

Mathews' attacks on *Tish*, the *Tish* poets' critiques of humanism—critical conceptions of twentieth-century Canadian poetry were dominated, at least until the late 1970s, by two closely related ideologies. One was the aesthetic/humanist ideology that assumes that the writing of poetry reveals and celebrates human creativity and the spiritual dimensions of a common humanity, and that the reading of it is morally beneficial through its enlarging of one's understanding of humanity. This was the view of many of the initiators of the institutionalized study of Canadian literature—Smith, Woodcock, and Frye in particular. The second was a nationalist ideology in which it is not merely a shared humanity that joins Canadian writers but a common humanity *as Canadians*.[6] This Canadianness signified *difference*, a difference from other nationalities (together with a potential to be oppressed by them), *homogeneity*, an identity with other Canadians, and *universality*, an impulse to national identification that the Canadian also shares with other humans. Thus while this nationalism was critical of the aesthetic/humanist ideology for being apolitical, it reinstalled many of its attributes—its valuing of cultural recurrence, its belief that art is morally and spiritually instructive—within national parameters. It is these values that those who now lament the apparent passing of poetry appeal to: Lane for the "fabled markets" of a Yeatsian Byzantium (4), Solway for a poetry "which honours the canons and attitudes of its masonic past" (130), the nationalist Lee for a time when Canadian poets all read one another (or at least identified with 'provinces'), the similarly nationalist Fagan for a poetry "spacious enough to embrace us" (10).

But, as Lee found, there now appear to be many poets who do not experience these sorts of categories. Like humanist nationalists, these poets are constructing difference and identity, perceiving conflict and oppression, but doing so within metaphors and grids other than national ones. There are even other kinds of nationalism, evident both now and as early as the 1960s—nationalisms which value the state as a field of discourse, or as a strategic social construction that enables difference and facilitates disparate social goals. One striking feature of the current national Canadian literature anthologies is that they have continued to be edited by poets and scholars of the humanist-nationalist generation. Meanwhile, the succeeding generation has constructed Canada and Canadian writing in terms of other tensions, identities, audiences, and discourses. This generation has produced numerous compilers of regional anthologies (Alan Safarik, Lorna Crozier, Antonio d'Alfonso, Mark Duncan, Andre Farkas), of feminist anthologies (Rosemary Sullivan, Mary di Michele, Betsy Warland, Frances Rooney, Judith Fitzgerald), and of racial or ethnic anthologies (Gerry Shikatani, Joseph Pivato, Pier Giorgio di Cicco) but as yet almost none for anthologies founded on the concept of 'Canadianness.'[7] It has constructed strong writers within the perspectives of those constituencies (Daphne Marlatt, Betsy Warland, Bronwen Wallace within differing feminist communities; Tom Wayman, Jeff Derksen, Steve McCaffery within certain left political communities; Dennis Cooley, Andrew Suknaski, Kristjana Gunnars within a prairie context; Dionne Brand, Marlene Nourbese Philip and Lillian Allen within the Toronto black community) but constructed none as before all else a national writer. When Dionne Brand writes "no language is neutral" she is writing of a Canada configured much differently from that envisioned thirty years earlier by Michele Lalonde when writing "speak white" or Margaret

Atwood when writing "This is my country under glass" (1968, 18). She is also imagining a much different audience.

With what appears to be at least the temporary diminishing in power of national literary constructions, and with the shrinking of a nationally-constituted literary audience, it has been extremely difficult for a Canadian poet not discursively affiliated with some regional, feminist, ethnic, racial, or otherwise ideological community to find audience, recognition, or identity. Affiliations with humanism that tied writer and reader throughout much of Birney's and Page's writing lives, or with a nationalist humanism in the case of Pratt, no longer seem to have the power to interpellate readers for writers whose fellow citizens are as preoccupied with difference as with identity, or who envision difference within more complex systems of conflict than such binaries as liberality-cupidity, French-English, female-male, colony-empire, or black-white. The one 'new' poet to rise to undisputed national prominence since 1970 has been Robert Kroetsch, who interestingly had already been constructed (in articles like Donald Cameron's "Robert Kroetsch: The American Experience and the Canadian Voice" [1972], or his own "Unhiding the Hidden: Recent Canadian Fiction" [1973]) by the early 1970s as both a theorist of Canadian culture and a novelist who wrote of 'Canada,' but who in his first books of poetry (*The Stone Hammer Poems* [1975], *The Ledger* [1975], and *Seed Catalogue* [1977]) quickly positioned himself in terms of both a regional 'prairie' identity and a transnational poststructuralist one.

The shift away from humanism and nationalism has been particularly difficult for lyric poetry, which has tended to be the default subgenre of anthologies of 'Canadian' poetry (in contrast, anthologies of other poetry subgenres like Ondaatje's *The Long Poem Anthology* [1979] or Barbour and Scobie's *The Maple Laugh Forever* [1981] have tended to efface their Canadiannness). The lyric's assumptions of transcendent inspiration run emphatically counter to the assumptions of historical and material particularity on which the power of new special constituency literatures rest. The lyric poet's reliance on humanism, that an individual voice can be accessible and valuable to others across all class, gender, and culture lines because poet and reader participate in a common humanity, appears to be colliding with a view of poetry in which it is co-authored by writer and constituency, and in which its value lies in the meanings it can produce for that constituency, or in the way in which it alters language so that it is more responsive to that constituency. The cry that 'poetry is dead,' in the case of Solway, Sanger, or Fitzgerald, may be more a cry that the lyric poem is in difficulty than the categorical declaration it appears to be. Again it is notable that among the younger Canadian poets who have found any recognition in the last twenty years, so few of them are lyric poets and so many have addressed their work to particular discursive communities (Wayman, Howard White, Marlatt, Warland, Gunnars, Cooley, Friesen, Arnason, McCaffery, Brand, Wallace, Suknaski, Dewdney), and have received their recognition within these communities. It is also notable that the theorists among this generation—Cooley, Godard, Shirley Neuman, Smaro Kamboureli, Gail Scott, Wayman—have by and large viewed language as a social construct historically shaped to favor particular classes, groups, ethnicities and regions, and not as the transcultural instrument of Smith, Frye, or even Louis Dudek.

Has Canadian poetry been in crisis? The answer depends on whether one understands 'Canadian poetry' to designate a national paradigm or merely poetry written in Canada. The latter appears in many ways to be as productive and disputed a thing as it ever has been. Although Canadian poetry may have lost its long-standing cultural utility as a delineator of national character (of what Alan R. Knight, in surveying Canadian poetry anthologies from Dewart to Atwood, has called "true and harmonious secular emotions" [148]), it seems to have found new use-value in elaborating or reifying the self-constructions of special-interest constituencies, and in implicitly arguing thereby the nation as an enabler of constituencies of equal value to itself. That is, Canadian poetry may only be in crisis to the extent that the national federation is in crisis. From Toronto, or from Ontario, where most Canadian poetry in other years was written, published or at least legitimated, it may well seem that poetry is in confusion or decline, or is extremely difficult to circulate nationally, much as it may also seem that Canada in the 1980s and 90s has been fragmented, and difficult to govern. But from within women's writing, or from Edmonton, or from one of the First Nations' presses, the current Canada may seem superior to a past one of Central Canadian consensus, and poetry may seem to have even more power to reify experience, validate lives, and define communities than it had in the past. The great problem at the moment may not be the writing of poetry, but the discovering of ways to get any kind of text to circulate between the constituent parts of the Canadian community. New non-centralizing national institutions may be needed in poetry as much as they are in national politics. Much like the currently makeshift 'anthology' of Canadian provinces, the Canadian poetry institution as we have known it—an institution which has assumed individual poets rather than poets radically imbricated in asymmetrical groups, discourses, or regions—may be incapable of facilitating the kinds of collisions and exchanges which will be needed to bring together a new 'national' gathering. Meanwhile, the groups which currently have the social power to legitimize the national circulation of texts may continue to invest their energies in much different, transnational affiliations.

NOTES

[1] In the overall structure of Canadian poetry publishing, the presses that receive Block Grants are a highly significant group. They are Canadian-owned publishers with resources to publish at least 6 titles a year, in editions of àt least 48 pages, and in print runs of at least 500 copies. In the last decade they have published nearly all of the prize-winning poetry titles. Although they range in size from McClelland and Stewart to presses that operate out of a postal box and publish the minimum required by the program, most would have gross sales of less than $100,000. The only poetry publishing presses that fall outside this group are the few branch plant publishers that publish Canadian poetry, and the numerous very small presses—'desktop publishers'—that publish chapbooks in relatively short print runs. Although the latter may distribute only within a single city, or sell mainly at cultural events or through a postal box, their persistence and ubiquity in Canada are also indicators that poetry in Canada is far from moribund.

[2] Karl Siegler of Talonbooks, Bev Daurio of Mercury Press, Margaret McClintock of Coach House Press and Paul Dutton of Underwhich Editions.

[3] Telephone interview, 1 March, 1991.

[4] Writing of the feminist essays of Gail Scott, Brian Edwards comments that "to theorize and address difference is to recognize its particularity at the level of individual production against the homogenising zeal of tourist guides to the territory" (154). The current preoccupation with difference within Canadian poetry, among writers, publishers and readers, makes it extremely difficult to construct tourist guides to it, or even to construct a knowledge of it that could be construed as 'Canadian poetry.'

[5] Although these four are trade anthologies in the sense that their primary market appears to have been commercial bookstores rather than college course adoption, this distinction is a fairly loose one in Canada where trade books are often adopted as textbooks and where publishers often design books to be sold in both markets. Often, as in the case of the Gustafson anthology in Canada, a book becomes trade title within a specific national market because of its failure to gain academic adoption. In poetry, the two markets can sometimes be distinguished by discourse, where the academic anthology conventionally presents itself in a empirical discourse (Newlove's *Canadian Poetry: The Modern Era*) and the trade

anthology presents itself in a discourse of excitement or persuasion (Al Purdy's 1971 anthology *Storm Warning*).

6 Although Canadian literary nationalists, through their arguing of the particularity of human social forms within specific national boundaries, have usually presented themselves as contending against the generalities of humanism, they have for the most part also been careful to maintain the compatibility of a Canadian national literature with humanism. Thus D.G. Jones argued that the Canadian imagination participates in "themes common to western literature" (6), and John Moss that it shares "objectives of art" that are "universal" (1974, 8). Such nationalism should be distinguished from others that view both the nation and humanity as social constructions.

7 In many of this generation's anthologies the nation is present merely as an implicit secondary category, as in anthologies of women's writing where the fact that the poets are all Canadian women (like Mary di Michele's *Anything is Possible* [1984] or Rhea Tregebov's *Sudden Miracles* [1991]) is left unstated, or generic anthologies (Thesen's *The New Long Poem Anthology* [1991]) where the fact that these are all Canadian long poems is unstated. In others the relegation of 'Canadian' to the subtitle announces it to be secondary to the category declared in the title (as in Fitzgerald's *Sp/elles: Poetry by Canadian Women* [1986].

English-Canadian Literature Periodicals

There are eight journals that focus principally on the theorization of English-Canadian writing. By theorization I mean not only inquiry into the relationship between texts and cultural practice, into the process by which meanings are constructed, or into the implicit and explicit assumptions of literary interpretation, but also explication, interpretation and evaluation, the processes by which the particulars of texts are assigned connections with epistemological categories, their meanings are abstracted, their cultural functions hypothesized. Eight is a large number by contrast to the absence of such journals that preceded the founding of George Woodcock's *Canadian Literature* in 1959, but not a particularly large number in terms of the geography of English-Canada, the 10 provinces and 15 or so large cities in which English-Canada has significant populations. Four of these journals define themselves in terms of Canadianism: *Canadian Literature* itself, *Essays on Canadian Writing*, *Studies in Canadian Literature*, *Canadian Poetry*; four define themselves in terms of language: *Line*, recently become *West Coast Line*, *Signature*, which very recently ceased publication, *Tessera*, and my own *Open Letter*. Two major semes operate at the far edges of these titles: that of unity under the sign 'Canadian,' and that of difference under, as might be expected, various signs of the open, the signature, the fragment, or the line. By geography three of these journals come from British Columbia, three from Ontario, one from New Brunswick, and one, *Tessera*, operated until 1992 managerially in British Columbia and Ontario, and editorially in British Columbia, Ontario and Québec. These are of course not all of the magazines and journals that attempt to mediate between texts and readers. There are the book review journals *Brick* and *Journal of Canadian Poetry*. There are various magazines that mix the occasional critical essay with other kinds of writing—like *Prairie Fire* or *Rampike*, there are polemic art and culture magazines like *What* and *Fuse*, and there are critical journals such as *Ariel*, *Mosaic*, and *English Studies in Canada* that from time to time publish essays on Canadian topics.

My personal connection with the eight journals I'm looking at is not limited to *Open Letter*. I was on the editorial advisory board of *Signature*, one of my graduate students at York University in the 1970s, Jack David, is co-editor of *Essays on Canadian Writing*, one of my office mates from my teaching assistant days at UBC, Bill New, is editor of *Canadian Literature*, one of the contributing editors of *Open Letter*, Barbara Godard, also a former colleague of mine at York, plays a major editorial role in *Tessera*, a current colleague of mine at Western Ontario, David Bentley, edits *Canadian Poetry*. Such a network of connections is not uncommon in Canadian literature, and points to the way in which those who engage in literary commentary in Canada, from whatever ideological position, not only enter into an existing institutional structure but become part of that structure, both shaped by what it enables them to do and shaping what it does. Friendship, the ongoing processes of professional interaction, and even respect for ideological difference can cause the boundaries between the periodicals to be less firm than their general focuses would lead one to expect. For example, I have published essays in all of these journals except *Signature* and *Tessera*; in 28 years of publishing *Open Letter*, I have also successfully solicited contributions by Bill New, Barbara Godard, David Bentley, *West Coast Line*'s Roy Miki, *Tessera*'s Daphne Marlatt, and *Signature*'s Stephen Scobie and Smaro Kamboureli.

The eight journals also intersect in their funding relationships: *Canadian Literature* receives funding from the Social Sciences and Humanities Research Council of Canada (SSHRCC), *Open Letter* and *Tessera* from the Canada Council (CC) and the Ontario Arts Council (OAC), *Essays on Canadian Writing* from the SSHRCC and the OAC; *Studies in Canadian Literature* and *Canadian Poetry* have both received SSHRCC funding and been recently denied continuation; *Signature*'s recent closing was due to two successive funding rejections by the SSHRCC. Adding to this intersection is the frequent participation of contributors to all eight journals on the juries of the funding bodies.

Much paranoia, anger, and suspicion can attach themselves to this process of interaction and intersection. Attacks on "establishment" (like John Sutherland's on A.J.M. Smith), accusations of conspiracy (like Robin Mathews' on George Bowering or Robert Lecker's on W.J. Keith), claims about exclusion (like feminist revisions of the Canadian modernist poetry canon), and challenges to canonicity (like Paul Stuewe's attacks on Grove and Callaghan) are all conventional gestures within the literary and criticism communities and characteristic aspects of their operations. For the overall literary institution isn't limited to the specifically-focused journals I'm looking at here, but ranges far around them through school and university classrooms, publishing houses of all kinds, literary quarterlies like *The Malahat* or *Quarry*, newspapers, trade journals like *Prairie Bookworld* or *Quill and Quire*, 'counter-culture' journals like

Fuse or *Ruebsaat's Magazine*, and government agencies like the Canada Council. Perhaps from a first publication in a high school newspaper, individuals enter wittingly or unwittingly into this institution's genres and conflicts, and sometimes re-position themselves many times within its manifestations. In no sense is there a firm boundary between the overall literary institution and textuality generally, or between it and the culture at large. For literary codes and conflicts are also cultural codes and conflicts. This is why some of us *care* about literary texts, why we intervene on behalf of some and not others, why we write articles or books like this one.

The critical journals of Canadian literature, of course, are a bit like those proverbial mills that grind slow but exceeding fine. When writers and book publishers think of interventions on behalf of a text, they often think of the kinds of short-term interventions that affect its immediate reception—radio and television appearances, newspaper and news magazine reviews that appear within the month of publication. The critical journals are not concerned with a text's short-term circulation but with its persistence in cultural memory, and particularly with its power to act within the intertextual field which students are initiated into during their ten to twenty years of primary, secondary and postsecondary education. Contrary to popular myth—a myth one can encounter from nearly any political position—the academy is not distinct from an equally distinct 'popular' culture; both are products of the general culture, and function equally both among its determinants and as each other's determinants. Those who protest against "ivory tower intellectuals" or "academic feminists" have themselves been produced by texts and discourses that have been disseminated through the academy both from and into the general media, and both from and into grade and high school curricula, as have the 'academics' for whom they declare mistrust.

My point is that the power of academic critical journals, while slow moving, is not inconsiderable. These journals occupy a crucial node in a network which both begins and ends with the educational formation of those who write, edit, and publish texts, and those who consume them. This network encompasses the publishing of new texts, the financing of this publishing, the entry of texts into the intertext of formal education, their entry into general cultural meaning, and their eventual re-publication as educational texts or 'classics.' Although this may seem like a series, it is indeed a network inasmuch as the causations within it are lateral, reversible and multiple rather than simply linear. An intervention to re-publish one text rather than another and in one edition rather than another—such as Malcolm Ross's to publish an abridged *Roughing it in the Bush* in 1957 in the New Canadian Library Series—can affect which texts can be placed on curricula, which are perceived as important for academics to write about, what story is told about literary history, what economic myths are acted upon, and ultimately how newly written texts are perceived.

◆◇

Earlier I noted how the eight journals I am placing in question tend to divide under the sign of unity on one hand, and the sign of difference or fragment on the other. This isn't as simple an opposition as it looks. One can find wide differences between journals in each grouping; one can find journals in each grouping gesturing to the sign of the other grouping; one can also rephrase the dichotomy in a number of ways—as culture vs. language, affirmation vs. interrogation, dominance vs dissent, the national vs. the transnational, each re-phrasing naming itself and the others both true and not-true. These are all constructions that are available within the journals, and that serve as devices by which they attempt to intervene in cultural debate.

Canadian Literature, Studies in Canadian Literature, Essays on Canadian Writing and *Canadian Poetry* all fly a national flag in their titles. Although their circulations range from approximately 2000 copies for *Canadian Literature* to around 350 for *Canadian Poetry*, all report a significant number of high school subscriptions. In the four year period 1987-91 these journals appeared interested primarily in the single author-name, either as the sign under which a number of texts can be brought together for discussion or as the sign of the person as 'writer.' This author-name appears in the titles of the majority of the articles published. The journals' coverage of authors was simultaneously wide-ranging and narrowly concentrated. A tally of the articles in these years shows them to have addressed the texts of 102 writers. However, very few writers—16 in all—received more than two articles: Atwood received 15; Davies 7; Bowering 5 plus 6 others in a special issue; Kogawa, Kroetsch, Munro, Roberts, and Klein 5 each; Gallant 5 plus 8 others in a special issue; Findley 4; Crawford, Pratt, Laurence, Lowry, Ryga, and Ondaatje 3. Not surprisingly, these were all writers whose work appears frequently in school anthologies or has been nominated for high-profile awards. However, a number of writers of similar qualification received only one or two articles: Mitchell, Hodgins, Wiebe, MacLennan, Livesay, Purdy, Richler, Wiebe, or—like Layton, Souster and Rooke—no articles at all. Overall, these statistics suggest a criticism that engages the work of a relatively large number of writers, that has a marked preference for living writers (9 of the favored 16), and that lacks interest in writers of the modernist period; Klein, Pratt, and Lowry were the only writers between the Confederation poets and Margaret Laurence whose work was addressed more than twice.

Another intriguing aspect of these statistics is the number of writers whose work was addressed by only one journal. In the 1987-91 period, in 9 regular issues *Canadian Literature* published 14 articles on writers whose work the other four journals ignored; *Essays on Canadian Writing*, in 8 regular issues, published 10 such articles; *Studies in Canadian Literature* in 8 issues published 16 such articles; and *Canadian Poetry* in 8 issues published 21. These figures appear to indicate a range of dissent, with *Canadian Poetry* the most likely to be sole intervenor on behalf of a text, and *Canadian Literature* most likely to intervene on behalf of texts already well endorsed.

However, 'range of dissent' is complicated by the fact that in these four years *Canadian Literature* also published seven special issues and *Essays on Canadian Writing* four. Two of *ECW*'s special issues—one each on Bowering and Gallant—merely extended an emphasis on famous living authors already evident in the essays of the regular issues. However two other *ECW* issues, one on writing from Atlantic Canada and one on the West Coast writing, offered essays on 14 writers none of the other journals addressed in the period. In the context of the regular issues' 'famous author' emphasis, these two special issues appear a kind of conscience-offering, a token compensation for a continuing exclusion. *Canadian Literature*'s seven special issues each focused on conceptualizations rarely examined in regular issues: on native writers, translation, popular culture, literature and visual art, and Slavic and East European influences. Many of the articles in these issues focused on understanding single texts, but many also focused on transnational matters—Kathy Mezei's "Speaking White: Literary Translation as a Vehicle of Assimilation in Québec," David Bentley's "Savage, Degenerate, and Dispossessed: Some Sociological, Anthropological, and Legal Backgrounds to the Depiction of Native Peoples in Early Long Poems on Canada," Audrey Thomas's "A Fine Romance, My Dear, This Is."

In this disjunction between *Canadian Literature*'s regular issues and its special ones, one can detect again a kind of compensation for things not ordinarily done. But one can detect also the presence of one of the major questions facing such a journal: is its business to be the aiding of the understanding of a text within the frame of its own devices (E.F. Shields' "Mauberley as Narrator in Timothy Findley's *Famous Last Words*" [CL 119]), or within the frame of an author's other writing (R. Alex Kizuk's "One Man's Access to Prophecy: The Sonnet Series of Frank Oliver Call" [CP 21]), or is it to understand the cultural and discursive formations within which various texts have been written and, once written, have exerted force? Does it intervene to mark the text as intrinsically meaningful, as special because of some internal complexity, or does it intervene to locate it within cultural argument? Does it construct the text and its author as isolated, 'unique,' praise-worthy or blame-worthy occurrences, or does it construct them as part of ongoing intertextual and discursive histories? Each of the four journals has some means of suspending these questions. *Canadian Literature* acknowledges both individual talent and cultural history, each special issue becoming a lavish token of kinds of criticism that have not occurred in preceding regular issues. Or perhaps in the special issues both *Canadian Literature* and *Essays on Canadian Writing* are merely responding to the kinds of submissions they receive, perhaps intervening to commission material in the special issues and responding more passively in the regulars (both journals appear to solicit submissions only for special issues).

❖

Through its numerous special issues *Canadian Literature* presents itself publicly as the most expansive and socially conscientious of the four journals. Yet the disjunction between these issues and the regular issues remains, despite the journal's practice of naming each issue as if all were 'special.' Many of these names for regular issues seem to have more to do with the practice of having an issue-name than to do with the content of the issue. The result is an ambiguity about whether the special matters have been set aside or specially attended—have they been severed from the ongoing business of the journal, and from the texts of that business, or have they been accorded special standing within that ongoing business? This question is important also because of the difference noted above between the kinds of criticism in the regular and special issues. All issues of *Canadian Literature* tend to have author-focused or single-text criticism; at least 52 of the approximately 90 articles of 1987-91 were of this type, with the most-favoured authors being nearly all contemporary—Atwood, Kogawa, Kroetsch, Lowry, Ryga, and Ondaatje. Most issues also offered anecdotal articles, reminiscences by authors, personal statements on writing craft. These articles—a kind which appear rarely in the other journals—both re-enforce the importance the journal gives to individual authors and very likely increase its appeal to non-specialist readers. But the articles in the special issues were often quite different. Although these issues still contained anecdotes and reminiscences, their numerous transnational articles were very often issue- and concept-focused investigations of a kind that appears rarely in the regular issues. The proportion of theory was often much larger in these articles. Thus the special issues raise another question about kinds of criticism, about whether conceptual and theoretical investigations are exiled to these special issues or acknowledged as too 'special' for the 'ordinary' pages of the other issues.

Essays in Canadian Writing in these four years offered no special issues on conceptual topics. It published the fewest articles per issue of the four 'Canadian' journals, although it often disguised this low number by listing book reviews on its table of contents as if they were articles and by mixing its reviews between its three-to-four articles. In some ways it appeared much more rigorously specialist than *Canadian Literature*, offering almost no anecdotes or reminiscences. Its articles had a similar emphasis on authors and single texts, but the authors here tended to be almost all twentieth-century. Apart from the special issues, only three authors received more than one article in the four years—Atwood received eight, Davies three, and Kroetsch two. Only 14 of approximately 70 articles over the four years investigated conceptual issues.

Studies in Canadian Literature in this period published no special issues. Its emphasis was even more on single-texts or individual authors; only 8 of 58 articles had a conceptual focus. Its concern with authorship was very frequently signalled by a possessive in the article's title: "Vanderhaegh's fiction," "Smith's Nature Poetry." Although this Fredericton-based journal used to be known for its interest in Maritime and nineteenth-century writing, in these years by far the majority of its articles were on twentieth-century writing and on canonical central and western Canadian writers—Atwood, Davies, Gallant, Laurence, Munro were its most favored English-Canadian writers. Like *Essays on Canadian Writing*, *Studies in Canadian Literature* published almost no anecdotes, but did publish from time to time polemic statements, complaints and grievances. It seemed to be the only one of the four journals that scholarly dissidents perceived as open to this particular genre.

Canadian Poetry, subtitled 'Studies, Documents, Reviews,' presented itself as the most specialist of the four—which may explain its also having the lowest number of subscriptions. One of its main characterizing features was numerous research notes, both within and without the 'Documents' section. Perhaps because of its emphasis on textual scholarship, none of its 39 articles over the past four years addressed a conceptual subject. Although these tended to focus on a single author or text, they were sometimes framed within social, political or economic issues: Dorothy Livesay presented as "Daddy's Girl," Oliver Goldsmith discussed within a context of imperial fortune. Its editorials and reviews suggested that its editors were more open to investigations of ideology and institutional politics than its articles implied. Its overall coverage tended to be as wide as the larger *Canadian Literature*; including twentieth-century and pre-twentieth-century texts almost equally. The poets to receive more than one article in the past four years were Avison, Klein, Livesay, Purdy, and Roberts—a somewhat different list from the 'favorites' of *Essays on Canadian Writing* or *Studies in Canadian Literature*. The contributions suggested that the journal was perceived as the most open of the four to research notes and pre-twentieth-century investigations.

In terms of a politics of intervention, the four journals were fairly different. The large-format *Canadian Literature*, with its elegant typeface and wide margins, its topical special issues, its emphasis in regular issues upon known authors, its attempts to make its huge book review section a comprehensive if belated publication news, and its regular inclusion of poems and frequent offering of author-reminiscence, appeared to attempt mediation of text to a broad range of readers—scholars, teachers, students, and friends of literature. This is a complex task, which requires every bit of the large format, large number of pages, frequent publication, and frequent special issues to bring off. This comprehensiveness was accompanied, as Lorraine Weir has amusingly documented (1989), by a chain of editorials offering humanistic good news about literary work. Literature, and presumably *Canadian Literature*, were extremely good for the human spirit. These editorials have continued even after publication of Weir's analysis, and have continued also to have remarkably little to do with the specific content of the issue to which they are attached, but much to do with its welcome to some general literary reader.

Compact and glossy, *Essays on Canadian Writing* presented itself as a much more business-like and instrumental journal. Its articles more frequently than *Canadian Literature*'s had a polemic edge—that is, the boundaries between articles and reviews tended to be broken down not only on the contents page but also in the rhetoric of the texts themselves. Its interventions mostly concerned current texts, and were directed toward a fairly narrow audience of teachers and readers of the more fashionable of these current texts, including eight articles on work by Margaret Atwood. On the other hand, it often seemed to be close to riding its polemic undercurrent further into ideological contention, but unsure what ideological direction it wanted to take. Its occasional iconoclastic articles from T.D. MacLulich, and its Fall 1987 issue, with articles on such trans-individual, transnational matters as postcolonial writing, thematic criticism and literary biography, offered promises unfulfilled by the overall run of the journal.

Studies in Canadian Literature, although making itself open to polemic messages from a variety of positions, seemed to perceive little role for itself beyond the polite explication. Its interventions appeared directed to those, like teachers and students, who might need interpretations of specific texts. Its message seemed mostly that certain texts are intrinsically worthy of understanding—it didn't argue on behalf of texts like *Essays on Canadian Writing*, or declare literature's individual and social healthfulness like *Canadian Literature*. The value of the texts themselves, and their cultural importance, was quietly declared self-evident. This message was reinforced by the lack of any book reviews, the presence of which in the other magazines at the very least signalled that literature is a matter of contention and audience a subject of struggle.

Canadian Poetry's interventions were more open. Canadian literature here was visibly a field of scholarly and political construction; book reviews, particularly those from editor David Bentley or frequently contributor Ian MacLaren, were wry, ideologically aware, and deliberately provocative. It was more elitist in its rhetoric than the other journals, however, giving the sense that these might be the private pages of an ideological cognoscenti who saw themselves working above the general naivete and enthusiasm of other journals.

◆

The second group of journals, *Signature*, *Line*, *Open Letter* and *Tessera*, overlapped a great deal with the magazines above. Their contributors, though much fewer in number, were also in many cases contributors to the other four. Many of the articles would not have looked out of place in the other journals. However, their having named themselves through language or difference, rather than through Canadianness, often directed these journals into conceptual areas that transcended both individual cases and national boundaries. It also signalled a partisanship and involvement in power that was usually concealed in the four 'Canadian' magazines. This partisanship or specialization was probably related to their low subscription bases, between 90 and 250, and to their few, if any, high school subscriptions. Publishing somewhat fewer and smaller issues than the other four, and a larger proportion of conceptual articles, these journals addressed the texts of 24 individual authors; however half of these were authors not addressed by the 'Canadian' four. Only four authors received more than two articles in the four years: Daphne Marlatt, to whom *Line* devoted most of an issue; Bronwen Wallace, about whose writing eight articles all appeared in an issue of *Open Letter*; Steve McCaffery, concerning whom five articles also appeared in a special issue of *Open Letter*; and Margaret Atwood, who was the focus of two of the only three author-focused articles to appear in *Tessera*. Three of these writers were among those receiving no specific attention in the four 'Canadian' journals.

Line, published from the Contemporary Literature

collection at Simon Fraser University, focused its interventions almost entirely on contemporary North American authors and their texts, and usually on only one or two writers per issue. The reproductions of holograph manuscripts that appeared on most of its covers emphasized the individual handcraft of writing, its production as a labor of penmanship and paper, and the operation of this penmanship as the major signifier of the writer as a person. Nearly every critical essay it published was accompanied by a text by the writer under study. The overall effect, however, was to make the magazine appear as one that attempts to intervene massively on behalf not of a single text, and not necessarily of an author as personality, but on behalf of an author-name as text—the text signified by the handwritten words on the cover. The readers implied by *Line* were ones interested in the transnational text, in the context of the transnationality of textuality, although not necessarily as a political textuality. Texts in *Line*, it appeared, could be formally or biographically powerful without being visibly active in cultural contest.

Tessera, published by an editorial collective of women writers, moved in a much different direction, offering very little foregrounding of individual writers. Its covers each announced a conceptual focus, also transnational in implication: translation, autobiography, feminist fiction theory, writing as reading, feminist narratology. The direction of the magazine was toward the future—toward texts being written or about to be written. Its politics were enabling and feminist; the implied audience women about to write. Its contents ranged from poems, journal entries, prose chapters ostensibly presented as testamentary or exemplary texts, to theoretical texts on how a writing might be done. They also included the kind of anecdotal text found in

Canadian Literature but with the important difference that all of these were directed in some way toward the problem of a woman's textual production. The rare analytical essays that focused on the work of single person often concerned someone, not always Canadian, doing work slightly tangential to literature—Julia Kristeva, Joanne Tod, Toril Moi. At the same time the sense of a local collective that *Tessera* offered—of a small group mostly from Montreal, Toronto, and Vancouver, who gathered material almost exclusively from Canadian contributors—implicitly signalled 'Canadianness' as an additional sign. This sign was accentuated for uninitiated readers by the lengthy contributors notes each issue contained—the most generous contributors notes in any of the eight journals. These notes tended to present the contributors within fairly detailed circumstances that foregrounded the multiple contexts of women's production. Thus instead of an emphasis on authors, on the already-written, which a journal like *Canadian Literature* or *ECW* offered, came an emphasis on writers, current participation and future production.

The internationalism of *Signature*, which in the four years published only three issues, was signalled almost entirely by the titles of its articles and the names of its contributors. *Signature* had the most austere and minimal packaging of the journals—each cover carried only its name, a list of contents, and the subtitle "A Journal of Theory and Canadian Literature." The conjunction "and" carefully elided and postponed the relationship between the theory and the Canadianness of the literature. In a sense one was returned here to the dilemma of *Canadian Literature*, the choice between Canadian texts intervened for as distinct texts and Canadian texts read in the context of transnational codes and conflicts, as well as to the implicit fear evident in all of the 'Canadian' journals that Canadian texts could be lost in the vastness and political power of transnational textuality. The first issue of *Signature* offered essays by Terry Eagleton, Linda Hutcheon, Barbara Godard, and Pamela McCallum. Eagleton's was on Schopenhauer and the Aesthetic, Hutcheon's on the politics of representation. Godard's was titled "Sleuthing: Feminist Re/Writing the Detective Novel," but focused on three recent novels by Canadian women. McCallum's perhaps exemplified the tensions and balances struck by the issue: her title, "Walter Benjamin and Marshall McLuhan: Theories of History." A similar balance was achieved in the second issue. The third offered an all-Canadian cast, and more attention to individual writers: Julie Beddoes on James de Mille's *Strange Manuscript*, Susan Knutson on Marlatt and Brossard, and E.D. Blodgett's "Ethnic Writing in Canadian Literature as Paratext," plus a response and counter-response concerning McCallum's earlier article. But an overall nod toward conceptual and transnational concerns was achieved by the subtitle to the Marlatt/Brossard article: "Writing Metanarrative in the Feminine." A tally of the articles in the three issues confirms this nod: eight more concerned with concept than with a figure or figures; four mostly concerned specific embodiments of theory.

I am perhaps the most and least qualified to speak of my own journal *Open Letter*. I can claim to have struggled with its subtitle, once "A Canadian journal of writing and sources" and for these four years "a Canadian journal of writing and theory." Here seems to lurk the same double-bind I suggested marked *Signature* and *Canadian Literature*. For *Open Letter* the modifier "Canadian" was only slightly precedent to its companion modifiers "of writing" and "of theory"; the possible "Canadianness" of both the writing and the theory were hinted but not confirmed. In this period five of the nine issues have a special focus, one being collecting essays on prosody under the bill bissett title "No-tation," one collecting essays on Steve McCaffery, two forming a collection of interviews with British Columbia poet-publishers entitled "B.C. Poets and Print," and the fifth collecting essays on Bronwen Wallace. The No-tation issue was the fifth issue to be published under this title, forming a issue-focused series within the journal. Overall, the four years showed an even split between 14 articles focused on individual writers, and 14 on concepts such as prosody.

•❖

Not everyone is served by these eight periodicals. The ones best served would appear to be those who serve themselves—like the women of *Tessera*, or the scholars who contribute to *Canadian Poetry*. Certain geographic and ethnic areas of Canadian writing are at best intermittently served, mainly because they have no direct representation among Canada's scholarly literary journals. The kind of secondary representation they receive in occasional articles or special issues remains politically problematic as long as the regular pages of the journals that announce themselves eclectically Canadian remain dominated by studies of about a dozen writers. The scholars who operate the journals are well-enough served, in terms of securing their standing within their profession, at least for as long as they can secure institutional funding to continue.

Only the journals funded by the Canada Council or the Ontario Arts Council are open to visible influence by special or minority constituencies. SSHRCC grants are awarded to these magazines by juries comprised of approximately five members each from a different academic discipline; representation on the jury is based on these disciplines rather than on gender, regional, or special constituency 'fairness.' Grants are made on the basis of 'contribution to scholarship' and maintenance of high numbers of subscriptions, with criteria such as gender balance among contributors given occasional mention. The juries for Canada Council and Ontario Arts Council grants, however, are normally designed by the councils to achieve equitable regional, gender, and minority representation. Jury decisions tend to reward both eclecticism—the representing of numerous constituencies—and high circulation, rather than any focus on special or even historically disadvantaged constituencies. Taken together, SSCRCC, CC, and OAC practices tend to operate to the advantage of journals that, while making a sufficient number of 'special' gestures to minority communities to retain their political good will, address overall a general audience—the general academic audience of high schools and colleges of *Canadian Literature* and *Essays on Canadian Writing*, which have enjoyed continued SSHRCC funding, or the general literary audience of *Descant*, *Brick*, and *Books in Canada*, each of which received $30,000 from the OAC in 1991. Such practices disadvantage journals that focus on special social or academic constituencies—the 1991 OAC grants for *Toronto South Asian Review*, *Open Letter*, and *Tessera* respectively were $7,000, $6,000, and $3,000. Council juries complain about being asked to finance 'cliques' and 'coteries'. *Open Letter* has been repeatedly urged by Canada Council juries to enlarge the range of its focus, and to increase its circulation beyond 600. *Canadian Poetry* was cut from SSHRCC funding for having fewer than 350 subscribers. *Signature*, with around 200 subscribers, was twice refused SSHRCC support, and operated for its three years on temporary funding from the University of Victoria. What seems to happen here in terms of jury politics is that the increased representation of women, regions, and racial minorities on Canada Council and Ontario Arts Council juries protects some minorities, so that their journals always get 'some' money, but works much more to the advantage of general and eclectic journals, with which a majority of the members of any jury may be able to identify. Power here tends to return to the general and canonical who previously held it. A similar effect seems to result from the disciplinary representation of SSHRCC juries.

The eight journals would also appear, at least on the surface, to serve adequately the scholarly community, perhaps because they exist in a reciprocal productive relationship to that community and to the expectations of scholar-jurors. That is, the kinds of criticism they publish would appear to reflect the kinds of criticism academics seek to publish. Many of us have heard legends about quantities of radical criticism in Canada that cannot find publication, or at least of quantities of theoretical, transnational, and conceptual criticism that cannot find publication. In my own experience as an editor who has searched for this homeless criticism, it does not exist. The editors of *Signature* tell me of similar experiences. The source of such legends may be the difficulty a handful of Canadians who write highly theorized dissident criticism do have in placing all of their production in Canadian journals. Canadian scholars appear by and large to be writing the criticism that the larger of the existing journals invite—that is, making critical interventions consistent with a generalist or inclusivist politics. What is difficult to know, of course, is what criticism waits to be written, or perceives itself uninvited by the existing journals.

For signs of the limitations of a criticism focused on

individual authors or texts do abound. On one hand, the exclusions this criticism creates fall with apparent inevitability into configurations that run across the 'Canadian' configuration inside which most cultural criticism in this country has been written. But on another hand that national sign appears to be the only thing holding back an engulfing tide of international textuality. And on a third hand transnational, conceptual textual discussion (founded on such things as gender, sexual orientation, ethnicity, race, class, political theory, etc.) of the kind *Tessera* and *Signature* have attempted seems to offer the most promising way to open critical discussion in Canada to marginalized textualities and to admission of the cultural and economic conflicts *Canadian Literature*, *Studies in Canadian Literature*, and *Essays in Canadian Writing* all in their own ways conceal. The project signalled by the problematic 'and' of *Signature*'s subtitle, to negotiate between the transnational and Canadian, to open the Canadian field of critical intervention without losing that field utterly, seems to me the most urgent area for specific intervention in this country. Funding opportunities for critical or theoretical journals from cultural minorities that might undertake such negotiation should be increased, perhaps by regional funding bodies that have a political interest in doing so. There are notably no critical journals in Canada that operate openly from ethnic, regional, or economic grounds. To date, the main beneficiary of eclectic generality has been generous humanism in national dress, and its main beneficiary generous humanist critics, with optimistic visions dangerously out of touch with the angers, challenges, grievances, and ambitions that fissure most Canadian writing. There is a need for more positions, and for many more primary representations.

The Conflicting Signs of *As For Me and My House*

The continuing power of Sinclair Ross's *As For Me and My House* to remain both high among curricular choices in Canadian literature and the focus of critical argument has puzzled at least a few recent commentators. Unlike *How Hug a Stone*, the novel proposes no radical revisions of history or social organization; unlike 'Phyllis Webb,' 'Sinclair Ross' has not become a site of contention for literary historians or social critics. Those most puzzled are those who have constructed the novel as realism, who have viewed its narrative as straightforward and repetitive, and who have therefore looked for explanations of its power less within the text itself than within the scholarly community which has continued to valorize it with critical attention. Morton Ross, for example, in his 1978 essay "The Canonization of *As For Me and My House*: a Case Study," argues that an increased interest in complex critical theory has led critics to "convert" a flawed but uncomplicated novel into paradox and ambiguity, and to 'deregionalize' its western Canadianness into a depiction of "universal themes" (205). Laurence Mathews, in the 1991 essay "Calgary, Canonization and Class: Deciphering List B," attributes the novel's high standing and its being rated the third most "important" Canadian novel at the 1978 University of Calgary conference on the Canadian novel to class anxiety among university teachers of Canadian literature. Again reading the novel as straightforward realism, "unremarkable with respect to technique," Mathews argues that it constituted a "safe" text for English department Canadianists, who found their field regarded in most departments as "less rigorous," "less disciplined and sophisticated" (he is quoting W.J. Keith here) than those of their colleagues. Mathews suggests further—again reading the novel as an uncomplex, linear narrative—that what he sees as Philip Bentley's struggle "to find some sort of fulfilment" was also useful to these Canadianists, in their attempts to legitimize themselves, because the story of this struggle replicated the humanist values of individual salvation that, from Shakespeare to Joyce, have been the stock in trade of the English literature curriculum.

While both Ross and Mathews here recognize (but deplore) readers' contributions to literary power, and how discursive change can alter how the signs of a text may be read, both are also naive in their assumptions of a metaphysical integrity in the text itself. Both assume that some of the first readings of *As For Me and My House*, by E.K. Brown, Edward McCourt, and Roy Daniells, as a novel that is 'flawed,' 'repetitious,' 'wooden' in its characterization of Philip, and "clearly in the realist tradition" (Mathews 158), are 'true' depictions of the text; both cast doubt on later readings of Mrs. Bentley as an unreliable narrator, and perceive Philip to be the text's 'main' character. They thus theorize a conflict between a text with stable meanings and a self-serving critical community that is willing "to convert flaws into enhancing virtues" (Ross 183) in order to legitimize either its own standing or its critical methodologies. Ross extends this dichotomy into a contrast between early critics, whose work he characterizes as "workmanlike" (171), "direct" (172), "appreciative," done with "fairness," a "concern for craft" (173), "economy, clarity, and a tactful concern" (171-72), and later critics whose work he characterizes as "excruciating" (174), "taxing," "militant" (176), "hilarious," and "misleading" (177). Both commentators disregard the discursive context in which the early readings of *As For Me and My House* were done, and the early construction of its meanings through that context—how "sympathy," "fairness," "economy," and "directness" were humanist and high-modernist elements in the critical discourse of the period.

In the case of *As For Me and My House* and its critics, there appears to be no conspiracy of self-interest—only a particularly vivid example of how literary power is socially constituted, how it is in the interaction between the signs a text deploys and the discursive context in which they are read that this power arises. The critics whom Morton Ross surveys are all reading a similar array of potentially powerful signs, but the meanings they perceive there, and the relative importance they give to them, have changed as cultural discourses and the readers within them have changed.

◆

Nearly all the criticism of the last two decades to which Ross and Mathews object has tended to read the selection and interpretation of events in *As For Me and My House* as specific to the character of Mrs. Bentley, whose diary entries constitute the entirety of the text (see Dooley, Cude, Denham, Godard). These readings have occurred within a literary criticism increasingly skeptical of authorial authority, attentive to aspects of narratology and reader-centred interpretation, and sensitive to the accusations that earlier criticism had privileged male-focused readings and male characters. While this criticism has indeed, as Ross alleges, shifted interpretation of the novel away from Philip and toward Mrs. Bentley, and constructed the text as more complicated than did earlier criticism, it has also had a further effect, unnoticed by either, of extending the early readings of *As For Me and My House* as a realistic novel, and of obscuring the novel's existence as a complex of textual signs that participate in the readerly construction of meaning. The novel tends to shift, in this later criticism, from being a realistic account of Philip's life, to being a psychologically realistic portrait of Mrs. Bentley, whose narrativizations construct her as a character. Such criticism has implicitly kept alive the misconception that the novel has a stable meaning, and unwittingly abetted Ross's and Mathews' less complex theories that whatever the power the novel currently possesses beyond its realism may be a self-serving invention of the critical community. This later criticism, that is, has continued to obscure the fact that Mrs. Bentley herself is a textual construction, by a male author living in a particular and time-bound regional Canadian culture, and that this construction is part of the semiotic field the novel presents for reader interpretation. She is not a free-standing agent whose 'personality' can explain the emphases and omissions of the novel but a textual effect partly produced by these emphases and omissions.

In reading a fictional first-person narrative text such as that constituted by Mrs. Bentley's diary entries, we are in the presence of at least a triple construction—a signator, Sinclair Ross, who has constructed a text which in turn constructs its narrator by constructing that narrator's construction of events. Resonating throughout the text is the fact that it is a male signator who has constructed not merely a female character but a woman's intimate discourse, her diary, through which her 'character' will come into being. Although many of the text's elements which I will examine—including its peculiar array of proper names, its lack of information about Mrs. Bentley's childhood, its silence on economic issues—are indeed open to 'explanation' in terms of her personality (she is Eurocentric, self-effacing, humanistic in cultural perspective), such 'explanation' does not remove them or her from the overall textual/social operations of the book. Someone else, who may share these characteristics himself or at least attribute them to some women, has chosen to give the text these elements. Further, a fictionalized first-person text is not entirely defined by the personality of its narrator. The overall context in which this narrator narrates, together with the discourses of the characters she encounters, are constructed, like her, by the text's signator. For example, Mrs. Bentley is not an etymologist, yet both Paul and his reflections on words become parts of the novel; she has little interest in ranching, yet the male sexuality the text and its signator locate in horses and at the Kirby ranch is still signalled by many of the names various horses and bulls in the novel carry. The text's presentation of itself as a diary, its killing of Judith West in childbirth, its construction of Steve as Catholic and "Hungarian or Rumanian," all occur outside of her own narrative choices, and thus evade recuperation by appeal to her personality.

My interest here is in the text and the kinds of constructions, signs, and power affiliations it offers, whether these be through its construction of Mrs. Bentley, through gaps, intrusions or contradictions it allows in her narration, or through other determinations. For the most part I will leave implicit but unstated how the text reflects in turn on its male signator and on the gender questions the presence of this signator raises. Unlike Margaret Atwood's "Notes Towards a Poem," or Daphne Marlatt's *How Hug a Stone*, discussed in the following two chapters, *As For Me and My*

House is not in any sense a lyric text that refers overtly back to its signator, or makes unambiguous claims on the signator's behalf. Nevertheless, one can also assume that the selection and arrangement of meanings in the text has at least the unwitting endorsement of "Sinclair Ross."

❖

As For Me and My House became in the early years of its curricular life, as Morton Ross has nostalgically documented, a representative Canadian novel and novel of prairie Canada. Even in 1957, when introducing the New Canadian Library re-issue of a book "unfamiliar to the Canadian public," Roy Daniells emphasized its Canadianness. It belongs to "the Canadian scheme of things," to "the prairie region, of which Saskatchewan forms the central expanse" (v). "Although precise dates, places and historical events are avoided, there is no doubt that these pages present the prairies of the drought and the depression, the long succession of years between the two wars." "There is even a brief holiday to the Alberta foothills" (ix).

Daniells' assertion of "no doubt" appears to rest more on unstated biographical information about Ross than on marks in the text: "Ross's little town," he suggests, is "a composite of, or rather an abstraction from, little towns he had lived with and endured" (vi). In fact, the absence in the text that Daniells notes of "precise dates, places and historical events" is so pervasive that it is only by geographical inference that a reader identifies the continent on which the novel is set; the text's national setting, and its regional ones such as "Alberta" and "Saskatchewan," are neither specified nor implied. Reverend and Mrs. Bentley have arrived in a "little prairie town" with a "Main Street"; he is a "preacher" for a "Protestant" church referred to throughout the novel as "the Church." He has been educated at a "little university city" in "the Middle West" (32). Here he met his wife, a music student who was "saving hard for another year's study in the East," and wondering "if she might even make it Europe" (16). Her only other suitor had been a violinist who "went to England shortly afterwards,....then made a concert tour of South America" (77). The North American place names offered by the text are the mostly small town names—Partridge Hill, Tillsonborough, Crow Coulee, Kelby and Horizon—that have referents only inside the novel. The Bentleys at the end of the narrative leave Horizon to operate a bookstore in "the little city" where they used to live "two hundred miles southeast." Thus although the setting is marked as 'not-Europe' and 'not South America,' it is not marked as 'not-U.S.' Both "Main Street," with its invocation of Sinclair Lewis, and "Middle West" suggest the United States, while "prairie," "coulee," "Protestant," "the East," "the Church" can mark either Canada or the United States.

The proper names that participate in semiotic systems outside the book tend to gather together under the sign of 'not-this-place.' These include England, Europe, South America above, Buenos Aires—named as the place from which Mrs. Bentley's violinist friend sends a postcard, the names of the composers—Chopin, Liszt, Debussy, Mozart—whose music Mrs. Bentley plays, and those of painters—El Greco, Romney, Gainsborough—she borrows in trying to characterize their dog. The text thus constructs a profound disjunction between a non-North America which possesses powerful 'non-fictional' names and referents and an immediate 'prairie' context which lacks not only names with resonant semiotics but from which all reference to specific North American place names and institutions has been excluded. The effect of this disjunction is to create a semiotic silence around the Bentleys and Horizon. He has worked in anonymous towns, they met and married in a nameless city to which they are about to return; he has preached for an unnamed church; she orders clothing from an unnamed mail-order catalogue, walks beside an unnamed railroad. Official systems of meaning appear to operate outside this area of silence. One of these is that of Art, embodied in the names of three eighteenth-century European artists, and outside of which Philip Bentley attempts his near-modernist drawings. Another is music, represented both by eighteenth- and nineteenth-century European composers and by the violinist's concert tour which originates in Europe, centres on South America, and reaches 'prairie' North America only by postcard. A third is language, embodied both in the books that Philip Bentley has inherited or collected and in the etymological musings of the Bentleys' friend Paul. Language for all of them is also from somewhere else—from distant places where books are produced and a distant time when the 'original' meanings of words prevailed. The Bentleys' ambiguous connections to the power of these official systems are two institutions in their nameless "little university city"—the university at which they meet and the books of Philip's study and of the bookstore he may eventually buy.

~

A number of critics have remarked on another powerful silence in the novel, that around Mrs. Bentley's name. Although she is the narrator of *As For Me and My House*, and although most of its male characters carry both first names and surnames, she is identified only as Mrs. Bentley. Within a feminist discourse, the implications here are inescapable; the woman who tells us she became Philip Bentley's wife by "yielding" her "identity" and by making her piano take "second place" (16), loses both her given name and surname on marriage. At the very least this loss creates a semiotic inequality between herself and her husband: a reader can construct him as "Philip" or "Philip Bentley" or "Reverend Bentley" and as occupying the various roles those names suggest, but can construct her as only "Mrs. Bentley." One can construct him as young or middle-aged, as a student or as a minister, but construct her only as a married woman. One can 'tutoyer' Philip, address him within an intimate discourse but, despite experiencing the narrative through what should be another intimate discourse, a diary, one must continue to consider her "Mrs. Bentley."

An equally profound but less widely noticed silence around "Mrs. Bentley"—and for me it becomes difficult at this point in thinking of the novel to envision her name outside of quotation marks—concerns her past. Again this silence creates a marked imbalance between her and her husband. The text offers some detail about Philip Bentley's birth, his childhood identification with his dead father, his defiant interest in art, and his struggles to become a writer and painter by becoming a protestant minister, but gives no information about Mrs. Bentley's birth, childhood, and only enough about her ambitions as a pianist to establish the negative sign of what she may have given up. This and the silence around her name are particularly ironic in light of the illegitimacy of Philip's birth and the instability—is "Bentley" his mother's or father's surname?—of his name. The name of the one born outside of institutional naming has his name confirmed by the text and his birth story preserved, but one very likely born within that institution has her story and name effaced.

Mrs. Bentley's relation to naming is shared by most of the women in the novel. There is "Mrs. Nicholson[,] the station agent's wife" (77), Mrs. Finley, "President of the Ladies Aid," Mrs. Wenderby, Mrs. Ellingson, Mrs. Lawson, "Mrs. Bird, the doctor's wife," (20), Mrs. Pratt, Mrs. Brook. Only one of these is allowed a given name by the text, Josephine Bird, who foregrounds the male-female issue by complaining early in the book about the "dominating male" and of having to live in "a man's world" (21). The only other married woman who retains her given name is the even more defiant Laura Kirby, whom the text—or its male signator, or a simultaneously envious and disapproving Mrs. Bentley—describes as "a thorough ranch woman, with a disdainful shrug for all...domestic ties," "a star attraction in rodeos fifteen years before" (93). In this disdain, she is a decided contrast to the women of the town, whose values she implicitly mocks when she mimics Mrs. Bentley "at a Ladies Aid meeting leading in prayer" (95). Interestingly, she is the only married woman whom Mrs. Bentley can manage to call by her given name, and the only one never called by the text "Mrs."

Laura Kirby's having given up an individual career to become a wife, child bearer, and worker on a ranch known in the text by her husband's surname gives her a history very similar to that of Mrs. Bentley. Unlike her, however, and unlike any of the other married women in *As For Me and My House*, she was once successful in a career and can still manage to found her identity upon it, being able to "break[ ] broncos and punch[ ] cattle a match for any cowboy." She seems to do so in part by inattention to three children which the text is reluctant even to identify as hers.

> Three half naked little girls file in and stand watching us eat, and the moment we leave the table make a rush for the sirup jug. The eldest is seven, the youngest two. They look so dirty and neglected I volunteer to wash them.... (93)

Laura has also visibly alienated her husband through a brief relationship some summers ago with "a big handsome cowboy." In addition to marking "thorough ranch woman" as a neglectful mother and a probably unfaithful wife, the text has Mrs.Bentley emphatically mark her identity as powerfully masculine. She is "a match for any cowboy." She has "a mannish verve." She wears "a man's shirt and trousers, and for riding fine leather chaps studded with silver nails" (93). In this regard Laura resembles all the married women in the novel, who have identities through their relationships to men and usually to men's activities. But although the text, at least as Mrs. Bentley interprets its details, appears to insist that Laura's ostensible independence rests on both her participation in highly sexualized male systems of meaning, the cowboy and the rodeo, and on her neglect of the traditional 'nurturing' female systems of meaning, mother and wife, it is relatively quiet about the married woman's role as unpaid labor in her husband's employment or profession. It says nothing about the economic basis of Laura's confidence. Only five pages from the end does it have Mrs. Bentley consider a career separate from Philip's, and this because she fears that if she helps him run his new bookstore she'll prove "so much more practical and capable than he is that in a month or two I'd be one of those domineering females that men abominate. Instead I'll try to teach" (160). Embarking on a separate career could be read as the text's recommendation to strong women as a way not of achieving personal fulfilment but of avoiding intimidating one's man.

⚫︎⬥

    His father had lived for a few months in the restaurant, and pushed out of the way in the little room that later they gave to Philip was a trunkful of his books. There were letters and

> photographs among them. When a lad still, Philip discovered his father's ambition to paint, that he had been as alien to the town and Philip's mother as was Philip now himself. The books were difficult and bewildering, more of them on art and literature than theology; but only half-understood, beyond his reach, they added to the stature of the man who had owned and read them. (30)

Although the connections the Bentleys retain with officially constituted systems of meaning may be tenuous, one should not underestimate the importance the text places upon them. As the above passage suggests, it is through books, through the printed word, that Philip Bentley is said to have legitimized himself. Lacking a legal father, he has grounded his identity on his biological father's books, on a textual father. When "a preacher who had gone to college with his father" comes to town and suggests that if he enter the ministry "the Church would educate him," one witnesses a convergence of related meaning systems. The "preacher," the speaker of authorized words, offers access to additional books at the university, another authorized keeper of words, through the mediation of the Church, the keeper of the Word. Although the church and university and university town may be nameless, they nevertheless still guarantee access to the word itself, to the Bible from which the novel's title is taken and to the bookstore to which the Bentleys eventually will move. From Philip the illegitimate will emerge both Reverend Bentley and Philip Bentley, Bookseller. Along the way he attempts to write "a book" (64), and later tries "an article for a missionary magazine":

> a sober discussion of a minister's problems in a district that has suffered drought and dust storms for five years—well written, all his sentences and paragraphs rounded out sonorously with the puffy imageless language that gives dignity to church literature, a few well-placed quotations from scripture, and for the

> peroration unbounded faith in the Lord's watchfulness over flocks and shepherds alike. (110)

The novel here has Mrs. Bentley emphasize the textualized quality of Philip's identity, the dignity constructed through "puffy imageless language" and the faith produced by the power of pastoral metaphor. Behind this and the other musings it allows her on the gap between discursive constructions and the experiences they attempt to represent, the novel repeatedly places the concept of hypocrisy—with its implications of a single and 'correct' text.

•❖

> It doesn't follow that the sensitive qualities that make an artist are accompanied by the unflinching, stubborn ones that make a man of action and success.
> ...
>
> Comfort and routine were the last things he needed. Instead he ought to have been out mingling with his own kind. He ought to have whetted himself against them, then gone off to fight it out alone. He ought to have had the opportunity to live, to be reckless, spendthrift, bawdy, anything but what he is, what I've made him. (103)

Although the novel presents Mrs. Bentley as frequently perceptive of the textual constructions of others, it also presents her as unaware of the constructions in which it has her participate herself. The most important one in the novel is that of art and the artist. Her usual notion of an artist is that above—"sensitive," "reckless, spendthrift, bawdy," a fighter, implicitly male. This romantic conception is an important part of her belief that Philip's being an artist is incompatible with his being both a minister and a husband, that his being both "[t]he small-town preacher and the artist" is a "compromise" (4), that "as an artist he needed above all things to be free" (33). It is also what moves her to begin gathering money so that he can move to a different career"—[f]or these last twelve years I've kept him in the Church....The least I can do now is help get him out again" (107). This conception sees the artist as both a rebel against institutions like the church and marriage, and simultaneously as linked to the institution of learning, to the university, books and the bookstore. This conception belongs as much to the text overall (and its signator) as to its construction of Mrs. Bentley. Philip draws not in a studio, but in his book-filled study; the conflict Mrs. Bentley imagines between the bawdy artist and the dutiful husband is enacted by his withdrawing from the domestic space of the house to his desk and books. When, with Mrs. Bentley's help, he imagines a way to escape the Church and small town and move toward acting more as an artist, he imagines himself back in the university town and owner of a bookstore. The bookstore has links back to God's book, to the power and authority of the word, and thus to 'the Church' that Mrs. Bentley perceives as in conflict with the bawdy artist.

This contradiction in the text is replicated by Mrs. Bentley herself, who wishes Philip to be the bawdy artist but is shocked when it appears that he has slept with Judith West, and whose first impulse is to construct this event in institutional terms—"what has happened is adultery... he's been unfaithful to me, ...I have a right now to be free" (124). She later turns to the "bawdy artist" concept, but without much conviction. "[S]he was there, that was all." "The man I see in the pulpit every Sunday isn't Philip. Not the real Philip. However staidly and prosily he lives he's still the artist. He's racked still with the passion of the artist, for seeking, creating, adventuring. That's why it happened"

(126). Four times Mrs. Bentley tells herself, in effect, that Judith "just happened to be there" (129), on the last occasion telling us "I've reasoned it out a hundred times, and the answer every time is the same: she doesn't really mean anything to him: she only happened to be there" (129-30).[1]

•◊

One of the best-known recent readings of *As For Me and My House* is Robert Kroetsch's structuralist interpretation in the essay "The Fear of Women in Prairie Fiction." Kroetsch locates the power of the novel in its encoding of a *horse vs. house*, prairie vs. town "'grammar' of the western novel" (1989, 76) in which male sexuality is founded on the rural— the horse, the cowboy, the coyote—and female sexuality on the walled and institutionalized space of the town. Although the 'cowboy' can never feel at ease within the female walls of the town, male and female can come together, Kroetsch suggests, in the "horsehouse" or "whorehouse." Such a structure can read Philip's encounter with Judith West as an expression of his cowboy maleness, while reading Mrs. Bentley's attempts to construct it through the codes 'transgression of marriage' or 'expression of artistic temperament' as female efforts of logical enclosure.

As For Me and My House does locate male sexuality at the Kirby ranch, not only in various male animals, notably the bull Priapus and horses like Paul Kirby's Harlequin, "temperamental" with a "histrionic dash," or the "spirited sorrel" and "rangy bay" that are rejected as suitable horses for Steve, but also in the "mannish" sexuality of Laura. And it offers as the site of Philip's marital transgression a young woman who is both linked through her surname "West" to notions of 'west' and 'wild west,' and from a rural family.

But it also locates male sexuality under the sign of the non-British ethnic. Steve Kulanich's father's liaison with another woman is "the only case of open immorality in the town." Steve, said at one point by the text to be "Hungarian, or Rumanian, or Russian" is described in terms similar to the horses: "[s]ensitive and high-strung, hot-blooded, quick-fisted" (36). These are also similar to terms used to describe the artist—"sensitive," "reckless" (103)—who is thus linked both to the Kirby ranch at which Philip paints with "strength" and "insight" and with the city in which Philip buys his bookstore. Male sexuality is also located in music, both in the "zest and urgency" (48) of the music of small-town dances and in the serious music of the concert hall. Mrs. Bentley remarks that "one of my teachers used to wonder at what he called my masculine attitude to music. Other girls fluttered about their dresses, what their friends thought about the pieces they played, but I never thought or cared for anything but the music itself" (151).

•◊

The signs deployed by *As For Me and My House* are powerful ones not because they are intrinsically powerful but because of the powerful places they have occupied within the history of Western discourse. The barren prairie, marked as empty, nameless, infertile, anonymous, and contrasted with the fullness of both the city and—through the Word—with the city of God, connects intertextually with the wastelands of Eliot, of Christian mysticism, and medieval grail romance. The latent sexuality of the novel is given similar intertextual resonance, with the god Priapus, with horses and bulls, and through these back to grail fertility myths, and forward to discursive constructions of artistic creativity, painting, and music. The complexity and dichotomy-refusing inconsistency of these signs make any binary reading of the novel in terms of male and female, town and rural, art and church, very difficult. Although Kroetsch's horse/house reading identifies two important meaning systems in the novel, the cowboy/horse and the marriage/house, it is silent about a third, that of music/art/university/concert tour/Europe which appears offered as an alternative to both horse and house and which the Bentleys choose at the end of the novel. It is also silent about one of the main sources of power and identity in the novel, the Word—the books on which Philip founds himself, the Bible, the male names which define almost all the women. The novel's conflicting meaning systems also intertwine and overlap; although Church and Art are conflicting systems within Philip's life, they both participate in the authority of the Word; although the sexuality of music is experienced more by the cowboy than by the small town churchgoer, it is also experienced in "the East" or in the cosmopolitan centres of Europe or South America.

The small town's view of Judith West is particularly illustrative of the novel's semiotic complexity. She is introduced to the reader by Mrs. Bentley in a paragraph which preserves the language of the self-important Mrs. Finley who is herself 'describing' Judith to Mrs. Bentley.

> On the church steps Mrs. Finley told us that she comes from a family of shiftless farmers up in the sandhills north of town. Instead of trying to help them, though, she went out working when she was about seventeen, sometimes as a servant girl, sometimes stooking in the harvest fields like a man. With her savings at last she set off to the city to take a commercial course, only to find when it was finished that little country upstarts aren't the kind they employ in business offices. Now Mr. Wenderby, the town clerk, gives her twenty-five dollars a month and board for typing his letters in the afternoon, and helping Mrs. Wenderby in the morning and evening. They encourage her

in the choir because she needs a steadying influence. In summer she's been heard singing off by herself up the railroad track as late as ten o'clock at night. Naturally people talk. (11-12)

Mrs. Finley is President of the church Ladies Aid. She stands here on the church steps speaking 'as if' from the male authority of the church. In fact throughout the novel Mrs. Finley attempts to adopt authoritative, quasi-theological positions—advising the Bentleys against adopting the Roman Catholic Steve, striking Steve during Sunday School when he fights with her twins, informing the Bentleys about decency and respectability when they buy Steve a horse. Her beliefs, that unsuccessful farmers are "shiftless," that children should help their parents, that women should not act like men, that people should not aspire to roles they are not born to, that 'steadiness' is a virtue, that solitary happiness is a sign of instability, that unconventional people are appropriately subject to gossip, are declared as 'natural' throughout the paragraph. The notable phrases in the paragraph "like a man," "country upstarts," "aren't the kind," "steadying influence," are part of a narrowly categorizing discourse that privileges the familiar and resists both challenges to role definitions and the hope of magnificent and empowering greatness which 'West,' City, Art, and the Word all promise. The story she tells parallels that of both Philip Bentley and Paul Kirby, "the ranch boy with a little schooling...[who] fits in nowhere" (20)—a journey by someone born on a farm or in a small town to the city in search of a more satisfying life followed by a forced return to the town. Judith's ambition to return to the city is the same as that of the Bentleys; her solitary singing connects with Philip's solitary painting, or Mrs. Bentley's solitary piano playing. Her having worked "like a man" connects with Mrs. Bentley's feelings that she will bring disapproval upon herself and her husband if she repairs stovepipes or digs her garden, with her "masculine" piano playing, and with the "mannish verve" of Laura. Her employment as secretary and as kitchen help places her in subservient roles familiar to women in Western culture and certainly visible in the novel in such concepts as "ladies aid" and "preacher's wife." The various codes of gender, art, farm, small-town, and city mix and compete in this passage. Judith is the girl who would transgress gender and class roles, who would refuse conceptions of the normal, the familial, who looks for "something more" (56) than what she has rather than attempting to defend, like Mrs. Finley, an inherited world.

The Kroetsch horse/house reading is also, like the novel itself, silent about the economic implications of the narrative, implications which are more than evident in Mrs. Finley's account of Judith West. The town of Horizon rests on one activity, agriculture. The industrial passes through it, like the railway track beside which Judith walks. The 'commercial,' which presumably includes the market context within which Horizon's agricultural products are priced and sold, is somewhere else, in the unnamed city. Signs of long-term economic distress appear throughout the text. When Philip was ordained fifteen years earlier he "had counted on a salary of at least fifteen hundred dollars...but hard years and poor appointments kept it to a thousand" (33). "Five years in succession" the farmers of the four towns he has served have "been blown out, dried out, hailed out" (19). Together these towns now owe him more than "twenty-eight hundred dollars" (106). The towns are marked by "broken sidewalks and rickety false fronts" (5), "ugly wretched faces" (17), "red chapped necks and sagging bodies" (19). Although the amount and decline of Philip's salary and the five consecutive years of adverse climate suggest the 1930 depression years,[2] no mention appears in the text of other than local economic factors. Economic adversity is displaced in the text to the wind, to which the farmers listen during Philip's sermons, "tense, bolt upright," "their faces pinched and stiffened with anxiety" (37). Repeatedly the wind brings to Mrs. Bentley her own economic plight, "the dust, the farmers and the crops, wondering what another dried-out year will mean for us. We're pinched already" (39). The Lawsons' son dies because he is unable to receive the care of "a city specialist." Judith West dies without hospital care, giving birth at home. The latter pages of the book are dominated by Mrs. Bentley's attempts to recover a thousand dollars from the twenty-eight hundred owed to her husband by the towns he has served; this thousand dollars becomes for her a measure of the value of her future.

The economic structures in the book appear particularly difficult for women, most of whom are presented as sharing the economic lives of their husbands. Mrs. Bentley's relationship to Philip's professional activities, relieving him of necessary domestic tasks so that more of his time may be available for his work, is that of all the married women. If these women have ever had their own economic lives, they have given them up like Mrs. Bentley claims to have given up a musical career, to "be a good companion," to do what "it seemed...life was intended for" (16). Unmarried, like Judith West, they have had their ambitions channelled into low-paying male-service occupations—typing and housework.

The horse, house, and university-city alternatives proposed by the text mark not only possible structures of sexuality and ideology but also economic possibilities. All three rest on powerful economic forces. Many of the values of Horizon—its disapproval of ostentation, its fear of the sexual whether enacted, as by Steve's father, or symbolized as in Judith's singing—appear founded on such things as shortages of money and the financial dependence of married women on stable marriages. The 'horse' cattle-ranching economy in the novel appears oddly prosperous, apparently little affected by problems of either drought or cash-flow. It can evidently accommodate a more extravagant dress code and—although the economic grounds for this aren't particularly clear—a more relaxed sexual code. The city economy, although barely visible, shows vague signs of specialization and scale; here one can take commercial courses and do "good business" in secondhand bookselling.

⁕

> Judith died early Tuesday morning.
> ....
> For me it's easier this way. It's what I've secretly been hoping for all along. I'm glad she's gone—glad—for her sake as much as ours. What was there ahead of her now anyway? If I lost Philip what would there be ahead of me? (161-162)

From what signs and positions does *As for Me and My House* speak? To what discourses or potential discourses? On the part of what community—that of horse, house, or some other possibility—does it enter into the conversation of Canadian texts? This passage occurs at a point late in the novel at which, according to a recent article by Barbara Mitchell, Mrs. Bentley "has been converted to empathy and honesty" (62). This passage also has interesting implications for the lives of women, who it suggests have such empty futures that if they give birth to illegitimate children or lose their husbands they are better off dead. It also offers a curious structural connection to Mrs. Bentley's relief at

Steve's being taken away from herself and Philip by the Catholic Church—she says then of Philip "It was good to have him to myself again" (118). Both Steve and Judith are constructed by Mrs. Bentley as competitors with her for her husband; in turn the novel and its signator appear to construct marriage as a narrowly focused relationship to which all outside parties, even children, are potential competitors.

With its large and interwoven array of enormously potent signs—primordial sexuality, wasteland devastation, industrialism, the Logos, the oppression of women, European high art, bohemian creativity, the City of God, nurturing motherhood, exile, legitimacy—and with the potential for these to engage with discursive change, the position the novel speaks from is both synchronically and diachronically complex. To a large extent it speaks from Mrs. Bentley's position, a position of multiple marginalization that is constructed by both her and the text as for the most part 'reasonable' and unchangeable given the time and place Mrs. Bentley inhabits. She is the woman excluded from economic productivity, the wife excluded from the role of biological mother, the musician excluded from most of the institutions of art and music, the citizen of Horizon who both accepts and refuses the narrow economic and sexual rules through which it manages its fragile family economies. She is the unnamed woman excluded from official discourse, the writer who works in a genre, the diary, of which the first mark is that it is unread. Although the novel sometimes casts irony on what Mrs. Bentley records—particularly on the feelings of superiority she has toward her husband and to most other women—it rarely dissociates itself from the views it gives her: that men and women are essentially different, that there's a "man's way" and a "woman's way"

(64); that men dislike visibly strong women (160); that the benchmarks of art and music are exclusively European; that art celebrates the human, celebrates "[f]aith, ideas, reason—all the things that really are humanity" (80). Mrs. Bentley's Eurocentrism, her humanism, her sense that men are stronger and less competitive than women, her rejection of both the small town and the ranch as suitable places for art, are if anything confirmed by the text overall. The text keeps all mention of Canadian or United States places and institutions out of the mouths of other characters. It gives her its last reflection on art, the comment that Philip "hasn't the courage to admit" the humanistic content of his drawings. It makes Judith's baby male, and causes her to die while giving birth to it, thus not only allowing Mrs. Bentley the son she has always wished Philip to have but killing off her competition for both it and Philip. It allows Philip to find and purchase the secondhand bookstore in the little university city which will become the site of the Bentleys' re-insertion into the cosmopolitan. These textual acts in turn reflect back on Sinclair Ross as the novel's signator, and become views which 'his' text places on the social record. In many ways they render ironic various feminist readings of the text as one which supports the struggles of women, for the things that the text has Mrs. Bentley struggle toward—"mannish verve," the right to produce a "masculine" music, and motherhood of a son—remain part of a male view of power and of liberated womanhood.

Canada in *As For Me and My House* is, like Mrs. Bentley, unnamed. In the place of national or regional indicators are a variety of contending meaning systems. There is the ranch/freedom/wilderness system of cowboy, coyote, wolfhound, horse, bull, and the cowgirl Laura; the rigid, heavily defended marriage-economy of the small town; and the Logos, the authority of the word, and all the "Eastern" institutions that flow from it: Church, university, art, music, Judith's commercial courses, Mrs. Bentley's mail-order catalogue. Within these are further contentions—art as 'bawdy' and ranch-like, 'raunchy' if you will, contends with the canonical art of El Greco and Gainsborough, and thus implicitly with other constructions like "business or family." Paul tells Mrs. Bentley "there was a French artist who decided one day he couldn't stand his business or family any longer, and just walked off and left them. It's a good sign" (128). The Church appears to conflict in Philip's life with art and letters. However, the text itself resolves these latter contentions within the figure "bookstore"—under whose sign Philip will be able to paint, shelter his family, operate a business, as well as re-enter European art and culture. This movement of the text away from the two Horizon choices Robert Kroetsch identifies and toward the "little university city" can be read as one not toward the whorehouse but toward Northrop Frye's implicitly Eurocentric "emancipated and humane community of culture" (347).

The text's endorsement of this unnamed university city becomes, by that non-naming, the signator's endorsement of a putative universal global over the local. This endorsement leaves the other contending forces of the novel powerless. Although sexuality has been linked in the text to art, and art to the bookstore, signs of the sexual are notably absent in the passages in which Mrs. Bentley foresees their city life. Woman remains through her namelessness a co-opted part of a global order that is, by its singularity, European, male, and canonical. She carries her husband's name, plays music composed by men, regrets not having born a male child, acts as mother to an adopted son. Judith West, the woman who attempted both to escape class and gender determinations and to gain sexual pleasure outside a marriage-economy, is obliged by the novel to die giving birth to this son. And behind these determinations still lurks the economic, disguised as wind, drowning "hymns and sermons," silencing Paul's reflections on etymology (38), covering books with dust (73), blowing so thickly one cannot "see beyond the town" (162). Behind marriage, childbirth, death, art, and the word, in some way the text leaves mysterious and unquestioned, lies money. The thousand dollars, earned through labor and wheat and railroads, through some Judith "stooking in the harvest fields like a man," which was the necessary precedent for the coming of Rev. Bentley's word of God to Selby and Coulee City, is also the necessary precedent to the Bentleys' return to art, book, and word. Again ostensibly conflicting signs intertwine. Here, as late twentieth-century Canadians face the approach of an apparently inevitable transnational city (and with it recurrent and most likely false promises of gender, race, and class liberation), is the most resonant and powerful of all the constructions of *As For Me and My House*. Our Canada too risks becoming unnamed. Our lands risk 'wasteland' sterility from the 'winds' of our own pollution. And we too have begun to journey, physically or psychologically, toward the city for which the Bentleys are leaving: the great global city of industry, wealth, authority, great concert halls and galleries—the postmodern and postcard 'village' of Mrs. Bentley's long-lost friend, the touring violinist. How the conflicting signs of this village will intertwine, however, remains as dusty and obscure to us, reading the novel or reading our futures, as the outskirts of Horizon on a stormy day. In *As For Me and My House*, although one can sometimes find shelter from the wind, the wind itself remains constructible only as "grim primeval tragedy" (59).

NOTES

[1] Some readers have suggested that because Mrs. Bentley does not open the storeroom door and verify her belief that Philips and Judith are in the throes of sexual intercourse, the text leaves doubt that the intercourse occurs. Unlike in the story of the disappearance of El Greco the dog, where the text offers signs that subvert Mrs. Bentley's interpretation, I can find no similar signals here that would invite a reader to doubt Mrs. Bentley's certainty. Although the text does have her seek ways to rationalize and mitigate the event—"[s]he was there, that was all"—it does not have her seize upon the more powerful rationalization, that the event did not occur. One can, of course, psychologize Mrs. Bentley as enjoying her betrayal and therefore inventing it, and as wanting both the excitement and power that adultery by Philip would give her. But one can equally move this argument back to characterize the text and its signator as 'wanting' the adultery, much like these can be argued to 'want' other events and signs in the narrative.

[2] A check of the calendar years for 1920 to 1940 shows only one period that is consistent with the dates given in the headings of Mrs. Bentley's diary entries, 1939-40. If these are indeed the years of the novel, they raise further questions about the novel's portrayal of its characters as oblivious to concurrent national and international events.

Agony Envy: Margaret Atwood's "Notes Towards a Poem"

The Margaret Atwood text "Notes Towards a Poem That Can Never Be Written" was published in 1981 in a book titled *True Stories* (65-70), in which the fourth page begins "Some of these poems have appeared in...." On four occasions here, specific genre conventions are foregrounded: three times they are affirmed—"notes," "*these* poems," "'*True*' *Stories*"; and once denied—"a Poem That Can *Never* Be Written." The text is published again in 1988 in an anthology titled *15 Canadian Poets X 2* (409-411), which is identified by its editor as a "teaching anthology of twentieth-century Canadian *poetry*." In both publications, the poem that can never be *written* is represented by 'notes' which, if not 'written' in the narrowest sense of the word, have at least been typeset, and classified as a 'poem.' This is a true story. Later an essay can be attempted, if not on the poem that can never be written, then on the notes which have been substituted for this poem, or have been presented with apparent success *as* a story or poem.

•◇

The visual signs offered by "Notes Towards a Poem That Can Never Be Written" indicate 'poem' somewhat more strongly than they indicate 'notes.' These signs include none of the signals of haste, incompleteness, or indecision that 'notes' connotes: no dashes, ellipses, over-writings, or erasures. Rather, they repeat the visual signs established by the surrounding 'poems' of the two books they occur in. The lines are arranged in stanza-like units that, in the *15 Canadian Poets* anthology, resemble the stanzas of "Five Poems for Dolls" that precedes it. The lines in both texts stretch one inch to about four inches across the page. Roman numerals interrupt both, arranging the 'stanzas' into sections which in one case appear to be the five 'poems' of its title and which in the other are possibly separate 'notes' or sections of notes. In *True Stories* the text is double marked as "notes towards" by being included in a ten-text section of the book also titled "Notes Towards a Poem That Can Never Be Written." These ten texts are visually and prosodically indistinguishable from all but one (which is written in prose) of the 28 texts that constitute the remainder of what the back cover announces is "Margaret Atwood's ninth collection of *poems*."

Other signs in "Notes Towards a Poem" also offer intertextual suggestion that it may be a poem. It begins with a dedication, which 'notes' rarely do but which literary texts do often. Its lines open in a syntax—"This is the place"—which is the syntax of the opening lines of numerous 'poems' that bear the Margaret Atwood signature—"This is a photograph of me" (*The Circle Game* 11), "This is before electricity" (*Procedures for Underground* 7), "This is the one song for everyone" (*You Are Happy* 38), "This is what you changed me to" (*You Are Happy* 30), "This is the plum season" (*You Are Happy* 93). In the anthology this syntax is echoed not only in the opening of "Game After Supper," six pages earlier, but also in lines within the other eight 'Atwood' poems the anthology includes "This is no museum" ("A Women's Issue"), "This is not a smile" ("Five Poems for Dolls"), "This is not order" ("Progressive Insanities of a Pioneer").

The title "Notes Towards a Poem That Can Never Be Written" denies the possibility of a written text but appears to leave other possibilities open. "Written" appears to invoke a speech/writing dichotomy: the poem that can never be written may be envisaged, imagined, perhaps even spoken or shouted. It is being at least imagined here, foreseen: "notes" are being proposed "towards" it. It can be known other than through a complex act of literacy. But the opening lines appear to move against such a possibility. "This is the place / you would rather not know about" they begin, "the place you cannot imagine" (65). Three times these lines repeat "this is the place," affirming place over cognition and imagination—the place that can make one "not know" or "not imagine." What, however, is this "you" that cannot imagine?—a generic 'you' that signifies humanity-in-general, a 'you-reader' addressed by the note-writing originator of the non-poem, or an intradiegetic 'you' within the text, within the recounted event, whose being addressed by the note-writing subject is witnessed by a 'third-party' reader? Does a reader encounter these "notes" in the second person or the third? Does the note-writer construct itself in the second person as well as the first?

Part two of the "Notes" begins "There is no poem you can write / about it, the sandpits / where so many were buried." There being "no poem" appears to mark a slight change from the title in which there was at least a poem which notes could be written "towards." Now there seems to be "no poem." But again, "poem" is modified—not "no poem" at all but "no poem *you* can write," or perhaps "no poem you can *write.*" What began in the title as a dichotomy between "notes towards" that could be written and the poem that could not, and a covert dichotomy between the envisioned poem, perhaps even the oral poem, and the written, now appears to have taken on a third contrast: between a writing-subject that can write at least "notes towards" a poem, and even pass them off as a "poem" we are reading, and an intradiegetic "you" that can write "no poem." Three dichotomies overlap imprecisely: written notes vs. unwritten poem, oral/imaginary poem vs. [un]written poem, a "you" incapable of writing vs. a writer capable of writing the words we are reading. These imprecisions leave unanswered questions not only about the identity of "you" and about the subject position from which a reader encounters the text, but also about poetry itself: is a written poem more "real" than one envisioned in "notes" but never written? or is a "poem that can never be written" unwritten because poetry itself is incapable of representing the horror of political torture, its buried victims, "pain still traced on their skins"? The third of this section's four stanza's suggests that incapability may reside in the kinds of texts that "we" employ to consider such victims:

> We make wreaths of adjectives for them,
> we count them like beads,
> we turn them into statistics & litanies
> and into poems like this one. (66)

Like the "you" of the first stanza, this "we" is ambiguous, potentially signifying only people like the writing-subject, or the writing-subject and the reader, or the writing-subject and the intradiegetic 'you.' But the signs associated with incapability are not at all ambiguous—they point directly to the conventionality of literature, its literariness: the classical praise of the laurel wreath, the religious gesture of the rosary, the twentieth-century's secular faith in statistics. They imply another poem which is somehow not literary, not produced through discursive conventions, but somehow more authentically produced, perhaps even 'unwritten,' through some unspecified, textually unmediated process. All three—wreath, rosary, and statistics—point also to death, and associate it with literary convention. They are followed by a fourth sign, "poems," and abruptly the "notes toward a poem" have become "poems like this one." But what kind of poem is "this one"?—a failure, no more effective than wreath or rosary? "Nothing works" (66), the next line reports. The "notes" may have inexplicably become a poem, but possibly not the one looked "towards" in the title.

❧

In part three, the first- and second-person pronouns of the opening parts yield to an impersonal narration about a woman who lies on a "wet cement floor" under "unending light" wondering "why she is dying." It is this woman's body, the writing-subject announces, "silent and fingerless," that is "writing this poem." Which poem, however, is "this poem"— the text we are reading, the one that will "never be written," the deathly 'non-working' poem of the preceding section, or the discursively unmediated one implied by the preceding section? Or are some of these the same poem? Or is the text indeed claiming this dying woman as its writer? The woman and the "poem that can never be written" are semiotically related, it unwritten, she "silent / and fingerless." But she is also, through oxymoron and metaphor, distinct from it and acting to negate its unwrittenness: "writing this poem" (67).

❖

Part four appears to recount the torture that the woman whose body "writes this poem" is undergoing. The writing-subject searches unsuccessfully for metaphors to describe the torture:

> It resembles an operation
> but it is not one
> ...
> Partly it's a job
> ...
> Partly it's an art. (68)

In its failure, the note-writer demonstrates the limitations of the kind of poetry considered in part two. It also suggests that art itself may harbour or conceal moral corruption: what is being done to the woman is "partly...like a concerto," and "partly it's an art." If torture can be in part a concerto or an art, it may perhaps also be in part a poem.

❖

Part five shifts to the first person singular. The subject responds to someone—perhaps the intradiegetic 'you' from before—who has accused it of flawed vision:

> why tell me then
> there is something wrong with my eyes?

This subject now presents its visions as if they also were conditioned by torture:

> "this is agony, the eyes taped open

> two inches from the sun
> ....
> The razor across the eyeball
> ....
> It is also a truth.

It addresses its interlocutor as if it, in contrast, had only indirect experience of physical abuse:

> What is it you see then?
> Is it a bad dream, a hallucination?
> Is it a vision?

Here what appeared to be the diegetic situation of the first parts of the poem—a privileged, untortured subject attempting vainly to write a poem about a helpless, silent, fingerless victim of politically motivated torture—seems reversed. It is the victim that now occupies the text's subject-position, and who addresses a naively troubled and privileged intradiegetic 'you': "Witness is what you must bear" (69).

◆

At the opening of the text, its geographic and political site was the torture chamber, and implicitly the oppressive, illiberal 'country' of the torture chamber.

> This is the place
> you would rather not know about,
> ...
> this is the place that will finally defeat you,
> where the word *why* shrivels and empties
> itself. This is famine. (65)

At the beginning of the sixth and final section, another major but concealed change occurs: the site changes to one far away from torture and violent political abuse, although the demonstrative pronoun—"this"—remains the same.

> In this country you can say what you like
> because no one will listen to you anyway,
> it's safe enough, in this country you can try to write
> the poem that can never be written. (70)

The shift works to re-confirm the writing-subject of the text as the "safe" untortured spectator who appeared to be the writer of the opening section, but it also subverts the specificity of the demonstrative. "This" can apparently denote either place, the unsafe or the safe, the place of torture or the place of immunity from torture. These two "places" construct the dichotomy that this concluding section develops, between a liberal country that has the appearance of political freedom because no one listens to anything that is said, and an "elsewhere" (hitherto, in part one, "this place") where words have the power both to inspire courage and to provoke extreme violence. The momentary ambiguity of "this" participates in a generalized ambiguity that recurs throughout the text: an ambiguity about who is speaking or writing, a torture victim or a privileged onlooker; about who is being addressed, a torture victim, a privileged onlooker, or the reader; and about what text we are reading, "notes towards a poem," the perhaps discursively unmediated poem the notes aimed "towards," the futile "poems like this one" of part two, or the "this poem" of the final section: "Elsewhere, this poem is not invention. / Elsewhere, this poem takes courage" (70).

The moral dilemma of the writer in the final section, free to write anything because nothing written from a comfortable, liberal democratic subject position is taken seriously, appears to lie behind much of this ambiguity. The poem "that can never be written" is among other things a poem that, if written, could have consequence, both to change society and to bring retribution upon the writer. The "notes towards" of the title indicate how distant the writing-subject believes itself to be from such a possibility. At the same time, the writer is unwilling to give up the attempt, and so begins writing what is formally, in line and stanza structure, a 'poem.' But after the opening gesture of "notes towards," how can this text gain the powerful standing of what from the beginning it has hierarchically privileged as a 'poem'?

The strategy the note-writing subject adopts involves appropriation, disguise, and ambiguity, in which the boundaries between notes and poem, writer and victim, and reader, victim, and writer, are rhetorically obscured. If the writer's text can claim authorship by the torture victim, or speak back to the safe-from-torture writer in the voice of the torture victim, it can perhaps claim standing as a 'poem.' If the text can be made to obscure whether its addressee is itself, its reader, or the torture victim, it may be able to effectively erase the difference between liberal and oppressive societies, and to appear to have a 'right' to write on behalf of subjects which it otherwise understands it is unable to represent—"Nothing works. / They remain what they are" (66). If it can blur the boundaries between its own mere "notes" and the poem those notes envision (or between them and the poem the torture victim, "elsewhere," might have written), or even imply itself to be textually identical to that poem apart from their relative positions in space—

"Elsewhere, this poem is not invention. / Elsewhere, this poem takes courage" (70)—it might be able to assume at least quasi-status as a poem. If the writing-subject can blur the difference between its own words and those of the victim, perhaps it can even become the victim, appropriate its subject-position, and relatively painlessly take for itself the victim's painfully acquired clarity of vision—"The razor across the eyeball /.../ Witness is what you must bear" (69).

A sort of rhetorical envy informs this ambiguity. The "notes" both foreground the modesty of the writer who would not claim priority over the suffering-earned poetic standing of the victim, and announce envy of the poem they would move "towards"; they both envy and hide themselves behind "this poem" which the dying and fingerless woman writes. The writing-subject envies the torture that qualifies the dying woman to write a poem that, untortured, the writer will "never" be qualified to write. The writer even envies the "country" of oppression, where words are consequential and powerful and poems are writable, and laments its own. "In this country you can say what you like / because no one will listen to you anyway."

◆

The dilemma enacted in "Notes Towards a Poem That Can Never Be Written" is presented as the dilemma of the contemporary writer in First World democracies: the writer who possesses great freedom to write and 'power' to publish, but achieves little political impact through this power; who covets the plight of the Third World victim as a means of recovering political impact, but has at best dubious authority to represent (politically and aesthetically) the victims of the horrendous oppression that occurs "elsewhere"—but from which the First World believes itself, for the moment at least, insulated. How can this writer act "on behalf of" the systematically electro-shocked, raped, and mutilated political prisoner, both when her or his own 'safe' position in culture, politics, literature, and discourse is so different from the position of that victim, and when even to presume to act "on behalf of" may be to commit a colonizing act of impersonation. Even if the poem envisaged in the title is construed as a possible, socially mediated text, and not as some unmediated and hypothetical entity beyond discourse, it can "never be written" both because its potential writer is dying, and because its available writer is an alien to its necessary discourses and intertexts.

Nevertheless, "Notes Towards" not only gets written and published, but becomes, in its own rhetoric as well as in the contexts provided by Oxford University Press, the poem it "never" could be. The text that is an "invention" and that it has not taken "courage" to write has become what Bowering has called the "poem for high school anthologies" (38). Its writing-subject, which at the beginning could only hope to write "notes," has legitimated itself through a series of rhetorical moves that culminate in its being able to claim the same "painful" vision as that possessed by a victim's mutilated eyes. The main device in this process is ambiguity of pronoun reference—the obscuring of who is writing, of how many positions "you" may include, and of where "this" place may be. Part five, with its blurring of first- and second-person pronouns, and with its paradoxical statements about the clarity of blurred vision, finally blurs any separation between the writer's vision and that of the victim. The concluding statement, "Witness is what you must bear," is made readable as a self-aggrandizing, 'liberal' statement about the writing-subject of the poem we are reading as well as an ironically figurative statement about the tortured woman. The writing-subject here is able to take on the authenticity of having been tortured—the "razor across the eyeball," "eyes taped open / two inches from the sun"— without suffering any of the incapacitating consequences. In a sense, the statement accomplishes an exchange of positions between the writing-subject and the victim: as the woman's actual torture becomes figurative, the writing-subject's vicarious or sympathetic pain becomes the literal "witness" that she must bear. The victim may die but the writing-subject acquires acute moral vision. The exchange is accomplished by the transformation of physical torture into a metaphor for the paradoxically acute moral vision of the writer. If one translates this process into an economic model, the victim's pain becomes—despite the deference the note-writer has tried to show toward the unwritable poem of the victim's suffering—the raw material for the note-writer's new vision, and her unwritable poem the occasion for the writer's notes to be seven times ambiguously termed "this poem."

Perhaps the most intriguing aspect of "Notes Towards a Poem That Can Never Be Written" is the effort the writing-subject makes to have its appropriation and conversion of the victim's physical suffering into its own aesthetically usable pain seem morally acceptable. It is primarily the marks of modesty and deference that the subject gives the text—an intermittent insistence that the text is only a poor attempt, mere notes, mere "adjective," something uncourageous that "invents" and "excuses" itself—that carries the burden of this effort. Although the text is repeatedly made to call itself a poem, it remains governed throughout by the title, "Notes Towards," so that each assertion that it is a "poem" remains incomplete and contradictory. The writer has it self-critically compare itself—"poems like this one"—to the 'unworking' conventions of "beads," "statistics & litanies." In the concluding sixth section the writing-subject writes cynically of the discourse of its own "country," and suggests that its own lengthy text may be paradoxically still unwritten. "Elsewhere you must write this poem / because there is nothing more to do" (70). But the paradox points at least as much in the other direction, a text has indeed been written, typeset, printed; royalties have been earned; the demonstrative "this" of "this poem" has been provided with a referent; something other than notes has been assembled out of notes towards a poem that the writer began by proposing, perhaps astutely, could never be written.

◆

"Notes Towards a Poem That Can Never Be Written" presents itself as a text about political oppression, and about the difficulty of powerful, effective protest against such oppression when the protestor is geographically located outside of physical danger. But it is also a text about literary power, a text which deplores a lack of literary power in Canada where, it argues, it is safe to "say what you like / because no one will listen to you anyway," and desires the power words have in countries where one can be tortured and killed for what one has written or said. At the same time, it participates in power it claims not to have, being linked discursively not only to similar texts—by Nadine Gordimer, Salman Rushdie, J.M. Coetzee, Gabriel Garcia Marquez, etc. and through these to internationally circulating discourses of social responsibility which *have* resulted in at least haphazard political pressure against apartheid in South Africa, and haphazard food aid to countries like Ethiopia, Somalia, and Sudan, but also through Atwood's signature to PEN International and its intermittent success in freeing abused writers. The text's claim, of course, is strategic: its immediate and literal reference, that Canadian texts lack literary power, both covers and discloses a tactical goal, that Canadian texts should gain more literary power than they presently enjoy.

The text's implicit envy of the power held by the oppressed who may lack, paradoxically, the means to deploy it, however, shadows other aspects of power and power contestation in Canada. There are oppressed individuals and groups in Canada as well as in Atwood's "elsewhere"— blacks, native peoples, gays and lesbians in particular—who have only in recent years managed to overcome some of the barriers oppression creates between themselves and printed discourse to write texts which previously could "never be written." The moral authority of their texts, no matter how marginal their sites of publication to generally circulating discourse, or how limited their readerships, is indeed 'enviable' by writers outside such groups, who enjoy the "safe" but socially inconsequential publication Atwood's text describes. One can detect this envy in Sharon Thesen's characterizations of "party line" feminism (16), in Alan Twigg's characterization of Mary Meig's *The Medusa Head* as being "for lesbians only" (6), and in the 1988 resistance of Women's Press to the charges by women of colour of systemic racism. Writers from such minority groups may not be widely "listened to," but what they write has had effect, both on the perceptions and strategies of their own communities and on institutional policies outside those communities. Their texts link communally and intertextually with Canadian native peoples' success in gaining entry to the 1992 Canadian constitutional conferences; with the influence of feminist lobbyists on federal Canadian gun control legislation, with the making by various minority writers groups of "appropriation of voice" into a Canada Council consideration in the awarding of grants. For writers unable to affiliate themselves with (or appropriate) such empowering disadvantage, such textual effects and consequences may indeed seem like "poems that may never be written."

Words and Stones in *How Hug a Stone*

How Hug a Stone begins with an introduction—"June 14, 1981. we fly to England...." This introduction offers what appear to be the circumstances of the writing of the text. The writer and her "Canadian-born son," "one 39, one 12" "fly to England for a month of visiting" the writer's "side of the family." The writer was last there thirty years ago, and before that lived in Malaya. On the present visit the son "will now meet" his English relatives, and the writer "perhaps... will come to understand" her mother.

An unsigned introduction such as this is by generic convention 'from' the signator of the book; in the case here the details offered connect intertextually with other materials associated with the signature "Daphne Marlatt"— particularly the journal/poem "In the Month of the Hungry Ghosts" (1979). The effect of this introduction is to mark *How Hug a Stone* as autobiography, that is, as a construction of its signator rather than of a persona or character. Inside the text this mark is repeated in five italicized passages that begin, like the introduction, with dates (14, 22, 42, 58 and 64). Each of these follows an interior table of contents and a reproduction of a highway map. On each highway map one or more elements are circled, and on some pencilled words have been added. The maps, like the introduction, insist on factuality, while the pencilled additions act both to insert the narrator into this factuality and to document that someone was actually 'there'.

The claim that these various pages repeat is one of

authority: that the signator "Daphne Marlatt" is represented by this text, that the text is not 'just' 'fiction' or 'writing,' that before it is these it is something which 'really' happened. Here too there are intertextual echoes of elements associated with the Marlatt author-name: the marks of journal and autobiography carried by *Rings*, *Zocalo*, *The Story She Said*, *What Matters*, the maps on the covers of *Steveston* and *Vancouver Poems*, the photograph of the author on the cover of *The Story She Said*. Beyond the claim of 'real' events is another insistence—that although there may be some ironic distance between the "Daphne Marlatt" i-narrator (the subject of its enunciation) and the "Daphne Marlatt" i-character (the subject of its enounced), the text as a whole is to be read as in no sense 'framed' or relativized by irony: a reader should construct no significant distance or 'disagreement' between the third "Daphne Marlatt," signator of the text, and the earnestness of the i-narrator.

●◆

Throughout *How Hug a Stone* various directions to the reader are strongly foregrounded—directions in how to frame, order, and interpret its narrative passages. The reader is given, in addition to the introduction, five section titles, a table of contents for each section, a map for each section, and following each map a set of dated and italicized summaries that re-inscribe the text within the section as 'journal.' "*June 22, Ilfracombe, Combe Martin where i stayed as a child, bits of intact memory but the overall terrain is different ...*" (42). Within the narrative texts there is further foregrounding. The first text "departure" ends with a question—"without narrative how can we see where we're going?" (15)—that is repeated both overtly ("*narrative is a strategy for survival*" (75), and covertly as a need for story, for narratability, throughout the book. The opening text introduces the concept of an imprisoning imposed 'script' or written narrative: the narrator's airplane journey that is a "plot we're in, wrapped up like knife and fork." It introduces in the Agatha Christie movie that is shown aboard the plane the notion that inside the imposed plot there is always an "enraged mother at the heart of it: lost." It begins an association of the narrator's son (whose first words are "i LOVE to go into that lab'ratory") with the power of positivistic science, with the "23,000 gallons of fossil fuel" that drive their airplane (15), and with masculine preoccupations with measurement and control.

●◊

> ground still rushes away from me though my step-brother has named every flower in all four directions contained by a brick wall. my host. reading the light of Reading read in pink petals overblown. overgrown. i am the child with chocolate smeared across her face. three frocks in a green wheelbarrow merely photographic the way he hauls us up in thirty years. i am the one who pushed. & she to whom we were hostage then, hostess & mother (his): o they are all right really. (17)

There is a sharp contrast in *How Hug a Stone* between the syntactic density and opacity of the text at the sentence level and the simplicity and visibility of its structural elements. Sentence by sentence the text is complex and plurisignative, marked as above by the co-presence of multiple narratives and narrative frames and by a narrative focalization that can encompass a variety of perspectives and times. In the above passage that focalization includes the narrator's present epistemological confusion ("ground still rushes away"), the step-brother's contrasting Adamic certainty ("has named every flower in four directions"), his reliance on the power of categorization and containment ("contained by a brick wall") and his control over her ('hauling' her up in a wheelbarrow when she was young and 'hauling' her out through childhood photographs in the present); this focalization moves also from the present ("my host") to thirty years earlier ("i am the child with chocolate smeared across her face"), and expresses itself in double significations such as the 'red'/'read' of "reading the light of Reading read in pink petals" and the positional contrast of "hostage"/"hostess." At the sentence level *How Hug* suggests the complexity and ambiguity of the meanings of experience, employing its own textuality to subvert and contradict the positivism of the step-brother who can dare to name "every flower in four directions." It suggests the insufficiency of simple binary contrasts: the narrator is both the same and different from her child self; her hostess is both 'hostess' and metaphoric 'hostage'-taker in different ways in both past and present.

On the structural level, however, *How Hug* offers meanings that are heavily systematized and, through repeated foregrounding, overdetermined. The outline of this structure is also visible above: a male-female dichotomy in which the male is active and positivist, naming, categorizing, hauling, and the female passive, being hauled, "merely photographic", subject to male gaze and activity. Historically, these constructions follow what Barbara Godard has described as the "American feminist...tradition of feminist activism, essentialist and non-theoretical in position" (1987, 4). These were the feminisms of Ellmann and Millett, and of popular understandings of Daly, feminisms which in the late 1970s were the ones most widely available in Marlatt's British Columbia.

under the moon a grown man now lures *moththe, math-*, worm.
with a white sheet spread on the lawn, with a bedroom lamp he
lures their bodies, heavy, beating against the walls. he wants to
fix them in their families, he wants them wing- pulled-open,
pinned on a piece of cotton, mortified. as then, i protest this play
as death—despite his barrage of scientific names, his calling to
my son, you game? as if he held the script everyone wants to be
in, except the moths. (17)

Here the step-brother's interest in moth-collecting becomes, through the phonological similarity of *moth* and *mother*, a male attempt to 'collect' the woman. His procedures are marked with domestic imagery ("white sheet," "bedroom lamp") as ones that are implicated in institutionalization of male-female relationships; the text constructs him as wanting the moth/woman sexually available ("wing pulled open"), humiliated ("mortified") and institutionally defined ("fix them in their families"). It links this view of women with empiricism ("his barrage of scientific names") and chauvinism ("as if he held the script everyone wants to be in"), and suggests it to be passed on from older men to younger ones ("his calling to my son, you game?"). It also associates it with writing, scriptedness, in contrast to the implicitly oral "narrative" (15) for which the narrator is ostensibly searching, and without which she fears to be lost.

The contrast between a duplicitous, ambiguous and apparently plurisignative immediate text and a systematic heavily determined general structure invites a reading that 'solves' the former and 'discovers' the latter, and that comes to rest in that discovery. The kind of heavily foregrounded thematic content that many 'didactic' texts carry in the immediate text is in *How Hug* deferred to the general structure. The interpretation the reader is likely to 'discover' is one in which a patriarchal system of empiricism, reason and mastery attempts to write woman, who has 'lost' her own (oral) story, into its script as a minor and exploited element. The patriarchal system enters the text in the son's interest in the "lab'ratory," is given detail in the portrait of the step-brother, of the uncle who is a doctor, "furious, driven" (33), of the rescuing grandfather (47), and of the similarly rescuing "blacksuited" British Rail official who efficiently drives the narrator back to the appropriate rail station when she misses her stop (62). It has its fullest depiction in the narrator's young son who is as avid in his determination to identify himself with Hero, Man and Father as his mother is in hers to perceive and acknowledge her "lost" mother. In a passage that echoes the step-brother hunting moths, the son attempts to construct himself as "Adventurous Marlatt" "in the jungle to stalk some wild animals" (36); he is said to be "happiest in the Lucky Penny counting hits or testing quickness of eye against sci fi enemy bombers" (48), to have an eye "impressed with target accuracy" (51). In a passage that precedes his mother's missing their station and having to be rescued by the Rail official, he recounts a long dream of leadership and confidence in which, when his home is invaded and threatened by belligerent teenagers because he has helped a few "homeless" children, he successfully and righteously confronts and defeats them (61). His dream, in which he gives himself a "big giant house" and the power to help the weak (ostensibly in compensation for a feeling that he is weak and "homeless" himself) and defeat the sadistic, contrasts with his mother's recurrent insecurities and her confusion about the route of their train journey.

The figure of the exploited woman is depicted mainly in the narrator's mother and in the other family women who are presented as having become conditioned by male 'scripts' into being agents of their own repression. The narrator's maternal grandmother, who years ago insisted on dressing her daughter as a glamorous debutante, now emphatically recalls that "she looked a *dream*". The narrator angrily comments,

> *her* dream, the one my mother inherited, *her* dress, my mother lending her body to it. as i refused, on a new continent suffocated in changing rooms thick with resentment: you don't understand, *everybody* wears jeans here & I *want* a job. refusing the dream its continuity in what i thought was no man's land....
> (29)

The narrator recalls herself as a young woman rejecting clothing that would have coded her as a marriageable woman, and dreaming of economic independence, and then learns from her amused grandmother that her mother had had similar desires immediately before surrendering to marriage:

> "We went to Penang and she said 'Mother, I'm so *tired* of this life, of just wasting my time going out dancing every night, getting engaged to play tennis, somebody ringing up and wanting to take me out to golf. It seems so futile. I want to learn dress designing and dressmaking. I've seen advertisements and I've written off to England. I won't be coming back with you when we go on leave.' This was when we were in the hotel in Penang sitting on the grounds facing the sea just where her wedding photograph was taken a few months later. Isn't it extraordinary?" (29)

Although the grandmother is oblivious to the semiotics of what she is reporting, it is implicit in the text that her daughter had asked to be the one who imagined and made the dress rather than the one who wore it, to be the one who did things in life rather than the one who waited passively to be danced with, telephoned, golfed with or married. Her surrender to her mother's "dream" script of dress and wedding picture led to her becoming the disabled person the narrator once despised—"furiously unable to budge"—who cried for her father when her children's game-playing threatened to crush the younger ones under a heavy dresser (47), who felt *"irresponsible, incapable"* when she allowed her children get trapped on the beach by the incoming tide (55), and who alone with her children in Bombay became paranoid with fear, "every cab... a possible abduction" (78).

•◊

The narrator's various re-enactments of her mother's incompetence, by missing the rail station, or by not knowing how to deal with the allergy attacks her son experiences intermittently during their time in England, suggest that her return to England has re-awakened for her the powerful scripts of female incapability that her mother several decades before had acquiesced to. She has herself entered those scripts and definitions within which men are authorities and managers and women agree to view themselves as decorative, child-bearing, easily flustered accessories to male power. The escape she constructs for herself out of this "little-mother" (66) script is both to complete her visit to England safely and to recover as much of the occulted *story* of her mother as she can for the somewhat more 'public' discourse of the autobiography she is writing. She would become *"free,...at home,...*be unnamed, walk unwritten, de-scripted, un-described. or else compose, make it say itself, make it up" (35). The terms 'free,' 'home,' 'unnamed,' slide into one another here, gathering *Genesis* connotations. The series of negative prefixes—*un, de, un—*accumulates and intensifies itself both as a desired cancellation of writing (writing which itself continues to resist, in "un-described," by appropriating and neutralizing one of the i-narrator's cancelling prefixes) and as a desired return to some condition *prior* to names, writing, scripts, description. As contrasting strategies for moving not only against writing through new writing but also to a position prior to writing, the narrator considers both imagination ("compose...make it up") and orality ("make it *say* itself").

Without such strategies, locked within the male script, her mother (and the narrator herself as mother) is merely, the text suggests, another failure, unsurprising in a woman, "the gull, unsettled, sad" (45), the one who "'seemed to enjoy setting people against her'" (66), the one paralyzed by "brooding silence" and a "sense of fatality" (76). Recovered by her daughter, she becomes an imaginer, one who would "wrestle with the angel authority of father, teacher, doctor, dentist, priest," the one "hated" for her "imagination, that *mad boarder in the house of the mind which alone can prevent a house from being built on safe, practical and boring foundations* (Sagan), that winged thing that flies off the handle, leaps out the window..." (67). A more vivid example of a personal exercise of literary power, to narrate a family member and oneself out of a scripted discourse of victimhood and into imagination, orality, and a story of empowerment, would be difficult, Sagan might say here, 'to imagine.'

In addition to re-imagination, the narrator's way out of the male script involves increasing attention to the landscape of southern England, a landscape that is slowly identified, through its lushness and dampness and its association with Bronze Age culture, with female sexuality and para-rationality. At the West Kennett long barrow and stone circles of Avebury the narrator imagines herself in contact with a different narrative, not a 'script' but an "old story" (73)—a narrative of the primal feminine, "*her tomb-body...built to contain that primary chaos".*

> this *kiel*, to *ku-* to, a hollow space or place, enclosing object, round object, a lump. mound in the surrounding sea of grass. *ku-, kunte*, to, wave-breaking womb: Bride who comes unsung in the muse-ship shared with Mary Gypsy, Mary of Egypt, Miriam, Marianne suppressed, become/ Mary of the Blue Veil, Sea Lamb sifting sand & dust, dust & bone, whose Son... (72)

> although there are stories about her, versions of history that are versions of her, & though she comes in many guises she is not a person, she is what we come through to & what we come out of, ground & source, the space after the colon, the pause (between the words) of all possible relation. (73)

This woman/narrative is located in silence, "between the words" that elsewhere the scripting authorities of "father, teacher, doctor, dentist, priest" control. She is "source" (69), the one who writes not in "words" but chthonically, "in monumental stones," "longstanding matter in the grass, settled hunks of mother crust," the "stone (mother)," "the old stone pulse beyond word" (75). The fragmentary stone circle of her 'speech' is presented by the text not merely as a lost mother, but as a lost plenitude, the collapse of which has opened the way to rigid and incomplete 'scripts,' to oppressing "words."

> ... that is the limit of the old story, its ruined circle, that is not how it ended or we have forgotten parts, we have lost sense of the whole. left with a script that continues to write our parts in the passion we find ourselves enacting, old wrongs, old sacrifices. & the endless struggle to redeem them, or them in ourselves, our "selves" our inheritance of words. wanting to make us new again: to speak what isn't spoken, even with the old words. (73)

The glimpse of this plenitude which the narrator believes she sees in Avebury becomes for her a possible movement *back* from script to story, from writing to orality, and from law to a state of being "free" (79), at the same time as it 'reveals' for the narrator a contrary movement in Western culture. The woman "story" once beyond words has become metaphorically for her Avebury's ruined circle, its missing "parts" simultaneously the parts of that circle, "parts" of and in the story, and the social/dramatic parts written in substitution for that story in the "scripts" which "old wrongs, old sacrifices" have, since the collapse of the circle, brought women to enact. The text's pun on "passion" marks women's 'roles' as having become "parts" also in a Christ-like sacrifice, at the same time as it creates the politically charged oxymoron of women having had their sexual/emotional passions scripted for them. Throughout this section, Marlatt's text constructs "words" as a barrier to 'redemption,' to woman's being made "new." The paradoxical "to speak what isn't spoken, even with the old words," echoes the Christian mystic goal of entering transcendent language, of 'speaking the unspeakable.' Grafted metonymically and intertextually to this passage, and contested by it, is once again *Genesis*: this time the fall from Eden, into law or scripture. The passage is placed not in some binary opposition to a patriarchal *Genesis*, but both parallel to it and in contest with it; it is posited as a similar but woman-focused Ur-condition, before language, before Law and Script, before a Fall from the perfect circle and into language, words, script, before a fall from a story that can "speak what isn't spoken."

How Hug a Stone, through its Avebury passages, is thus able to place beside a categorizing, collecting, and scripting masculine a transcendent feminine inside which, a few pages later, the narrator can "stand in my sandals & jeans unveiled,...dance out names at the heart of where we are lost, hers first of all, wild mother dancing upon the waves" (78). This is, again through metaphor, simultaneously the "*maere*" mother—the sea mother and moor mother, associated with blood, dance, "wild beating," the dinosaur-descended bird, "wild-wandering dove" (79)—and the also 'lost' but now redeemed mother of the narrator. The "ruined" mothering circle (story) implicit in "the squat stone mothers of Avebury" (64), is 'regained' in the narrator's dance of repressed "first love" (78), to exemplify woman's story amid the gaps, contradictions and fractures in masculine discourse. The "lost" daughter/mother thus can relocate her own self as 'narrative' in the 'lostness' of both her mother and the wild dancer of the stone circle.

❧

While this overall figuration of a kind of anti-*Genesis*/woman's *Genesis* is constructed by the text as both dramatically effective (the narrator ends the text amid a discourse of freedom—the text's last words are "free we want to be where live things are"[1] [79]) and narratologically complete (the barren ice floes of "departure" [15] have become the plenitude of the narrator's dance; a woman "without narrative" [15] has become one with "a possible world" [78]; a patriarchally scripted woman has become "unwritten, de-scripted" [35]), they are not without conceptual limitations. For one, the text remains one made of words. The writer/narrator, who from the beginning has associated word and text with masculine power, continues to effect whatever power she has through the printed words of *How Hug a Stone*, despite her assertion that the female speaks in a "mutter of stone" (75), in "old words," in "the pause (between the words) of all possible relation" (73). She may write about dancing, and about affirming dance over words, but is able to construct that dance and that affirmation only in the words on the text's pages. For another, the stone mother remains despite the various etymological (*ku-*, *kunte*) attempts to imply its originality, or to associate it with some primal "M" ("matter," "matrix," "moth," "moor," "*maere*," "material," "mother," "mutter," "Mary Gypsy, Mary of Egypt, Miriam, Marianne suppressed, Mary of the Blue Veil"), a rhetorical and social construction.[2] Alliteration remains a linguistic device which can signify belief but a dubious means for transforming Bronze Age religious and funerary practice into archetypal principle. The reader remains in language rather than with some "first love that teaches a possible world". Moreover, the i-narrator herself seems aware of this tension, and often, as when describing the i-character's goals as "to be unnamed, walk unwritten, de-scripted, un-described. or else compose, make it say itself, make it up," seems to want both possibilities: a woman who composes herself in the social medium of language, and the woman whose self is revealed to her by some transcendent source.

Another place of conflict in the text is the narrator's son, whom the text claims expresses a "jubilant ego" at Avebury and loses his allergy at the moment his mother makes contact with the "stone (mother)" of Avebury. But other elements in the text suggest something different. At Avebury, in fact, the son is constructed as continuing in a phallic love of "target accuracy": "& small toy pistol in one hand, cupped, & sheltered by the pelvic thrust of rock, jumps, gotcha mom!" (74). This phallic inscription of his mother into his war game appears little different from his grandmother's inscription by a phallic society into marriage and motherhood (although presumably narrator reads this as more understandable in a boy than in a woman). At the end of the text, when the i-character is entering even more jubilantly into the "wild beating" she claims to believe she has discovered in the lithic mother, the son complains "i want to go home...where it's nice and boring." The implication here is that the narrator views the son as limited by his sex to a life of positivism, despite his mother's belief that she has recovered a primal female story.

•◊

How Hug a Stone confronts the exploitation of woman in western culture, her exclusion from meaningful labor and from the construction of social narrative, and her being named as beauty, wife and mother, and counters this with a discursive affirmation of female difference. It groups its male characters under the sign of the phallus—the inscribing pen, the targeting gun, the assertion of single meaning—and proposes for women the sign of the "wave-breaking womb"—sensuous, dancing, imagining, between the words of patriarchy. Despite several places in the text where the narrator deploys the concept of female "imagining" as if it signified the ability of women to collectively construct their own culture, the chief sites of women's reality in the poem remain this "womb" and the Avebury "stone mother." Like the narrative of God the Father that supports patriarchy, the Avebury counter-narrative of a primal feminine is a metaphysical one which locates the human outside of social action in an archetypal predetermination. "free we want to be where live things are" announces the text in its final words, but this "where live things are" has already been defined as "unveiled" and thus as in oxymoronic relation to the "free" (79). Rather than unambiguously contesting the use of gender as a basis for structuring society, or arguing that this use has been a social choice rather than a biological inevitability, *How Hug a Stone* both asserts the role of socially-constructed "scripts" in gender relations, and accepts what Mary Ellmann has called the "gender analogy"—to the point that mother and son at the text's end appear destined to gender-based separation. "i want to go home, he says." "i can do nothing" she replies (78).

Yet the possibility that such destiny is a social choice remains nevertheless inscribed in Marlatt's text not only in its intermittent use of the "script" metaphor but also in its own emphatic construction of male-female difference. This overdetermination of the male-female dichotomy, marking the male exclusively with guns, the electronic war games played by her son, the step-brother's 'moth' collecting and with the roles of "teacher, doctor, dentist, priest," while marking the female who has thrown off patriarchal constructions of women equally exclusively with "imagination," "dancing" and the "wild" suggests a 'culture/nature' distinction as rigidly constructed as the positivisms of train schedules or "big business" (64). Although its combining of a plurisignative difficult-to-interpret immediate text with a highly directive unambiguous general structure gives a reader the illusion that the latter has been immanent in the former, the general structure itself remains a power construction signed by "Daphne Marlatt" and qualified by that signature. The possibility of more than two constructions of a mother named as "Edrys who was also Tino" (7) is—despite the concluding rapture of "wild beating, blood for the climb, glide, rest, on air current" (79)—not foreclosed. That is, the very constructedness of *How Hug a Stone* that announces its function as a power-contesting text (the power to re-write Neolithic history, family history, personal history) implies that further numerous power-contestations are also possible.

Figurations of power and powerlessness occur on nearly every page of *How Hug a Stone*. At the opening, power is mostly technological, and 'masculine'—the power of the aircraft that takes the narrator to Britain, of the "pater familias" (24) uncle who keeps a "doctor's schedule" (23). Women are shown working to maintain patriarchal scripts— the aunt who see herself as "a doctor's wife" (27), or the grandmother who imagines her daughter as a beautiful bride—or they are figured in the passive voice: 'lost,' 'scripted,' 'tired,' 'electrocuted,' 'abducted.' Toward the end power begins to be figured as enduring and primordial, as at Avebury, "mutter of stone, *stane, stei*-ing power" (75). The pun on "mutter" (barely audible orality, German for 'mother') connects these figures to an even larger power move, to install a 'great mother' narrative alongside the patriarchal *Genesis* narrative of establishment Christianity. Intertextually this connects Marlatt's project with similar feminist 'power' projects—Christine Downing's *The Goddess* (1981), Janet Farrar's *The Witches' Goddess* (1987), Carolyn Edwards' *The Storyteller's Goddess* (1991)—in which a great mother deity is posited as alternative to the authorizing God the Father of Western metaphysics. A narrative of a search for personal power, for the narrator to become personally 'unlost' and non-selfdoubting, is also an affirmation of the *presence* of woman-power, posited against history as a revealed power at East Kennett and Avebury. The political quality of this affirmation is evident in its lack of curiosity about the actual material circumstances of the women buried in the West Kennett long barrow (their ages, causes of death, positions in the burial chambers), or of the material conditions associated with the kinds of monumental, tribally celebratory structures such as the

Avebury circle or the nearby Silbury Hill.

The potential power of Marlatt's text to compete with the attempts of materialist feminists to locate women's struggles within history and society, rather than in a fight for ownership of transcendent authority, has been reflected somewhat in the extent and terms of *How Hug a Stone*'s reception. For example, Barbara Godard's essay, "'Body I': Daphne Marlatt's Feminist Poetics" (1985), focuses on the dense and punning plurisignation in Marlatt's writing, on its "excess of signification," and argued that this excess called "attention to the materiality of the signifier." Constructing comparisons between Marlatt and Julia Kristeva and Hélène Cixous, whom Marlatt has cited, Godard argues that the "phenomenological" emphases of Marlatt's *Rings* and *Steveston*, and the etymological associations of *How Hug a Stone*, operate not to signify idealisms but to peel patriarchal metaphysics from language and to declare a faith in the multiple materiality of language itself. "Without *an* author, texts are unauthorized, subversive" (481). Godard's argument requires her to overlook the selectivity of Marlatt's readings of Kristeva and Cixous, of how she takes from them not so much their emphases on linguistic materiality, or their attempts to render the female body an active, semiotic signifier,[3] as their ambiguous gestures towards transcendence; it leads her also to omit discussion of both the idealism implicit in phenomenology and the search for absolutes implicit in Marlatt's "calling into question the possibility of representation" (481). To passages in which Marlatt's skepticism about the potential accuracy of language seems to imply the need for a transcendence beyond, Godard adds her own swerving supplement, to make that skepticism veer away from metaphysics and back toward language. Quoting from Marlatt's "In the Month of the Hungry Ghosts," she writes

> Writing becomes problematic: "How can I write of all this? What language, or what structures of language can carry this being here?" (p. 52). No single one, of course. (493)

Similarly, in commenting on the Avebury passage in *How Hug a Stone*, Godard chooses to ignore its explicit search for metaphysics and to argue that "[t]o hug the *stane* brings the speaker back to her venerable maternal language, old English, to discover the root meaning of words, hidden meanings, the knowledge of the goddess repressed and buried in the his-tory of the words." For Godard, Marlatt's goddess *is* a goddess of Avebury and Stonehenge—"ancient places sacred to the Great Mother," and concurrently *not* a goddess at all, but an effect of language—"only *differance*, deferral" (494). She accepts an anti-historical argument that Avebury was "sacred to the Great Mother," while also continuing to read *How Hug* as replacing metaphysics with the material effects of continuously circulating discourse. Her counter-historical argument that the Avebury *stane* represents "Old English," Marlatt's "maternal language" (Avebury was built, most likely by Gallic speakers, approximately 2000 years before Old English speakers reached Britain) similarly leads to the suggestion that its lithic words are simultaneously "sacred" *and* historically connected to Marlatt's family past.

This 'both-and' figure appears in Godard's argument to be part of an effort to synthesize a politics in which differences within feminism can be blurred so as to achieve an appearance of unity. Figures of blurring and non-conflictual multiplicity run through Godard's text. The source of Marlatt's poetic is said to be "a holistic blurring of boundaries" (481); For Marlatt, "truth is...multiple, polyvalent" (481); her poems are "meandering, pointless" (483); her "text becomes multiple through the manifold interpretations it invites" (494). This depoliticizing of Marlatt within feminism is reinforced by Godard by carefully selected allusions to feminist theorists—to Kristeva and her theory of the semiotic which Godard summarizes as positing a "Women's speech...outside the codes of language,....a flux of shifting connections articulated through ellipsis and parataxis"; to Cixous, whom she quotes as saying "[a] feminine textual body is always without end. It is aimless, endless and pointless...an infinite circulation of desire..." (483); and to Chodorow, whom Godard summarizes as proposing that to write as a woman is "to write from a position in which there is no single authoritative view, no proprietorial and authenticating signature, but many voices" (489). These allusions repeat the conflict-erasing figures of liquidity and multiplicity through which Godard characterizes Marlatt's writing. Godard's discussion includes no comment on where Marlatt's own theory or practice diverges from or contrasts with those of these theorists—most likely because 'divergence' and 'contrast' are figures not possible within the blurring and unifying discourse Godard has adopted (ironically, exclusion itself is "denounced" in her final paragraph as a figure of "dominant discourse" [494]). The political positions of Kristeva, Cixous, and Chodorow within the debates of feminism are also not mentioned by Godard (for those one would read her essay of the same year, "Mapmaking: a Survey of Feminist Criticism").

●◆

Although in her 1989 essay "Daphne Marlatt: Writing in the Space that is her Mother's Face," Lola Tostevin does not refer to Godard's essay, the issues of difference and contradiction which are the 'unsaid' of Godard's essay become emphases in hers. Tostevin argues that Marlatt's use of etymology in her writing not only proliferates meaning but also constructs a reliance on "originary/original meaning" which conflicts with the project of French feminism's *écriture feminine* to locate meaning within textual play and difference.

> This genealogy, the *filiation* of a direct line leading back to a fundamental original signification, parallels the search for the lost mother on which traditional Western philosophy and literature are based and contradicts the open-endedness and new beginnings of *l'écriture feminine* which attempts to displace and exceed authority, truth, and the illusionary essence of origins. Marlatt's theory differs from Hélène Cixous' theory of *écriture feminine* which also emphasizes textual play and language as presence, but which does not maintain a source.... (35)

Tostevin goes on to argue that *How Hug a Stone*, *Ana Historic*, and other recent Marlatt titles have a "utopian vision" and maintain metaphysical gender distinctions by making a simple reversal of phallogocentrism for "vulvalogocentrism" and maintaining "the traditional concept of binary opposition" (38). The utopianism offers insufficient "solutions to complex social problems" while the binary construction of male/female suppresses "not only the multiple differences that exist between men and women, between women and women, but perhaps most importantly, within each woman" (39). For Tostevin, solutions to gender bias must be found in society rather than in transcendent norms, and difference must be acknowledged throughout society, even among feminists, rather than only between men and women. Tostevin's political position is in some ways similar to that of Godard's: she locates value in the social and material rather than in the transcendent. But in terms of feminist politics, she acts to assert difference rather than to elide it, and to distinguish Marlatt's text rather than to appropriate it for materialist feminism.

●◆

The implicit debate among Marlatt, Godard, and Tostevin was continued in 1991 by Lianne Moyes in "Writing, the Uncanniest of Guests: Daphne Marlatt's *How Hug a Stone*," an essay which addresses an essay by Dennis Cooley, an earlier draft of the present essay (in *Line* 1989), as well as Tostevin's critique. Moyes in this essay follows Godard in placing emphasis on the passages in Marlatt which cast doubt on the representing powers of language, rather than on those which express desire for origin and presence, and on arguing similarities between Marlatt's understandings of language and those of French feminism. Moyes advances three key arguments against Tostevin's readings of Marlatt. One is Luce Irigaray's thesis that a decentering feminine origin exists silently within traditional arguments of patriarchal source. A second is that Marlatt's use of etymology destabilizes current meanings, and exposes the social constructedness of meaning, rather than pointing back to original meaning. A third is that Marlatt's punning, morphologically metonymic style creates "differential relations [which] structure [its] presentation of family relations" (210) and gender relations.

Moyes curiously does not follow up her first argument, and its implications that an attempt, such as Marlatt's, to recover in gaps and silence signs of a feminine origin co-present with the masculine could be a strategy to discredit 'origin' itself, since 'origin' is by definition singular. Instead she relies on the second two arguments, to suggest that "Marlatt's return to the mother is a return in language, a return that is non-originary in so far as language is a system of *repeatable* terms" (219), and that, in its focus on unstable and differential meaning, it explores "the largely unrepresented and perhaps unrepresentable *material* contingencies of beginnings" (203). Moyes' thesis rests on employing the rich plurisignations of Marlatt's text to perform extensive readings-in of deconstructionist meanings. In one instance, she re-reads a short Marlatt sentence so that it can deny the possibility of transcendent knowledge by affirming Derrida's conception of the always already writtenness of knowledge. The sentence reads "host and guest fixed in the one script, the prescribed line of relationship." Moyes translates this sentence "host & guest fixed in the one script, the [always already written] line of relationship," and then comments "The notion that the script is prior to the written implies that writing is preceded only by writing; no underlying principle outside the field of writing regulates the play of differences" (208). In another instance she cites Marlatt's

> out of nowhere we are near the source. a shallow brook ripples by a few crosses at fords, a few stone walls for leaning up against—the Thames, really? not that one. wellspring. dayspring. home—when the walls come down, what kind of source? (Marlatt 69)

She then comments,

> Here, the ghostly mother 'materializes' in the words of text; "home" is linked to "womb" by the term "walls," and "river" is linked to "womb" by the term "source." The text de-idealizes and demystifies the origin by writing it in the terms of the source of a river. Thus, if the mother is a "source" or an "origin," her status as such cannot be read outside the material contingencies foregrounded in this passage—the materiality of the signifier that allows the meanings of "source" and "walls" to proliferate and referential adjacencies and similarities that subtend the home-womb and source-womb metaphors. (217)

While the metaphorical linkages Moyes points to indeed appear to operate, there is no necessity for them to operate as she constructs. Moyes construes these linkages as fixed and balanced pairs, rather than as—an equally likely possibility—chains of 'links' that move toward one of the linked terms, here sequentially from "brook," to "spring," to "home," and finally to "source." Intertextually subtending all these terms are the mystical and Christian connotations of water, and of 'source,' the term on which the increasingly less material and more abstract interrogations of the passage comes to rest. Any "material contingencies" that are foregrounded by the punning significations of the passage can be read as undercut by the movement of the text itself upstream toward "source,"[4] and by the additional meanings it attaches to "walls" as barriers—between language and origin, or humanity and "source." That is, other intertextual echoes than deconstructionist ones can operate here, including the yearning for transcendence of an old African-American 'spiritual'—"and the walls came a-tumblin' down."

•◊

Almost concurrent with Moyes' new reading of *How Hug a Stone*, Marlatt published her own reply to Tostevin in the self-interview "Changing the Focus." The interview takes the form of brief italicized questions, mostly skeptical ones that ask Marlatt if there are not problematic instances of anger, binary oppositions, and unitary construction in her writing, and lengthy 'replies' in Roman type. In her first reply, Marlatt asserts considerable authority over the meanings of her writing, declaring anger "at having my values or my sense of reality—what i feel are the real conditions i write out of—ignored, denied, passed over as unimportant in their specificity" (127). Many of the subsequent 'replies' provide an interpretive supplement to her writing, mostly to *Ana Historic*, and seem generally aimed at placing emphasis on the social relationships that text constructs among women, and at thus indirectly discrediting Tostevin's characterization of it as "vulvalogocentric"—a characterization Marlatt does not otherwise contest.

Noticeable throughout the self-interview is a strongly foregrounded binarism. The alternating question-answer, italics-roman passages offer but two points of view, the skeptical interrogator and the patient but strong writer. Marlatt takes on and controls both these roles, much as she does the two kinds of textuality—plurisignative sentences and overdetermining general structure—in *How Hug a Stone*; here she gives the respondent the fullest, most sensitive and reflective interventions, and the last words— "her own specificity which won't be denied" (132). Marlatt's explanation of *Ana Historic* is founded on gender opposition, "to look at a range of female presence in relation to women rather than in relation to men" (129), and on centre-periphery contrast, the affirmation of "woman-centredness." The latter affirmation lends some irony to her accusation a few sentences later that it is readers like Tostevin who are mostly responsible for the perception that there is "oppositional thinking" within *Ana*.

The later sections of the interview, however, operate more openly to defend binary constructions, "identity politics," and the idealization of 'wholeness' critics such as Tostevin have argued to be difficulties in *How Hug a Stone* and *Ana Historic*. On binarism, Marlatt asks "How do you think differently in a language structured by male domination where one term in any comparison has to come out 'on top'?" (130). On "identity politics" she says "i know

[it] is considered essentialist in theoretical circles. But a sense of identity is very important to us [lesbian writers] exactly because it's so often objected to, erased, or denied in the feminist movement as a whole" (130). On the "evolution of a single unified identity" implied by the narrative movement of texts like *How Hug* and *Ana* toward idealized self-awareness, she begins uncertainly, suggesting that both the linear conventions of the novel and her own not yet having learned to "avoid" a "narrative line" may be responsible. But she quickly moves to defend this narrative movement as one that is accurate to her own experience, as a movement toward an embracing of "something you knew dimly, somewhere, was always a possibility" (131). This double-argument, a qualified denial followed by reassertion, occurs again when she asks herself if a desire "to prescribe a certain kind of reading" is not evident in her work. Here she first makes the conventional disclaiming gesture, "the work goes out into the world and has to speak for itself" (which if she believed, she would perhaps not be writing the present text), but soon adds, "Still, you want people to read the work on its own terms." A few sentences later, addressing the push for thematic articulation in some "feminist and lesbian writing," she constructs another doubly-moving argument, writing "On the one hand, there is the seductiveness of language...[a]nd on the other hand, there is what we experience as authenticity (as the authority of subjectivity) of the i that writes" (132)—here moving from the duplicity and "uncanniness" of language that Moyes argues to be the characterizing property of Marlatt's texts to the phenomenological "authenticity" of the writer's experiencing consciousness. What is interesting here is not only the latent binary structure of these arguments, but how each comes to rest in an assertion of a strategically or

personally necessary, but epistemologically dubious, authority or authenticity.

While, despite the examples of Irving Layton prefaces and Margaret Atwood's *Survival*, it is still regrettably[5] unusual in Canadian literature (perhaps even to some in 'dubious taste') for writers to compete openly with critics over interpretations of their texts, Marlatt's intervention is quite understandable in terms the explicit power contestations in which a text like *How Hug a Stone* is affiliated. Marlatt candidly frames her remarks in the context of feminist and lesbian attempts to secure greater textual/social power, and of the political difficulties of lesbians within feminism. Most writers, whatever their politics or 'lack' of politics, do something of this kind of 'adjunct' textual activity, if not writing and publishing discursive prose, at the very least granting interviews, or commenting about their work during public readings. Writers openly committed to working through their writing for social change—MacLennan in the 1940s and 50s, Layton in the 1950s and 60s, Atwood, Lee and Acorn more recently— will like Marlatt explicitly identify their supplementations of their 'literary' texts as contestations for textual/social influence and power. What is of particular interest here is the strikingly different agenda Marlatt has from those of any of her commentators. She does not wish the elaborate defenses from charges of 'essentialism' and didacticism that Moyes constructs for her, or the defense from phenomenology that Lorraine Weir constructs in another essay ("Daphne Marlatt's 'Ecology of Language'"); she does not care whether her work is perceived as prescriptive, idealizing, authorizing, or identity-focused. Throughout her remarks, she stays firmly with a theory of stable, unitary textual meaning, a theory which both Godard and Moyes work hard to modify or conceal: one should read a work "on its own terms" (132), it is written out of "real conditions," it represents an authorial "sense of reality" which should not be "denied" (127).

•◊•

Daphne Marlatt is a powerful writer, with readers throughout Europe and North America, whose texts 'matter' to women because of the potential influence they can have in debates and dialogues among them. These texts, with their recurrent searches for a lost mother, their metaphorical implication of a lost "Great Mother," and intertextual connections with feminist anthropological programs to recover a lost great 'Goddess,'[6] have strong essentialist implications which, despite the strategic value feminists like Fuss have perceived in essentialism, do little on their own to assist socially and linguistically based feminisms. One strategy to enhance the political usefulness of Marlatt's texts is to confront and challenge them, as does Tostevin. Another is to attempt to translate them into a large, fluctuating, differential, semi-homogenous feminist project, such as the strategy taken by Godard. A third, already implicit in Godard, is to attempt to claim Marlatt's texts for a socially and linguistically operating feminism that is opposed to the metaphysics which they recurrently affirm—the strategy of Moyes. The power of Marlatt's writings within feminist constestations is arguably indicated by the length, elaborateness, and ingeniousness of the devices Moyes deploys to capture them.

But this power is exerted not only within feminism but within society generally. That is, the contestations between feminist theories have impacts outside of feminism, as I've suggested in previous chapters, on the activities of women writers who do not construct themselves as feminist, and on male writers who are also seeking readership and social influence. While male writers are not participants in these contestations, they are also not merely spectators or bystanders. The outcome of dialogues within feminism has the power to alter both the contexts in which literary texts circulate and the shape of society generally. Speaking here from only what I see as my own male perspective, I suggest that men have a large stake in the success of constructionist feminisms because these locate women's lives within a social sphere to which all human beings have access. Essentialist feminisms, while offering understandably attractive separate worlds for those who can identify with and enter into them, reduce and empoverish the social sphere by reducing the range of its potential relationships and interactions. But men's stake here offers no ground whatsoever for intervention. Materially, these are women's arguments. The only useful power that rests with men in such a scene of gender politics is to shape their own lives and social actions in such ways that women continue to find it possible to interact with them politically.

NOTES

[1] My editor suggests that this line, the concluding one of the book, should be read as "we want to be free, where wild things are" rather than, as I have read it, as "[having become] free, we want to be where wild things are," and argues that the line therefore suggests that they are not presently "free." The plurisignative sentence structure of the poem often allows such ambiguity. Here the ambiguity does appear to allow two contrary meanings to be present, much like the poem overall allows both an understanding of women re-scripting themselves and of women discovering a transcendent and liberating Ur-script to be asserted. I find my reading to be the more plausible in the context of the celebratory, dancing mood that immediately precedes, but agree that the poem leaves space for a politically different interpretation.

[2] Marlatt's construction of the West Kennett long barrow and the Avebury circle as 'female' contrasts sharply with the archaeological evidence that the latter was built by a Neolithic culture in which newly emerged patriarchal, hierarchical and possibly totalitarian social organization permitted the undertaking of large-scale public constructions requiring up to 800 workers laboring for up to ten-year periods. See Caroline Malone, *Avebury* (London: English Heritage, 1989). While it could be argued that it is against such kinds of 'patriarchal' empirical thinking as that of archaeology that Marlatt is writing, it can also be argued that it is this kind of incidental 'factual' evidence (railroad timetables, maps, objects in living rooms and gardens) which she attempts to 'read' for occulted meaning in *How Hug a Stone*.

[3] Despite the promise of the "Body 'I'" in Godard's title, she offers little explicit discussion of Cixous's theories that a writing-woman may produce language 'from' her body processes, thus producing a language that is 'material' as well as cerebral. Instead she implicitly uses 'phenomenological' as both a synonym for Cixous's "circulation of desire from one body to another" (qted 483) and as the more familiar philosophical term. Rather than focussing on the potential materiality of a 'body-i' language, she focuses on the blurring effects of its "abundance, flux" (483) and overflowing. Overall, Godard's discussion of Cixous seems to have been constrained both by the wide range of her essay—most of Marlatt's writing, including all of the early work in which intertextual gestures to Merleau-Ponty appear frequently but ones to feminist theorists not at all—and by the persistence of the idealism of phenomenology in Marlatt's writing long after the beginning of her influence by feminist thought.

4 While 'source' is not necessarily a word announcing assumptions of transcendence—it could be merely something materially prior to another thing, as is the material source of Moyes' material spring—the mystical context Marlatt constructs around the word troubles such a reading. The disparity between Marlatt's idealized Avebury, as offering in its "stone (mother)" "the old slow pulse beyond word," and the material Avebury of monumental public architecture also works against Moyes' suggestion that Marlatt attempts to explore "the *material* contingencies of beginnings."

5 I write "regrettably" here not because I see the writer as the determining authority on the meaning of their work, but because such interventions can often elaborate the position of this work within the general text of society, and enlarge the numbers of intertexts of immediate relevance to the work. They foreground the social role that writing plays.

6 There has been a proliferation of interest in a feminine transcendence in recent years, from Christine Downing's *The Goddess: Mythological Images of the Feminine* (New York: Crossroad, 1981) to Marija Gimboutas' *The Language of the Goddess: Unearthing the Hidden Symbols of Western Civilization* (San Francisco: Harper and Row, 1981) and Jennifer Woolger's *The Goddess Within: a Guide to the Eternal Myths that Shape Women's Lives* (London: Rider, 1990). An ecstatic discourse of goddess-recovery links many of these to *How Hug a Stone*.

The Struggle for 'Phyllis Webb'

> ... the Phyllis Webb whose poems I read interacts in... complex ways with the Phyllis Webb whom I visit at her home on Saltspring Island. In neither case would I have the confidence to say, unproblematically, that 'I am encountering, let us say, Phyllis Webb.'
>
> (Stephen Scobie, 1989, 17)

In 1971 Talonbooks publishes *Selected Poems 1954-1965* by Phyllis Webb, edited and introduced by John Hulcoop. The dust jacket copy begins "Phyllis Webb is one of Canada's major poets." Before publication of this volume Webb has contributed to *Trio* in 1954, and published *Even Your Right Eye* with McClelland and Stewart in 1956, *The Sea is Also a Garden* with Ryerson Press in 1962, and the chapbook *Naked Poems* in 1965. *Selected Poems* is an ambitious publication for Talonbooks, which has grown in Vancouver's 1960s counterculture from the poetry magazine *Talon*, into an irregular publisher of esoteric volumes of poetry (often undated, and sometimes reproduced from typescript) but which is now attempting to legitimate itself through photo-typefaces and the publishing of already-known texts and authors. In 1969 it publishes James Reaney's *Colours in the Dark*, in 1970 George Ryga's *The Ecstasy of Rita Joe*, and in 1971 Reaney's *Listen to the Wind*. In 1972 it publishes Connie Brissenden's *Factory Lab Anthology*. The Brissenden and Ryga titles carry the first cover endorsements printed on a book by the press, quotations from reviews by *The Ottawa Journal*, *The Vancouver Sun*, *The Toronto Star*, and signed by such celebrities as Nathan Cohen and Urjo Kareda.

Like the *Factory Lab Anthology* and the other drama titles, *Webb's Selected Poems 1954-65* differs from earlier Talon titles in documenting work that had already been made public and certified by public appraisal. The publisher emphasizes this certification by prefacing the volume with a lengthy introduction by John Hulcoop, who teaches Victorian and early modern British literature at the University of British Columbia, and who has published the first academic essay on Webb's writing in 1967. Hulcoop, perhaps overly influenced by his British training in the work of canonical authors (he has emigrated from England in 1956, after writing a dissertation on Browning), is also concerned to mark Webb as a "major" poet. His opening paragraph begins with a quotation from Northrop Frye, Canada's best-known critic of the time, and continues by indirectly associating Webb with D.G. Jones, who had published *Butterfly on Rock* with the University of Toronto Press the year previously, and with Canada's most influential poetry anthologist, A.J.M. Smith. His subsequent outline of her biography lists the various famous writers she had "met," whether meaningful or casual encounters: Earle Birney, Roy Daniells, F.R. Scott, John Sutherland, Irving Layton, Louis Dudek, Eli Mandel, Leonard Cohen, Miriam Waddington, Charles Olson, Allen Ginsberg, Robert Duncan and Robert Creeley. A twenty-page interpretation of her poetry then elaborates this association with canonicity and celebrity. Here Hulcoop observes that her love poetry "is often reminiscent of Matthew Arnold's sequence of poems to Marguerite" (21), compares her suicide poems to Camus's *The Myth of Sisyphus* (19), and her early world-view to "that of the Magi in Eliot's poem" (22); he proposes that her poems of enchantment offer "the same sense of wonder that overcomes Ferdinand when

Prospero conjures up his mask of Isis" (25); that her concern with madness recalls Aristotle and Keats (26); that "several of her major poems... say[ ] in her own way what William Carlos Williams says in his, in *Paterson*" (27). These connections in turn recall for him Nietzsche's "story of Midas's search for Silenus" (27), and lead him to quote Nietzsche on the futility of human action and observe "The resemblance between this last statement and Phyllis Webb's "Sitting" is striking" (28). As Hulcoop continues, the reader is told that Webb's world is "different from that of Shakespeare's tragedies," that "[l]ike Auden, she believes that 'poetry makes nothing happen,'" that "Nietzsche, like Kierkegaard, and Miss Webb herself, is 'an intuitive existentialist'" (29-30).

To a small extent, Hulcoop is led to these juxtapositions by Webb's writing. The poems Hulcoop is collecting do repeatedly link themselves by direct or indirect allusion to well-known author-names—Kierkegaard, Rilke, Joyce, Marvell, Dostoevsky, Williams, Yeats, Shakespeare—and invite some of the comparisons he suggests: "With Rilke, compare the following 'naked poem' by Phyllis Webb" (41). But while Webb's writing employs these names to evoke concepts which it reconsiders and occasionally challenges, Hulcoop's preface uses them much differently, as the parallel syntax of many of his pairings indicates. One use is simply legitimation: if the Webb name can be easily placed in parallel with names like Shakespeare, Keats, Arnold and Eliot, then there should be little doubt that she is a "major poet." A second is to demonstrate intellectual seriousness: Webb seems to be an eccentric, she writes about having considered suicide, reveals "impulses towards self-indulgence and self-pity which... constantly threaten to sweep away the poet and her poetry." Hulcoop cannot risk having the poems he and Talon are investing in swept away, and so he anchors them with weighty names. A third is to place her in the Canadian canon: she is one of "*Canada's major poets.*" Except for Cohen, all of the Canadian poets he associates her with are older poets; except for Sutherland and Waddington, all have apparently secure places in the canon. The few American poets he names—Williams, Olson, Ginsberg, Duncan, Creeley—are also older and widely known to have had influence in Canada.

The most useful aspect of these names for Hulcoop, however, is that they locate Webb within modernism. In a general sense to so locate her is not difficult—Webb's associations within Canadian poetry, with F.R. Scott and with Contact Press, involved some of the most influential writers of Canadian modernism. But Hulcoop has another agenda: to associate Webb with a modernist current largely unrepresented in Canada—that highly emotional, subjective despairing modernism with its roots in the failure of Kant's systematic philosophy and general collapse of European metaphysics, that displays itself in various ways in the writings of Kierkegaard, Sade, Dostoevsky, Nietzsche, Baudelaire, Kafka, Artaud, Arp, Ball, Gide, Rilke, Camus, Sartre, and Beckett. This is the modernism that will redeem Webb's excessive despairs, her "self-indulgence and self-pity," and redeem it under the then still fashionable sign of existentialism. Moreover, when Hulcoop quotes Webb as saying she was "an intuitive existentialist," that even before she read existentialist writers she "just knew all about [it]" (30), he is insisting on the absolute legitimacy of this sign: she is not merely someone who has read William Barrett's *Irrational Man* in 1960 and begun wearing black clothes and makeup, but has genuinely suffered; *existence* has indeed preceded *essence*; moreover, she is major, and she is

Canadian. Hulcoop's achievement of this is direct: no Canadian poet is mentioned during his lengthy analyses of Webb's poems; instead the poems are repeatedly explained by reference to continental modernist philosophers and writers. Webb's poems fall 'naturally' into their company.

◆

It was this *Selected Poems* that initiates the second extended examination of Webb's poems, by John Bentley Mays, entitled "Phyllis Webb (for Bob Wallace)," and published under my editorship in *Open Letter* in 1973. Mays comes to Webb's writing with none of the concerns about legitimacy that informed the Hulcoop/Talonbooks production of *Selected Poems*. He too has recently emigrated to Canada, believing he has a teaching position at York University, but has settled for a position as cultural advisor and 'animateur' in the administration of one of York's colleges. Considerably younger than Hulcoop, he comes not from British historical criticism but from a progressive United States school of cultural studies. At the University of Rochester, he has studied with Norman O. Brown, been influenced by Brown's and Merleau-Ponty's phenomenological writing strategies, taken part in protests against the Viet Nam war, and read widely in the influential texts of the 1960s American counterculture—the *Kabbalah*, Blake, Marx, Sade, Celine, Artaud, Jung, Marcuse, Ginsberg, Genet, and Burroughs. He has considerable curiosity about the art and culture of his new country, and finds himself most intensely engaged by those areas of Canadian culture that carry forward discourses familiar to him in the U.S.—the International Image Exchange network and the activities of Michael Morris and other Western Front artists, the conceptual art of General Idea on which he will write an article for *Open*

Letter the next year. He joins the board of the artist-run gallery A-Space, and begins helpful friendships with Victor Coleman and Marian Lewis. And he begins reading contemporary Canadian writing. If there is a central motif to his activities, it is to locate himself in relation to Canadian culture, and to historicize himself within it.

Mays's experience of "Phyllis Webb" is somewhat different from that of Hulcoop. Hulcoop had met Webb in 1960 within a small gay community at UBC and corresponded with her when she had left to work for the CBC in Toronto. During his decade and a half in Canada before editing her *Selected*, he had familiarized himself with some aspects of contemporary Canadian literature, and could locate her publications within Canadian publishing practices, where her two collections, a chapbook, and a selected poems constituted a significant achievement. For the newly-arrived Mays, however, the same array of books appear much less impressive: "she has contributed to or published only four small books,... a few poems in odd places, a review in *Poetry* (Chicago), and a couple of popular articles in *Maclean's*" (11). For Hulcoop, while the similarities of her writing to existentialist and decadent romantic European writers operated to legitimate it, her poems were still to be inscribed within Canadian modernist poetry. But for Mays, these similarities are the features of her writing that most connect it to the 'decadent,' existential, and phenomenological writing he is familiar with; they inscribe it within a tradition.

A major stylistic difference between Hulcoop and Mays tells much about their assumptions regarding the European texts invoked by Webb's poems. Hulcoop quotes them at length, and explains their meaning, as if they would be unfamiliar to his colonial readers. Mays merely offers names—Gerard de Nerval, Rimbaud, Simone Weil, Jacob Boehme—as if they signified intellectual texts shared by himself and other modernist readers. Hulcoop writes from a place to one side of these names and texts, and attempts to explain the strangeness of Webb's poems by quoting Frye's "the existential movement... seems to have had very little direct influence in Canada" (41). Mays declares the influence of "decadent" and "gnostic" European texts to be "without question the most compelling and sheerly interesting feature of contemporary North American culture" (26). Behind this declaration is a New-York centred American cultural milieu in which Genet, Robbe-Grillet, Beckett, Henry Miller, and Alexander Trocchi are headline names for Grove Press, New Directions, *The New York Review of Books*, and *Evergreen Review*, in which Timothy Leary and Alan Watt have become folk-heroes, and in which the romanticizing of both self-destructive quests for transcendence and amoral violence is becoming characteristic of new fiction—Burroughs, Rechy, Hubert Selby Jr., Mailer, Hawkes, Kosinsky among others. The distance between Hulcoop and Mays is the distance between *Canadian Literature* and *The New York Review of Books*, and between the different 'worlds' on which each is attempting to found its cosmopolitanism.

Later commentators will attempt to represent Mays's essay on Webb as mean-spirited, vituperative, and destructive; such a representation, however, can only be made outside the general frame of reference which Mays invokes, a frame in which self-destruction, deliberate failure, a neo-Gnostic risking of death and damnation are 'goods' of which to be 'proud' and 'fascinated.' The essay begins with a scene in which an "English Department" scholar considers his years of research on "the damned": "Sade, Gerard de Nerval, Hart Crane, Celine, Simone Weil, Artaud, Sylvia

Plath, Pound" (8). The scholar is pleased to have kept himself detached from "the ideas or projects of self-annihilation that had damned each to his particular torture." The "interminable formal descriptions" of his criticism "had tamed the lunatic or self-deprecating exemplars of modernist sensibility into 'classics.'" He had achieved scholarly success, "his 'opportunities' and 'future,'" had realized "his solid respectable dreams of quiet acquisition." Yet he is still dissatisfied, and finds the "source" of that dissatisfaction "at the very bottom of his card-box":

> ... the indiscrete, ugly things he felt: his dark fascination, not so much with the 'works' he was being paid to describe, as with the brilliant careers of the damned, the heroism of their obscenity, their extravagant hatred of all the critic had come to cherish. The memories rush back upon him: he remembers how the splendid proportions of the tormented souls' vulgar attacks on self and society had, if only for an instant, made his solid, respectable dreams of quiet acquisition seem puny and cowardly by comparison, how the theatre of cruelty that was their lives made his own life in home and department seem a boring soap-opera of flabby ambition. He remembers how a deep lust was quickened, a proud lust for the world-cancelling insanity and hatred that had made the damned a population of inescapable presences. (8-9)

This scene frames the essay within a binary opposition, not uncommon in romantic theory, between the open and the closed, the conventional and the risk-taking, the clichéd and creative. This opposition also articulates one between constrained, empiricist criticism such as Hulcoop's and open, subjective, phenomenological criticism such as that of Mays. The scholar is cautious, materialistic, and self-serving. Collocated with him are a series of words that gather a particularly negative charge by their association with him: career, detachment, irony, classroom, ambition, status, civilized, respectful, cool, detached, tasteful, solid, respectable, puny, cowardly, home, boring, flabby. The "damned" writers are fiery, transgressive, and self-annihilating. Collocated with them are a very different series of words: sin, repulsive, torture, lunatic, brilliant, obscenity, heroism, extravagant, heroism, tormented, splendid, vulgar, cruelty, lust, insanity. The conventionally 'positive' words in this series—brilliant, heroism, extravagant, splendid—are heavily ironized by being bound in oxymoronic pairs: "brilliant careers of the damned," "heroism of their obscenity," "extravagant hatred," "splendid proportions of... vulgar attacks" (8). The conventionally 'negative' words in this second series are positively charged through their association both with creativity and with the resonant names—Sade, Nerval, etc.—with which the scene began. The oxymoronic aspect of the series further associates its terms with the discourses of alchemy, Christian mysticism, and Jungian psychology. The cumulative weight of the scene is to define words like career, detachment, irony, civilized, respectful, and tasteful as 'bad' and terms like sin, repulsive, lunatic, obscenity, tormented, vulgar, cruelty, lust and insanity as 'good.'

The second step in Mays' essay is to valorize Webb by associating her with the second set of terms and inscribing her syntactically into the lists of "distraught, indiscreet artists":

> It is not possible to turn creators as various as Norman Mailer, Andy Warhol, Allen Ginsberg, or Leonard Cohen, Michael Morris, or Phyllis Webb into classical exemplars of dead sensibilities; their witness is too immediate and too vigorously alive to be monumentalized. (9)

This step adds monumental to the list of negative terms, and leads to a discussion of the ways by which critics attempt to reduce "dangerous, uncontrollable" artists by associating them with a 'civilization,' "tradition" or "an archetypal role." This, Mays argues, is what Hulcoop has done in the introduction to Webb's *Selected Poems* when he characterizes her as a "priestess'" and asserts that "civilized 'good sense' is an unmistakable element in Miss Webb's more mature poetry" (11). Mays reveals the cautious scholar of his essay's first two pages, anxious to confine a lunatic poet within his detached discourse, to have been Hulcoop. Simultaneously, through the subjectivities of his own phenomenological strategies, he distinguishes his own criticism from that of Hulcoop and associates it with his construction of "Phyllis Webb."

The strength that Mays locates in Webb's poetry is not in its offering "good sense" or its comforting the reader with the triumph of creativity—"it refuses to assume the shape of greatness" (11)—but precisely in its refusing to attempt such things. The poetry thus succeeds in confronting its readers with their own inadequacies and vanities:

> Her passions are ordinary (they are ours), her failure is familiar (it is ours), her hopes are the familiar ones our passions relentlessly engender, and her refusal to accept the phoney solutions proffered by suicide, madness, or the pose of Sisyphus is nothing other than unremarkable intelligence's unwillingness to accept nonsense. To go through the looking-glass of Phyllis Webb's writing is suddenly to find ourselves, not in a magical world of dream or realm of transcendent meaning, but in the same history we thought we had escaped, alone with the familiar problems of our world; *the same.* (12)

This proposition enables Mays to make the crucial link between the culture he left behind in the United States and Webb's writing, to read the latter as a familiar sign amid the strangeness of his new country. The proposition that Webb's failures are "our failures" allows him to read within her poems his own history of disillusionment with the radical student movement of the 1960s, and to read the people of both his old and new countries as existentially condemned to the absences of meaning lamented, cynically celebrated, or raged against by writers from Sade to Trocchi. The remainder of his essay is a chronicle of his own fall from metaphysics and utopian hope together with the collapse of the Marxist idealism of both the generation of Lukacs and Adorno and that of the 1960s U.S. student movements, and a celebration of Webb for having risked psychic devastation to confront and accept "the devaluation of all value" (22). The essay thus is able to locate Mays's own Southern post-bellum reconstruction background and student movement activism in relation to the larger context of twentieth-century Western metaphysics and political theory, and locate Mays in Canada through Webb's own emphatic preoccupation with the contradictions and failures of this metaphysics. The terms of Mays's celebration of Webb become the ones marked for approbation in the opening contrast between self-interested and respectable critic and tormented, damned, paradoxical and brilliantly lunatic writer. Her writing demonstrates "a *commitment* to sexual, intellectual, literary failure." It is "irresponsible, indiscreet." It possesses a "small, tacky theatricality... that *compels* us" (15, my italics). In a subtle allusion to Webb's poem "Sitting," which ironically considers the social value of bathers who "sit emptily in the sun... only remotely human" (*Selected Poems* 101), Mays concludes with a second dichotomy that echoes the one with which he began: a dichotomy between "the great mass of canadian [sic] humanity who, even as I write this summer day, are sitting emptily in the sun,... the motorized swarm that will take to the highways for their cottages this weekend, for the oblivion of beaches and resorts," and "us who have not yet found, any more than she, just how to render ourselves remotely human, oblivious to... the monstrous, meaningless, pointless questions" of metaphysical perplexity. Again Mays offers only two choices—to be philosophically naive and self-interested, like his English Department critic and swarming "canadian" vacationers, or to be tormented by questions which render "our" lives hollow and absurd. In the earlier parts of the essay Mays's use of the first person plural was ambiguous, often ironic, and usually included all western twentieth-century subjects and their 'empty' lives regardless of whether they attempted, like the academic scholar or the vacationers, to hide this emptiness under respectability, or like Rilke, Cohen and Webb, 'dared' to live in open contemplation of the abyss. Here, however, Mays emphatically shifts the meaning of "we" and "us," disassociating it from "the great mass of canadian humanity" and restricting it "to *us*, the dwindling minority" (his italics) who agonize over "monstrous, meaningless, pointless questions" (32), thereby decisively affiliating himself, his essay, his readers and Webb with the second possibility, and with the intellectually courageous—Kierkegaard, Nietzsche, Genet, Lukacs—to which he has tied it.

•◊

The next year I write a short entry on Webb for my guidebook to English-Canadian literature since 1960, *From There to Here*. While Mays's persuasive essay (persuasive to me, at any rate—perhaps because Kierkegaard, Nietzsche, Dostoevsky, Jaspers, Unamuno, Heidegger, Henry Miller, Camus, Gide, had been fashionable out-of-class undergraduate reading for 1950s North American arts students like myself) is very much on my mind, the context of my writing is considerably different from that of Mays's essay. In *From There to Here* I am setting out to distinguish much of the new Canadian writing of the 1960s from modernist writing and to claim for it the name of "postmodernism." This project gives my book a governing dichotomy, but not the caution vs. breath-taking failure dichotomy of Mays: mine opposes modernists who would prefer "to control both their world and their art" with postmodernists who "seek to participate in anarchic cooperation with the elements of an environment in which no one element fully controls any other" (20), modernists who believe in transcendent truth and postmodernists who attempt to believe only in subjective, phenomenological constructions. It is only by emphasizing the negative side of Mays's argument—that Webb's compelling gambles with nothingness are founded on profound dismay at the collapse of metaphysical certainty (and by concealing the ways in which his construction of Webb as extravagant and risk-taking resembles some of my own constructions of the postmodern)—that I am able to argue that Mays's readings of Webb are congruent with my own project. Although my phenomenological assumptions at this time are similar to those of Mays (and also, I should mention, to those of Marlatt in books like *Rings*, *Our Lives*, and *Steveston*), my arguments are based on formal and diachronic readings of her poems, rather than on his thematic and synchronic ones. These readings link the pessimism identified by Mays to "a restraint of image and a directness and economy of language" that increases, from the *Trio* poems through *The Sea Is Also a Garden*, until it becomes the silences and blank spaces of *Naked Poems*. My readings reduce the generously constructed melodramas perceived in Webb by Mays to "small melodrama and failures," and repeat Mays's suggestion that Webb's philosophical outlook is "Gnostic in seeking both transcendence without elevation to a celestial kingdom and purification of the soul by abasement of the body" (262). The "Phyllis Webb" of *From There to Here*, however, is not to be the suffering gnostic who will link Canadian writing to a disillusioned United States counterculture; it is to be an exemplar of the 'death' of modernism. My concluding paragraph begins:

> Phyllis Webb's poetry stands at the juncture between the modernist and post-modernist sensibilities. In it the modernist's rejection of the secular and the material and his campaign to purify the language have reached their ultimate end. Beyond lie only suicide and silence. From the fragments and silences of this end, however, the post-modern recognition of a vast, disjointed, but sufficient cosmos can begin. (264)

●◊

The struggle for "Phyllis Webb"—for whether this name would be a synecdoche for humanism, gnostic modernism, the end of modernism, or for some position on experience and value—takes yet a fourth turn in 1978 with Jean Mallinson's "Ideology and Poetry: an Examination of Some Recent Trends in Canadian Criticism." Mallinson, as her title hints, is concerned about "ideology" in literary criticism, and opens her essay with an argument that non-ideological criticism is a "possibility."

> I would like to examine three separate instances of what can be called ideological criticism of Canadian poetry: examples from a body of criticism which not only interprets but also ignores, rejects, and misreads poems and judges poets on philosophical or quasi-philosophical grounds. This kind of criticism, in spite of the professed good intentions of those who practise it,
> undermines the possibility of a sympathetic understanding of the variety of contemporary Canadian poetry. (93)

The non-ideological criticism, of which her own essay is implicitly to be an example, is to be inclusive ("understanding of variety"), and to avoid not only conflict with the texts it considers (being "sympathetic") but perhaps even the 'ignoring'or 'rejecting' of texts. Mallinson repeats these arguments in her conclusion, arguing that "[d]octrinaire criticism is baleful because it misinterprets the poetry which exists [sic], thus misleading readers, and because it is prescriptive in its directives about desirable attitudes and poetic modes, thus tending to limit the variety and scope of our literature" (109).

The notion that criticism should be non-philosophical or non-ideological is itself a fairly transparent ideological position, a doctrine of 'fairness' similar to that of Canadian multiculturalism in its assumption that conflict among cultural elements should be minimized and that "variety" should be a higher value than "philosophy" or selection. There is a pervasive lack of clarity in the syntax of Mallinson's argument which facilitates her development of this doctrine. She describes the criticism she opposes as one which "not only interprets but also ignores, rejects, and misreads poems and judges poets on philosophical or quasi-philosophical grounds," leaving it not clear whether she objects to the ignoring, rejecting, misreading, and judging per se or whether only when these are done on "philosophical" grounds. Her insistence, however, on not limiting "variety" suggests that she is against judgement absolutely. So too does her parallel listing of "ignores, rejects, and misreads" and "judges" as equally undesirable activities. Yet her principles about defending the variety of poetic texts do not extend to critical texts: she can oppose the rejecting of poems but she can herself vigorously reject an essay such as Mays's "Phyllis Webb," calling it "malevolent," "self-indulgent," "irrational," "venomous" (93), "hysterical" (94), and "savage" (95).

The focus of Mallinson's anger with Mays is apparently his having approvingly associated Webb's writing with the European literature of existentialist despair. In representing his argument, Mallinson makes no mention of how Mays establishes a neo-gnostic reversal of the connotations of the major evaluative terms he will employ—of how he makes his opening narrative of the cautious scholar, eager for career security and respectability, who carefully distances himself from the obscene, self-destructive extravagance of writers who fascinate him, operate to redefine terms like *failure, lunatic, vain, melodramatic, unhealthy* into terms of positive value.[1] Thus when she quotes passages in which Mays praises Webb, they appear indeed to be as mean-spirited and vituperative as she describes them.

> a poet whose whole desire goes out, finally, to the barbarian silence and lithic insensibility of things: whose poetry does not 'mature,' but merely changes as her tactics of self-destruction vary; whose work is as vain, sectarian, as without acme or distinction, as distorted by her lusts, and as inconclusive as any in the recent career of literary modernism.
> (Mays 11, as quoted by Mallinson 94)

> It is crucial to see... [her questions] for what they are: cries of pain camping as ideas, gasps for air too desperate for metaphor, yet set out in pleasing language *anyhow*, wilfully, against all reasonable expectation of what poetry can be expected to do. This unreasonableness... is radical to Miss Webb's poetic decisions and is that mental characteristic to which we can ascribe the melodramatic hollowness and overwrought stageyness of her poems.
>
> Such writing is a symptom of unhealth...
> (Mays 14-15, as quoted by Mallinson 94)

In the case of both quotations Mallinson conceals the implications of the concluding words. In the first what she conceals is Mays's repeated and favorable comparisons of Webb to writers like Genet, Plath, Artaud, Rilke (if she finds these comparisons belittling and 'malevolent' toward Webb, she omits to say). In the second quotation, her concluding with the word "unhealth" leaves the impression that Mays wishes that Webb were "healthy," and that he deplores "unhealth." In Mays's text, the words that follow "Such writing is a symptom of unhealth" declare the very opposite.

> Such writing is a symptom of unhealth—but were Phyllis Webb a *healthy* writer, it is doubtful that we could find much pleasure in her. (Health in literature, no less than in life, is very boring, and the only modern writers who can be read with much enjoyment are those whose works offer obsessive documentation of loss, disease, perversion, and self-destruction, or who, like Phyllis Webb, have demonstrated publicly a commitment to sexual, intellectual, literary failure. (15)

It is through these concealments that Mallinson reveals much of her own ideological agenda. The "Phyllis Webb" that she wishes is "lucid" (94) and healthy. She is not in conflict with societal values, and not dismayed by life, not driven by dismay to aberrational concepts like obsession or self-destruction. To view "Phyllis Webb" texts otherwise—to associate them with the "exuberant creativity [of] the Gnostic exemplars and... the 'decadents' of modern times, from Rimbaud and Baudelaire to Genet and Burroughs and the New York Dolls and General Idea" (Mays 26)—is to be venomous and vituperative. Where Hulcoop carefully explained the work of such writers, and Mays invoked their names as if they would be familiar to his readers, Mallinson keeps all of their names out of her text, as if they were somehow irrelevant to both her "Phyllis Webb" and the reader. She makes a similar omission in discussing my entry on Webb in *From There to Here* which she characterizes as passing on Mays's views in a further "castigation of a poetry of melodrama and failure." Here too her conceptions of "castigation" and "condemnation" (96) are strange: my writing in that entry much more closely resembles the "detachment" which Mays lamented in his "respectful" academic critic.

> The culmination of her work has been the brief, understated and ironic *Naked Poems* (1965) and the seven years of silence that have followed. Her distrust of materiality had always included a distrust of the efficacy of language; in *Naked Poems* this distrust brings about a language so private, cryptic, fragmentary, and 'naked' that it almost abandons communication. (262)

If the lucid and healthy "Phyllis Webb" were the only one in Mallinson's essay, the work would be of relatively little interest—another humanistic defense of the critical discourse of civility,[2] refusal of ideology, and Hulcoop-like attempt to define "Phyllis Webb" in familiar and comfortable terms rather than in the uncomfortable and alien ones offered by Nietzsche, Genet, and Artaud. However, on at least two occasions in her essay Mallinson speculates that Mays's alleged vituperation may have been directed toward Webb because of his "culturally determined expectations about the nourishing and comforting attitudes that it is thought appropriate for women to express" (94). This is one of the earliest attempts to construct a feminist "Phyllis Webb." Although it is founded on a male response to Webb's writing rather than on the writing itself, and mistakenly founded, this attempt will become a reference point for many subsequent feminist readings.

In 1980 Webb publishes *Wilson's Bowl*, her first new collection since 1965, dedicated to John and Sally Hulcoop. W.J. Keith's lengthy review in *Canadian Literature* acknowledges the "desperation of... consciousness," "unbearable loneliness," the "mind pushing towards the extremes into areas of perception both fascinating and dangerous, a mind never far from the end of its tether," that both Hulcoop and Mays had observed in her writing and had firmly associated with existentialist and decadent modernist textuality. Keith, however, associates this with the *person* "Phyllis Webb": the desperation is not in her texts but behind them: "the tension between the lucidity of her tone and the desperation of the consciousness behind it is perhaps the most remarkable quality of her poetry" (100). Of the existentialist and decadent modernist intertexts to Webb's poems named by Hulcoop and Mays, Keith mentions only Dostoevsky and Rilke, and in the context of Webb's poems about them.

In the earlier criticism there had been no firm distinction between person and text. Although Mays in particular emphasized the textual sources of the anguish and pessimism of Webb's poems, both he and Hulcoop had treated her poems also as personal utterances (quite possibly because many of the poems contain signs inviting readings of them as 'personal'). Commenting on her poem "Lament," Hulcoop had even altered one of its pronouns so that it could refer to "Webb" rather than to a persona; the change enabled him to say that Webb "has grown increasingly conscious of some readers' exasperation with what she calls 'the petulance / of (her) cries'" (24). Mays had more openly remarked on her "testimony, as a woman and a writer, of decisive, unmitigated failure" (12). In his review, Keith considers the possibility that the text should be regarded as a construction separate from its maker, and dismisses it as both inapplicable to Webb and possibly non-feminist—a particularly ironic suggestion in the light of later feminist discussions of Webb:

> Eliot's famous modernist dictum, 'the more perfect the artist, the more completely separate in him will be the man who suffers and the mind which creates,' in no way applies to her. She would see it, I imagine, as a characteristically masculine response. Her mind creates by brooding almost obsessively over the woman who suffers—or over others, men or women, who have suffered. She may concentrate her attention on the lives and dilemmas of others, but the personal voice, however varied and modulated, always reveals the personal strain. (100)

Keith finds her poems "frighteningly subjective" and "chilling." However, his positing that this personal, subjective element is *behind* the text rather than in it, allows him to construct a new high modernist "Phyllis Webb," one in which "[t]he tension between the lucidity of her tone and the desperation of the consciousness behind it is perhaps the most remarkable quality" (100). This "Phyllis Webb" is a craftsperson, a creator of balances and tensions. She has undergone "a long apprenticeship"(101), has achieved "a firm poetic discipline" (100), a "consummate clarity of tone"(101). "The balance" of her lines "is beyond praise." They demonstrate "a smooth assurance," and "a hard-won serenity" (102). She is the modernist who overcomes chaos by piling fragments against ruins, constructing stays against confusion. She overcomes the "dark, extravagant, abhorrent sectors" of John Bentley Mays's poet by attaining the detachment and control of his academic critic.

Two years after *Wilson's Bowl* Talonbooks publishes a second Webb selected poems, *The Vision Tree*, edited by Vancouver poet Sharon Thesen. This selection contains poems from Webb's earlier collection as well as new poems from the concurrently published chapbook *Sunday Water* and previously unpublished new work like "I, Daniel." Sharon Thesen's introduction gives little attention to earlier critical constructions as it sets out to create its own "Phyllis Webb," the "'West Coast writer.'" 'West Coast' poetry for Thesen presupposes "the consciousness of language as physical, a materiality prior to the devices of content; and... stance, an abandonment of the dubious privileges of the poet's ego" (9). Her references to "stance" and "the dubious privileges of the poet's ego" cryptically invoke Charles Olson's 1951 essay "Projective Verse" and its influence on Vancouver writers during the early 1960s and publication of the *Tish* poetry newsletter.

The first half of Thesen's introduction attempts to focus Webb's poems through various aspects of poetics. The opening short section, "Voice," argues the oral quality of the poems, while the next sections, "Line," "End," and "Desire," work with the line and line-break as both technical resources and thinly-veiled metaphors for themes:

> The attentiveness to the process of shaping, the curve and stretch of the voice of her line across the grid of the lyric is what constitutes Webb's formality. ("Line," 10)

> what we are often most grateful for are the poem's open completions, which do not stop the poem, but which cast their strange felicity back over all the other lines, so that the whole poem is gathered into a unity without proposing a closure. ("Ends," 10)

> It is from the line-breaks that all the inventiveness of the poem springs, that is, that point at which all energies re-gather,

inspire. In this way, the poem is re-formed at every instance of a new line, composing the energy of transitions, rather than an enthusiasm for an expressible idea. ("Desire," 11)

Thesen's vocabulary is considerably different from Keith's, but the "Phyllis Webb" she ultimately constructs is very similar. Her concern with poetics repeatedly places emphasis on formal elements and on the achievement of wholeness and unity: "shaping," "formality," "felicity," "unity," "re-formed," "composing." The fifth section of the introduction is entitled "Decorum," and the sixth "Composure"; the latter concludes "While Webb's concerns are passionate, her poems are never linguistic or ideological battlegrounds: whatever they might be saying, we are aware of an energy composed inside the diction and consciousness of the poem. In this "Phyllis Webb," passion, ideology, and conflict are restrained by composure, decorum, and the formal achievements of poetics.

The ethical dimensions of such terms become more visible in the later stages of Thesen's remarks about both Webb and her critical reception. "Webb has not been a prolific writer, but neither has she written carelessly or presumptuously." Webb critics have taken "some curious looks into her psyche, some decidedly more competent and respectful than others" (15). "It is true that 'murder, ignorance and lust' often shadow the poems, but they shadow the poems in the same way they shadow our lives: the darkness simply figures, as presence, in most responsible minds" (16). With presumably unwitting irony, this vocabulary reverses the dichotomy with which Mays framed his essay. The good is now the values of his academic critic: care, respectfulness, responsibility; the bad is the transgressive: presumptuousness, lust, darkness. Thesen's concluding section is titled "The Vision Tree," and argues that in her recent poems Webb performs "as poet... the shamanic role of interpreter, to the living, of the knowledge of the dead" (19). "The vocation of the shaman," Thesen explains, "—transcendence, propitiation, magical flight, healing, and enchantment—is earned by suffering, isolation, dream, ecstatic trance, and song." Far from celebrating the "unhealthy" against bourgeois notions of conventional healthiness as did the Mays "Phyllis Webb," this "Webb" is a healer whose suffering helps her pass "'great dreams on / to the common good'" (19).

◆

These wide variations in what "Phyllis Webb" may be are not merely the products of critical perspective, desire, and ideology. It is not merely that Mays admires risk and extravagant failure, Keith tradition and formal quiet, Thesen healing, responsibility and composure, or that various discourses of romance, civility or reason operate through them. There is another player active among these constructions, a historic Phyllis Webb who writes an introduction to *Wilson's Bowl* in which she alludes to her "critical wounds," and who agrees there with Mallinson's feminist interpretation of her situation by writing of "the domination of a male power culture in [her] education and emotional formation." This Webb gives the fragments of poems with which the volume begins the ironic title "Poems of Failure," and writes the various post-1974 poems on which Thesen can construct her poet-as-healer interpretation. In a 1983 interview with Eleanor Wachtel, incorporated into an article by Wachtel in *Books in Canada*, Webb appears to make a further intervention into the evolving conflict. Summarizing Webb's response to her critical reception, Wachtel writes,

> ... most devastating to Webb was a cruel 25-page attack by John Bentley Mays in *Open Letter* in 1973. The string of vicious epithets—vain, distorted by lusts, a writer of tacky theatricality—formed the core of Frank Davey's more damaging (because more widely circulated) depiction of Webb in *From There to Here* (1974) as utterly desolate, despairing, despondent. (9)

This appears to be someone's memory and representation—Wachtel implies it is Webb's, although much of the representation is of course also Wachtel's. Wachtel herself has apparently not checked either the Mays essay or the *From There to Here* entry—of "the string of vicious epithets" that Wachtel writes form "the core" of the entry, "vain" is the only one that actually appears there. She goes on to comment that "to label the poetry, like the poet, neurotic, is simplistic and one-sided," further suggesting she is unfamiliar with the criticism (even Mallinson had recognized that Mays was perceiving his "Phyllis Webb" to be something more extravagant than "neurotic").

Later in the article Webb tells Wachtel that resolution of various medical problems in the 1970s have left her much changed. "I have an inner personal buoyancy I never had before and a kind of solidity that I could never count on. It's allowed me more freedom in poetry, to flash around, out of a different personality." She also indicates that she "has been an 'intuitive feminist' since the 1950s"—the phrase recalls her telling Hulcoop in 1969 that she was an "intuitive existentialist"—and that her new feminist consciousness has made her aware of how the history of Canadian literature has been "sexist" and of how her early loss of her father through divorce had led her to "gravitate[ ] to men, to fatherly figures" (14). From these comments and Wachtel's reflections emerges yet another "Phyllis Webb," one that appears partly constructed and asserted by the historic "Phyllis Webb," one whose early pessimistic poetry is partly the product of ill health, divorce, the cultural domination of men, and who now, because of growing awareness of feminist analysis, moves—in Wachtel's words—"increasingly away from a preoccupation with delineating loss and towards subjects that are essentially more nourishing to the creative self" (8).

•◊

In the later 1980s four more substantial readings of Webb's writing are published—by George Woodcock, Cecelia Frey, and two by Stephen Scobie. Frey's essay, "The Left Hand of Phyllis Webb" (*Prairie Fire*, Autumn 1986, 37-48), responds to the late 1970s shift in American feminism from a focus on equal rights to one on valorizing women's mythology, history, and social practice, and to Webb's own feminist comments in her preface to *Wilson's Bowl*. Frey reads Webb's 1984 collection *Water and Light* as revising "both a central literary text of male authority" and "her own early conventional text of despair." Her "Phyllis Webb" has a career which moves from "the destruction of the enclosure of the public self" (43) to seeking "the way to wisdom... through nothingness," ridding "herself of all excess baggage, male text, male language, male garments" (44), finally achieving "a different female voice, one that is part of the text of female community" (46). While the metaphor behind this account is that of Christian mysticism, the feminism is a simplistic version of the feminism of Elaine Showalter and Gilbert and Gubar, with its assumptions of radical and originary gender difference. Frey's "Webb" "reverses her expectations" of patriarchal authority. In "I, Daniel" this 'Webb' brings about "the intertransformation of opposites, of female and male, of 'I' and 'Daniel,' [to] bring into play qualities which are associated with the female principle, qualities of impermanency, fluidity, adaptability" (47). She "moves... away from the convent and the father's garden to the open sea and its surging female power" (43).

In Frey, Thesen, Keith, and Wachtel, a new plotline for Webb's writing develops, but does so within different discourses and interpretations. For Keith, it moves from terror, fright, and subjectivity to craftsmanship, lucidity, and control. For Thesen, it moves through suffering, propitiating pain, to care, respect, and the shaman's healing vocation. For Wachtel, the career follows Webb's own parallel journeys from illness to health and from patriarchal oppression to feminist insight. For Frey, the visionary language which led Mays to associate her texts with those of Blake and Baudelaire, and the collapse of metaphysics, indicates a struggle to locate an alternate metaphysics—"nun, priestess, prophet—trace a growing sense of female energy and power" (39) Mays's "lunatic" becomes Gilbert and Gubar's "madwoman in the attic" (40), and presages sisterhood with Lilo Berliner of "Wilson's Bowl"—and ultimately "female community" (46).

Both Woodcock in his "In the Beginning Was the Question: the Poems of Phyllis Webb" (1987, 246-265) and Stephen Scobie in "Leonard Cohen, Phyllis Webb, and the Ends of Modernism" construct a similar plotline by beginning their discussions with my argument in the *From There to Here* entry that Webb's "poetry stands at the juncture between the modernist and postmodernist sensibilities" (264; Woodcock 246, Scobie 59). After making some substantial reservations about my book, Woodcock writes "[a]t the same time I accept... Davey's... placing Webb at the point where modernism, as it was manifest in Canadian poetry, expands into a field whose variegation of talents and approaches made it more complex and sophisticated" (247). Woodcock in fact finds a narrative of change and development extremely useful in a book in which he describes Canadian literature primarily through metaphors of growth and expansion. His book's subtitle is "the flowering of Canadian literature." It reports that Canadian literature came "to maturity...during the past quarter of a century" (11), that Margaret Laurence left for Africa and returned "changed and culturally enlarged" (14), that "Canadian poets seemed to flower in the atmosphere of renaissance...that came into Canadian writing during the 1960s" (192). For Woodcock, Webb's writing provides evidence "that we have a mature literature" (246), showing overall "growing maturity" (248) and "poetic progression" (254). The brevity and silences of her *Naked Poems* and the fifteen years without publication that followed "enabled Webb to go forward with sureness into even better work than she had done in the past." Her next book, *Wilson's Bowl*, shows "she had moved into more expansive views and more complex forms." What Woodcock's "Phyllis Webb" grows into, however, is merely the modernism of Keith and Thesen. Her writing, Woodcock proposes, reflects commitment to "perfection of the craft" and "the rightness of the line" (249). It achieves an "equilibrium of force" and "a strange Pythagorean serenity" (255). For "the clarity of her vision and the dedicated impeccability of her craft," Woodcock concludes, she deserves "a first place not merely among recent Canadian poets but in the whole poetic tradition of our land" (265).

In "Leonard Cohen, Phyllis Webb: the Ends of Modernism," Stephen Scobie connects his "Phyllis Webb" even more closely than Woodcock to my distinctions between modernism and postmodernism. Building on the fact that my *From There to Here* entry was written in the middle of

Webb's fifteen-year publishing silence, Scobie has his "Webb" become in her poems of the 1980s and 90s an oxymoron, "a postmodernist in the trappings of modernism" (59). He builds a contrast between a recently 'enshrined' Canadian modernist canon and a "postmodernist alternative canon...which has made much more limited inroads into the popular view of Canadian literature" (58); his sardonic comments about the modernist canon—its "deification" of Atwood and Davies, the "exalted heights" of the ECW journal *Essays on Canadian Writing*—suggest some desire to delegitimize it. His conclusion, however, in which he declares the "hope that the breaking down of the modernist/postmodernist distinction, so evident in recent criticism, will be reflected in the evolution of canon-formation: and [that] in this process the examples of such writers as Leonard Cohen and Phyllis Webb will be...useful" is much more equivocal, lacking even the recommendation that Webb or Cohen be considered canonical.

What seems to be reflected in this understated, minimal conclusion is the failure of an attempt by Scobie to deconstruct a binary opposition between modernism and postmodernism, employing "Phyllis Webb" as the third term that dissolves the opposition. Throughout the essay, Scobie's re-definition of "Phyllis Webb" as modernist/postmodernist has focused not on her poems but on the cover-blurbs of her recent books, and on Robert Kroetsch's comments on Webb in his essay "For Play and Entrance." Webb is modernist/postmodernist for Scobie because she has been read in both "modernist terms" (68) (by Frye, Atwood, an D.G. Jones) and "postmodernist" terms (by bpNichol and Kroetsch). This double reading of her work becomes the foundation of the phrase "so evident in recent criticism" with which Scobie qualifies his "breaking down of the modernist/postmodernist distinction." There are a number of reasons for the failure of the attempted deconstruction, none of which bear directly on this new construction of "Phyllis Webb" (although they may bear on the reticence of Scobie's conclusion). One is that the argument structure Scobie presents is Hegelian rather than Derridean; a modernist/postmodernist "Phyllis Webb" provides a synthesis of the opposing terms rather than a deconstruction. Another is that Scobie's concluding argument confuses logic with politics: the modernist/postmodernist antithesis is a political as well as logical construction—its "breaking down" as a political construction will depend on conflicts among social forces rather than on abstract analysis. A third is that the conflictual structure "modernism / postmodernism" is not a true antithesis—it is always already deconstructed; it possesses a non-exclusivity similar to that of other 'pairs' of interpretations in Webb criticism—Frey's essentialist feminism and Keith's formalism, Mays's existentialism and Woodcock's liberal-humanism.

Despite the title of the essay, Scobie's "Phyllis Webb" is not to be an affirmation of either modernism or postmodernism. Mays's reading of her as "in the lineage of Sade, Artaud or Plath" is for Scobie an "accusation,"[3] and remains one when Scobie suggests that I make use of it in *From There to Here* to argue "the advent of a postmodernist literature in Canada" (64). Scobie's own use for "Phyllis Webb" is openly signalled here only once, in the one textual reading he makes from Webb. This reading invokes both postmodernism and deconstruction, and argues the 'post' of the former to be a deconstruction of modernism.

> *Naked Poems* begins with the lyric impulse, in its starkest, most minimal form ('naked'), but the very conditions of that minimal lyric force it towards the extended sequence, and towards its

final, open-ended question, 'Oh?' 'Compelled *out of* lyric *by* lyric,' the sequence enacts the way in which the postmodern emerges from the end(s) of modernism. The 'post' of postmodernism does not indicate mere temporal sequence; rather, it is what Derrida would call a deconstruction.... (69)

This is the overt agenda of Scobie's previous essay on Webb, "I and I: Phyllis Webb's 'I, Daniel'" (1985): to figure "Phyllis Webb" as a deconstructing force which proposes and dissolves dichotomies. By calling the verses of "I, Daniel" anti-ghazals, he argues, Webb is "simultaneously affirming and denying the connection, doubling her own form as a definition and its negation" (63). Her poem, he proposes, repeatedly creates doubles and problematizes both their identity and apparent contradiction.

> 'I, Daniel' casts every term into doubt. Whether it be the documentary Daniel insisting on his Hebrew identity in the Babylonian captivity; or Webb confounding 'I Phyllis' with her fictional persona; or the fundamental doubling whereby every instance of 'I' becomes problematic in the very act of writing, Webb's title opens up gaps and divisions which lie at the very centre of contemporary writing and theory. (68)

This argument in turn connects with Scobie's thesis in his book-length-study of bpNichol, in which Nichol's use of ostensibly deconstructive strategies in poems like *The Martyrology* becomes for Scobie a link between modernism, postmodernism, and poststructuralism.

> Deconstruction has been implicit within modernism right from the start: within Saussure's distinction between the signifier and the signified; within the self-reflexiveness of Stein's "Rose is a rose is a rose is a rose"; within the cubist analysis of the syntax of painting. There could be few more exact illustrations of what Derrida calls "nonlinear writing" than Stein's *Tender Buttons*, and her erotic poetry celebrates what Barthes and Kristeva would call the *jouissance* of the text. The kind of writing

prefigured in Stein, given a theoretical base by poststructuralism, and (to a great extent) realised in bpNichol is writing which, according to Roland Barthes, "unsettles the reader's historical, cultural, psychological assumptions...." (22)

Scobie's modernism—defined through Saussure, Stein, and cubism—is different yet again from the various modernisms of Mays, Keith, Woodcock, and Thesen. From Saussure it can be constructed as evolving into deconstruction specifically and poststructuralism generally, enabling Scobie to write of "the 'deconstructionist' criticism of recent postmodernism and poststructuralism" (9). Like his "bpNichol," Scobie's "Phyllis Webb" is a means not only by which postmodernism can be revealed as the 'true' fulfilment of modernism (pushing into marginality the 'mistaken' modernisms of Kafka, Eliot, or Pound) but also by which both modernism and postmodernism can be dissolved into Derridean term 'deconstruction.' Deconstruction in turn is the central critical term of Scobie's *bpNichol* and his 1990 *Signature, Event, Cantext*.[4]

•◆

The most recent event in the struggle for "Phyllis Webb" is the publication of a special issue of *West Coast Line*, subtitled "a Festschrift for Phyllis Webb." Of the previous contestants in the struggle, only Scobie and Thesen contribute, Thesen through a poem, and Scobie through diary entries, a text which he, in a poststructuralist self-critical gesture, terms a "standard 'deconstructive reading'" of Webb's "Breaking." Many of the other contributions are celebrations of Webb, by Fred Wah, Aritha van Herk, Heather Pyrcz, Margaret Atwood, George Bowering, Gary Geddes, Erin Mouré, Roy Kiyooka, Timothy Findley, Libby Scheier, and Daphne Marlatt. There are interviews with

Webb by Smaro Kamboureli and Ann Munton, and four critical articles, by Susan Rudy Dorscht, Brenda Carr, Douglas Barbour, and Janice Williamson. Barbour follows an ambiguously modernist/postmodernist course in reading Webb's *Water and Light* as an "open...generous and innovative text" whose openness rests in part on "its feminist poetics." Rudy Dorscht examines the pronouns of *Naked Poems* to speculate on why it has been only recently read as a lesbian narrative,[5] and to reconstruct Webb as a feminist whose poems "are like the 'flower' which is 'held out / and placed on the shell of Venus'" (62).

While there is a recurrent giving of emphasis in the festschrift to the feminism of Webb's recent work, in the interviews and celebrations as well as in the essays, it is the essays of Carr and Williamson, and Pauline Butling's introduction, that make the largest contributions to the possible constructions of "Phyllis Webb." Carr focuses on Webb's relationship with the lyric, and on recent theories of the 'death' of lyric poetry and of the long poem as a postmodern genre. Her "Phyllis Webb" becomes a pretext for addressing current feminist difficulties with the theorizing of subjecthood and agency, and the conflict between poststructuralist problematizings of the free-standing self-present subjecthood, and feminist desires both to celebrate female subjects[6] (such as the "Phyllis Webb" celebrated by the festschrift) and to intervene as subjects in social debate. Her "Phyllis Webb" is a poet who "negotiates a third possibility [between the binaries of a fixed subject or no subject]—a strategically constructed provisional subject" [68]. In effect, Carr appropriates "Phyllis Webb" for use in an ongoing conflict within feminism, over whether essentialism can be recuperated from poststructuralist critique and 'saved' for feminist deployment. Her phrase "strategically constructed provisional subject" echoes the "strategic essentialism" theorized by Diana Fuss in her *Essentially Speaking*. This construction of Webb also has a use for Carr in its strengthening of similar arguments she and others have made in defending Daphne Marlatt texts from characterization as essentialist.

Williamson's essay on "the feminist suicide narratives of Phyllis Webb" begins with assumptions that identity is "a fast-forward shadow-play" and that a "distinction between the poet and her work" should be maintained by critics. These assumptions appear to lead away from the critical construction of a "Phyllis Webb" which seems to become the usual work of the Webb critic. However, Williamson chooses as framing texts for her essay John Bentley Mays's 1973 essay and my endorsement of it in *From There to Here*, which she sets out to contest as constituting both false inventions of "Phyllis Webb" and as unfortunate collapsings of the distinction she has proposed between "poet and her work," and which she cites in her conclusion as a "Mays/Davey discourse" (172) that has now been refuted. Yet another "Phyllis Webb" emerges from the essay—a victim of critical and "cultural misogyny" (156) who writes her way to "transformation and acceptance" (172).[7]

There are at least two difficulties that Williamson encounters in her attempts to dispute "Mays/Davey." The first is that the Mays essay was written on the basis of texts Webb published between 1941 and 1970, while Williamson's is based almost entirely on *Wilson's Bowl* of 1981. Williamson's own theory of identity as a "fast-forward shadow play" suggests that the 'Webb' of 1941-71 may be different from that of 1981; her insisting on measuring Mays's essay by the later work contradicts her identity theory by implying that there is a stable "Webb" identity which Mays in 1973 should have both known and foreseen in its 1941 to 1990 totality. A second difficulty is that Williamson seems to read the Mays essay only through Mallinson's 1978 representation of it, and through Mays's response to Mallinson later that year. The only passages she cites are ones cited by Mallinson, and thus like her she fails to note the framing antithesis of academic critic and courageous writer with which Mays re-defines the terms he will employ or, even more importantly, the ironic voice he recurrently deploys when discussing the powerful desires such a critic experiences to regularize and 'rehabilitate' Webb's troubling writings.

The most troublesome Mays passage for Williamson and Mallinson occurs in two paragraphs at the bottom of page 11 and top of page 12 of his essay, where he addresses, with bitter and pervasive irony, the "refusal" of Webb's writings to satisfy the bourgeois desires of frightened readers for some pretext under which they could recuperate or "transvalue" her work as "great." "Despite her admirers' best attempts at rehabilitation, her work sprawls and breaks and refuses to assume the shape of greatness; she has not given this culture another Name with which to counter its pervasive sense of inferiority" (11), Mays begins this passage. He begins the second paragraph by adopting the voice of these "admirers," parodically mocking their desire to 'rehabilitate' or "transvalue," even employing an ellipsis to emphasize that the first-person "we" of this voice is a persona and not the voice of his own critical discourse: "Perhaps we could transvalue this failure...[his ellipsis] if only she had given us one monumental poem, or had she loved or hated heroically, or shown evidence of courage toward one besetting sin" (12). Williamson follows Mallinson in reading these desires non-ironically, as Mays's own—even changing his syntax from the conditional to the indicative mood: "we could transvalue this failure... if only she had given us one monumental poem..." (Williamson 156). She follows Mallinson again in not noticing that "heroically" here is no longer contained in the "heroism of...obscenity" oxymoron through which Mays earlier had collocated it with the "compelling" texts of Artaud, Rilke, and Kafka, but instead is left collocated with "monumental," "great," "tasteful," and the various other bourgeois values of the nervous academic. Ignoring as well Mays's recurrent praise of writers who refuse greatness, she goes on like Mallinson to interpret the phrase "if only she had loved or hated heroically" not only as Mays's personal wish but as a characterization of Webb as the ungiving female, for Williamson "La Belle Dame Sans Merci."

Pauline Butling's introduction to the festschrift endorses a number of arguments made by Williamson; in addition, it echoes John Hulcoop's wish of twenty years earlier when Butling declares her hope that her work will "attest to [Webb's] status as a major Canadian writer." Butling presents a narrative of Webb criticism as a narrative of progress, from "handful" and "homogeneity" to challenge, increase, fluidity, and variety:

> Webb criticism divides, roughly, into two periods. The first twenty years (from about 1955 to the early seventies) consists of a handful of reviews and articles.... The criticism of this period is fairly unified, reflecting the relative homogeneity of the literary establishment.(14)
>
> The first reviews to question both the liberal-humanist and gendered values in Webb criticism appeared in 1971-72. (15) Some reviewers continue to extend the now familiar narrative of Webb as the suffering, sensitive individual....

> However, feminist and other critics have challenged that construction: Webb as female writer working to transform male traditions and forms is now a familiar alternative narrative.
>
> Increasingly, too, there is more talk about language processes.... (16)
>
> Yet another recent approach is to discuss Webb's texts in relation to other texts. [...] With these critics, a static Webb persona is replaced by a fluid and variable I/eye: ironic, mocking, affirming, despairing, playful, erotic, intellectual, subversive, questioning answering. (17)

Butling follows Wachtel and Williamson in giving special emphasis to the need for criticism to acknowledge a "separation between the writer and her work," arguing that criticism will otherwise "be reductive" and lose any sense that the selves presented in literature "are constructed of and in language." This is a particularly ironic claim for an editor to make after having assembled a collection that collages critical essays with personal letters, interviews, the reminiscences of friends, tributes, and photographs of Webb with her mother, her books, her cat, and on the Salt Spring Island beach gazing at the petroglyph "Wilson's Bowl" (in its collecting of poems, reminiscences, and personal photos, the festscrift goes far beyond the practice of *West Coast Line* and its precursor, *Line*, to publish and investigate archival materials). A 'feminist' program to locate the personal so that it can be political, to establish and valorize what Williamson approvingly calls a "network of women" (171), " female friendship and authorship" (172), appears to collide in both Butling and Williamson with another 'feminist' program not to "conflate[ ] a woman's body with a textual body" (Williamson 157).

Butling gives special emphasis also as a subnarrative to Mallinson and Williamson's characterization of the

"Mays/Davey" commentary on Webb and, with subtle shifts in viewpoint between sentences, parenthetical interpolations, and the occasional omission of quotation marks (as around 'critical misogyny'), elaborates and endorses it as her own.

> Jean Mallinson's 1978 article on ideological criticism is the first to raise the issue of gender bias in Webb criticism. She points to the gendered definitions of value which inform John Bentley Mays' critique of Webb in a 1971 issue of *Open Letter*. He faults Webb's lack of the heroic (read male) vision "if only she had given us one monumental poem, or had... loved or hated heroically" (12). He also laments the absence of the earthy (read female) figure who "sings the song of dwelling" (33). Janice Williamson's 1987 dissertation chapter, published here in revised form, further explores the problem of critical misogyny and notes the resulting "limited and destructive reading of Webb's work" by critics such as John Bentley Mays and Frank Davey. (16)

This account of Mays is somewhat more misleading than Mallinson's. It not only ignores Mays's ironic attribution of the wish that Webb be "heroic" to his academic critic, but also manufactures an alleged lament of "the absence of the earthy"—ostensibly so Butling can complete the balance of her "read male," "read female" characterizations. No reference to 'earthy' occurs in Mays's essay. The phrase "sings the song of dwelling" doesn't occur on page 33 or on any other page of Mays's essay, but in his later essay on Daphne Marlatt which Mallinson cites in another part of her critique. Like Williamson, Butling is apparently depending on Mallinson for both quotation and interpretation of Mays.

◆◇

This already perhaps too lengthy survey touches on only the more substantial and consequential episodes in the continuing struggle for "Phyllis Webb." It omits numerous book reviews, Desmond Pacey's high modernist entry on Webb in *Creative Writing in Canada* (1961), John Hulcoop's "Phyllis Webb and the Priestess of Motion" (1967), "Webb's Water and Light" (1986), and booklet *Phyllis Webb and Her Works* (1981), Laurie Ricou's duplicitous "Phyllis Webb, Daphne Marlatt and Simultitude: Journal Entries from a Capitalist Bourgeois Patriarchal Anglo-Saxon Critic" (1986), and Pauline Butling's "Phyllis Webb as a Post-Duncan Poet" (1988). It omits also several interviews with Webb in which she makes additional interventions into the struggle. Although it contains events that occur on a line of history, it is not precisely a narrative, with teleology and metaphysical completion. The plots recur. Rival contestants remain undriven from the scenes, and contend again, if not under earlier names in similar discourses.

The struggle for "Phyllis Webb" is particularly instructive in showing the extremes contestants will go to in the struggle for literary power, and the shifting relevance of various scenes of power for specific contestants. "Phyllis Webb" is not a term to be claimed in any vigorous way by women critics until Mallinson in 1978, but by the 1991 festschrift male commentators (outnumbered sixteen-to-seven) appear almost as guests within a women's project. For John Bentley Mays in 1973 "Phyllis Webb" is a means both of bridging a gap between his birth and adopted cultures and of valorizing and disseminating concepts of phenomenology and eschatology within the Toronto arts scene. For Mays in 1992, "Phyllis Webb" is a sidebar to a critical discourse he has developed as art critic of the *Globe and Mail* on the basis of both contemporary Canadian and European art and the decadent modernist exemplars he cited in his earliest published essays.

Mays is probably correct in hypothesizing that Webb's modernist critics of the 60s and 70s feared the excesses and passions of her poems: figures of control predominate among both the criticism and praise of Pacey and Hulcoop. These figures, which return in Keith and Woodcock's essays in the 80s, are not merely 'modernist' or 'humanist' figures; they are also symptoms of the reader's own fear of the psychological depressions and metaphysical absences into which Webb's writing has often—both ironically and melodramatically—inquired. Webb's own interventions in the wake of Mays's essay, her apparent report to Wachtel of its damage, her allusion to her "critical wounds" in *Wilson's Bowl*, suggest that the excesses of her work may have offended her too—at least in the heightened form in which the extravagances of Mays' own admiration and textual productions returned them to her. For his "Phyllis Webb" remains—despite the perceptions of the many readers who feared its power to the historical person Phyllis Webb—a textual construction, formed out of the discourses of her poetry, the powerfully disturbing writers cited within it, the phenomenological strategies of his criticism, and the decadent 'black romantic' strain in 1960s counterculture writing from which Mays had come. Women respondents' attempts to represent it as a 'personal attack,' and to use it as an argument to insist on a "separation between the writer and her work" (Butling 15) are not only overlooking that all "Phyllis Webbs," even the "Phyllis Webb" of the person or "writer," are textual constructions, but also theorizing a simplistic relationship between texts. Although Mays's text can influence the construction of other texts (like those of Mallinson or Williamson), it has not the direct causal power that they fear. It and the discourses it contains can become part of the general discursive field in which Webb and others live and write; it cannot, as Mallinson in particular seems to fear, control that field. Such a fear ultimately returns to that of Hulcoop, and to the also powerful, containment-producing fears of the high modernists, becoming not a fear of Mays but of discourse itself.

Mallinson's essay, with its hyperbolic epithets and wilful misquotation, displays in extreme form the powerful fears discourse, Webb's poems, and responses to them can evoke. Her quotations from Mays come to rest on the word "unhealth," transferring to him her own distress at "unhealth" by concealing his endorsement of it which begins in the very next phrase of his text. It is for a *healthy* "Phyllis Webb" that Mallinson struggles—one both constructed as healthy in literary criticism and healthy in life. At the very least she will counter this notion of "unhealth" by constructing Mays as unhealthy—as "hysterical," "malicious," "malevolent." Within three years, in *Wilson's Bowl*, Webb's own counter-constructions appear. These too gesture toward the figure of health. She has been engaged in "great struggles with silence." She has not been reclusive, she has "a desire for privacy." She is embarrassed by the "dominance of male figures" in some of her new poems—her "embarrassment" here reaches intertextually to Mays's essay and the litany of overtly suffering male names with which he had associated hers. Moreover, Mays's comments on the bleakness of her poems on suicide are answered with the book's title. Wilson Duff and Lilo Berliner have suicided, Berliner has left her suicide note on Webb's porch, but Webb has contemplated these acts and completed out of them a remarkable poem. Wachtel's article follows, itself filled with Mallinson's indignation, concern, and focus on health. Its subtitle reads "Once threatened by 'the terrible abyss of despair,' Phyllis Webb has moved beyond mysticism and anarchy to a curiously domestic isolation," leading the reader from terror to domesticity, from despair to curiosity. Throughout, Wachtel will recurrently return her text and reader to healthy figures of the practical, domestic and organic.

> Phyllis Webb is standing in a drizzling rain in front of La Québécoise Restaurant in Vancouver....she looks elegant in tweeds—sweater and skirt—and dark boots. There's an impression of textures—silver jewellery nestled amidst layers of wool. (8)

> Webb is outside on the porch.... There are flowers everywhere, inside and out, tomatoes ripening on the windowsill of the sunlit kitchen. The wicker-topped table is positioned between two windows—one looking out on the garden and the other facing the harbour, toward which Webb gestures with long expressive fingers when referring to her Victoria childhood. (13)

> It began as an exercise. Webb would sit at her kitchen table every morning to work, writing the poems on file cards. [...] "I was thinking today, why do I write here? [...] But I was also thinking more, do I feel particularly comfortable where I cook and wash the dishes? Open and close the refrigerator?" We're sipping almond tea in the dusk. (14-15)

Webb's own role in arguing constructions of "Phyllis Webb" shows the direct and even unwittingly effective role an author can sometimes have in the processes of literary power. When she refuses Mays's admiring association of her with the extremes of modernist angst, she makes no visible effort to become the ikon of feminist struggle she will later become. She seems mainly to wish to become productive once again as a writer—to have poems "born" from her struggles with silence (WB [9]). Neither has she any visible interest in becoming an exemplar of poststructuralist poetics, even though her explorations of the uncertainties of identity will lead to Scobie's persuasive reading of "I, Daniel," as a poststructuralist text. More importantly it shows the role discursive change can play in power constructions. Mallinson's 1978 suggestions that Webb criticism reflects male disapproval of her unwillingness to play the "nourishing and comforting" woman (94) arises out of an emerging discourse of American feminism by which it is at least partly constructed. Webb's own comments in 1980 about "domination" of her writing by men arise similarly out of this discourse, and will join with those of Mallinson, Wachtel, and Frey in a growing network of interpretation whose latest manifestation is the *West Coast Line* festschrift.

The rival interpretations of "Phyllis Webb" were part of similarly wide-spread discourses and their struggles for interpretive power in our culture. Those of Hulcoop, Keith, Thesen and Woodcock were parts of high modernist discourse, with it emphases on conserving received values and defending the civilized against 'confusion' and excess. Conceived from its earliest appearance in Arnold as a defensive discourse, protecting the class prerogatives of the bourgeoisie against social change of all kinds (whether socialism, commercialized mass-values, ethnic, gender, and racial challenge), this discourse becomes increasingly defensive as the twentieth century proceeds. Its vocabulary of moderation, balance and common sense is especially stylized when it attempts to construct a 'balanced' and 'craftsman' "Phyllis Webb." My own dramatic interpretations of Webb in 1974, together with later and more nuanced ones by Kroetsch and Scobie, work out of the emerging discourse of a political postmodernism, with its program of valorizing the 'open' in order to delegitimate hierarchies and centralisms and establish alternate values based on regional, ethnic, gender and class specificities.

The stakes of these discursive assertions are high— higher perhaps than the 'person' Phyllis Webb, whose poems are becoming one of their sites of conflict, may have wished. At stake is both how a culture may be led to perceive its internal relations—as hierarchy, network, centre-margin, isolated regions, separate populations—and what constituency or alliance of constituencies will be perceived to have priority within the power structure of received perception. The competition between some feminisms and postmodernism here is particularly intense: Canadian postmodernism is a coalition of constituencies each with a stake in the opening of culture to alternatives to bourgeois, centralist Arnoldian 'common sense' assumptions. Its constituencies include western regionalists, cultural decentralists, socialists, various kinds of feminists, and racial, ethnic, and gender-orientation activists, who themselves often seek to advance conflicting agendas. Individuals may find themselves, from ideological conviction or strategic pragmatism, within one or more conflicting postmodern constituencies. Or to rephrase this, the individual constituencies, because of conflicting intertextual links between them, often overlap, or appear to overlap.

However, among feminists of various kinds, as Linda Hutcheon outlines in her *The Politics of Postmoderism*, the conviction has frequently appeared that postmodernism's challenges to authority are often more aesthetic than political, that they are male-dominated, and that they are done within a complicit relationship to existing power systems—that whereas feminisms have clear and intentional political goals, postmodernism contents itself with the production of gamey, parodic, marketable texts that challenge authority without threatening it. (In part this conviction has stemmed from United States postmodernism, arguably much less political and more market-driven than the Canadian variety, and from United States feminists' perceptions of that postmodernism.) In the case of recent Webb criticism, there has been a strong sense among women critics that Webb 'belongs' to feminist criticism more than to either postmodernist or high modernist criticism. Male critics, whether these be Keith, Woodcock, Mays, or Scobie, are cited here only to be disputed; they are either wrong or irrevelant. I say this not as an accusation, but in appreciation of what I regard as an understandable and reasonable political strategy, particularly on the part of less powerful constituencies. From this general strategy, I believe, come some of the excesses, deceptions, and strange strategic alliances in recent Phyllis Webb criticism—the recurrent attempt to construct Mays's phenomenological essay as destructive rather than endorsing, to construct postmodern constructions of Webb as 'misogynist,' to change the figure of health from being a cultural figure to being the literal well-being of the historic "Phyllis Webb." Butling's *West Coast Line* festschrift enacts this conflict, both in her introduction in which a relatively inclusive postmodernism yields to a certain kind of feminist need to invent a Webb rescued from men by women, and in the strategic abetting of this enterprise by more generally focused postmodernists—Bowering, Wah, Scobie, Barbour, Kiyooka, Tostevin, van Herk, Kamboureli—thus keeping alive their own claims to "Phyllis Webb."

The inclusion of these was most likely in some sense conditional. Under the editorship of Roy Miki, *West Coast Line* has been becoming much more aligned with disadvantaged social groups than his earlier *Line* magazine, which tended to reflect the manuscript collections of Simon Fraser University library. The Fall 1992 issue featured racial minority writers Miki had met at a conference of The Racial Minority Writers Committee of The Writers Union of Canada in the previous May; the Spring 1993 issue was partly focused on papers given at a November 1992 conference organized by Miki entitled "Inglish," a conference on "marks of domination, of intimidation, of the pressures to conform to a language not one's own" (Miki 5); the Spring 1994 issue is to be entitled "Colour: an Issue." A few days after the March 1992 appearance of the Webb issue, I sent a four-page letter to *Line* outlining most of my objections to the Williamson article that I present here. *West Coast Line*'s not publishing that letter was very likely an appropriate response given the network of power relations within Canadian literature. Someone like Frank Davey has ample opportunity to present his views; many of the writers whose work Miki is explicitly working to represent have much less.

This essay—as 'you reader' must have long ago recognized—is also very much an intervention in the "Webb" struggle, aimed to keep "Phyllis Webb" alive as a contest of multiple constructions, to contextualize these contending constructions, and to defend and keep in circulation my own views. A politically active, postmodernist "Phyllis Webb" remains of interest to me ("useful," Scobie might say), to my own writing, and to my various constructions of Canadian literature and culture, much as a paradoxically marginalized and major "Webb" remains of interest to *West Coast Line*. Like Hulcoop, Mays, Keith, Mallinson, Wachtel, Butling, and Williamson, I also admire and appreciate "Phyllis Webb." However, given the disagreement over what this "Phyllis Webb" may be, it may not be generally useful—or effective—for any one of us to say so.

NOTES

[1] In a reply to Mallinson's article, Mays repeats this distinction between an academic critic "who has definitively left his human wholeness behind him...out of touch with his own urgencies," "a disembodied intellect," and a transgressive writer who "bursts...expectations asunder." Academic critical writing is characterized by "timidity and narrowness" while poetry touches "the dark, extravagant, abhorrent sectors of ourselves." Mays implies here that Mallinson is practising academic criticism by refusing to recognize and respond to the "extravagant, abhorrent" elements in Webb's poems. In her response to Mays, Mallinson claims not "to understand" the point Mays is making or its relevance to her article. One can only speculate on whether she has forgotten the scholar-writer dichotomy with which Mays' essay opened or whether she is merely pretending to do so.

[2] See Lorraine Weir, "The Discourse of 'Civility': Strategies of Containment in Literary Histories of English-Canadian literature." Weir's focus is on how critical discourses which insist on values of tradition and reasonableness operate to keep ideologically disruptive writers on the margins of the Canadian canon. In the case of Mallinson, her emphasis on 'civility' lies in her understanding of a canon as inclusive and non-conflictual, and her refusal of Mays's attempt to have disruptive values—vanity, self-destruction, failure—established as criteria for canonicity. Her canon of "variety" requires that Webb be constructed not in terms of conflict and rupture but of 'style' and 'lucidity.'

[3] This word, together with his terming Mays's essay "bizarre" and "tedious" (64), conflict with the otherwise neutral summaries Scobie offers of it and my guidebook entry, and appear gratuitous to his general argument. There may be a shadow here, I suspect, of the historical Phyllis Webb's own generally known unhappiness with the Mays essay. See also note 7.

[4] It seems also possible that Scobie wishes to dissolve the critical conflict between modernism and postmodernism in order to make space for his own poetry, which unlike that of Bowering, Kroetsch, or Nichol has not found a highly visible place within Canadian postmodernism. Of the two poets whose canonical 'usefulness' he urges, Cohen has been largely forgotten by postmodernism, while Webb has been often adopted (by Nichol, Kroetsch, Barbour, Wah among others) into postmodernism as ambiguously both precursor and colleague. Webb's construction as either

postmodernist or feminist would do little to achieve the kind of canon-alteration which he urges.

5 Rudy Dorscht is probably asking the wrong question here, or perhaps asking only one of a number of possible questions. Most of Webb's early critics, certainly those who knew Webb in the Vancouver literary community, were aware that *Naked Poems* concerned a lesbian love affair. It was in part the polite conventions that governed literary criticism at the time, rather than reading practices, that lay behind the 'not speaking' about lesbianism, just as it lay behind the not speaking of homosexuality in discussions of various male poets. Another factor for some may have been concern that attention to the lesbian aspects of the poem could have unfortunate social or employment repercussions for Webb.

6 This conflict resulted in a particularly poignant moment at the 1983 New Poetics Colloquium in Vancouver, when arguments by various male poets—Steve McCaffery, Ron Silliman, Charles Bernstein among others—that in the wake of Barthes' "Death of the Author" and Derrida's deconstruction of *presence*, the self-present free-standing subject was an illusion no longer available to writers, provoked Daphne Marlatt to protest that just as soon as women writers had the opportunity to construct female characters as self-present Cartesian selves, male writers declared such a self obsolete. Marlatt at this time was writing *Ana Historic*. Her implication was that deconstruction was, at least in its effects, an attack on the still fragile resources of feminism. In recent years, some theorists have suggested that deconstruction offers both women and men the important political project of constructing their own subject positions in discourse.

7 Again the shadow of the historic Phyllis Webb's construction of the Mays's essay may be visible. Four years earlier, while being interviewed by Williamson, Webb had welcomed her characterization of the essay as "particularly nasty," and had applauded her attempt to summarize Mallinson's response.

> JANICE: Mallinson describes a particularly nasty John Bentley Mays article as 'ideologically biased.'
>
> PHYLLIS: To put it mildly.
>
> JANICE: Mallinson then goes on to dismiss Mays's article as an 'extravagant, malevolent, and self-indulgent...venomous

attack...a maligned combination of rhetorical self-advertisement and desperate, irrational ill-will.

WEBB: Wonderful, wonderful! Isn't that great? (Williamson 1992, 333)

Webb had gone on here to tell Williamson that she had been "genuinely pained and damaged by the Bentley Mays article" (334). This shadow may well extend to Pauline Butling's introduction to the *West Coast Line* festschrift.

Contesting 'Post(-)modernism'

> ... almost every writer on modernism and postmodernism now seems to be devoted as much to blurring the distinction as to sharpening it. The 'post,' we are told, does not really indicate temporal sequence; the two movements are implicated in each other. When I use them in this essay, then, they should be understood as having a Derridean mark of erasure hovering over them....
> (Stephen Scobie 1991, 56)

> Derrida has at times resorted to the device of putting key words 'under erasure,' in order to show that, while their continued use is indispensable, no firm assumptions can be made about their status or meaning. Frequently, one feels that almost every word in poststructuralist discourse should be used under erasure....
> (Scobie 1989, 8)

I, 'Frank Davey'—to make the self-distancing gesture which Stephen Scobie suggests lies "at the very centre of contemporary writing and theory" (1985, 68), and which Linda Hutcheon argues underlies "the postmodern view of representation as a matter of construction" (1989, 41), helped begin the history of the word 'postmodern' in Canadian literature by deploying it in 1973 as one of the organizing concepts of the guidebook I was undertaking on Canadian writing since 1960, published the next year as *From There to Here*. The "under erasure" gestures above are not merely playful: 'Frank Davey' and similar signifiers have had numerous doubles offered for them since 1973 as the political contests around 'postmodern' have grown. The 'I' and 'Frank Davey' who deployed the term are both text and constructions of memory to the 'I' etc. that writes this chapter. The latter, however, through both history and present circumstance, continues to have a stake in that deployment.

In 1973 postmodern was a term that had only recently entered literary use in the United States. Its entry had been accompanied by numerous retrospective critical texts that had attempted to construct and summarize modernism—Irving Howe's *The Decline of the New* (1963), Cyril Connolly's *The Modern Movement* (1965), Harry Levin's essay "What Was Modernism" (1966, one of the earliest texts to use "post-modern"), John Barth's "The Literature of Exhaustion" (1967), Monroe Spears' *Dionysus and the City* (1970), Joseph Chiari's *The Aesthetics of Modernism* (1970), Ihab Hassan's *The Dismemberment of Orpheus: Toward a Postmodern Literature* (1971), George P. Elliott's *Conversions: Literature and the Modernist Deviation* (1971). Although these studies offered at least as many versions of modernism as recent commentary has offered of postmodernism, the most recurrent one was one summed up by Spears:

> Most serious writers and artists of the present century have...regard[ed] the break with the past as disinheritance or Fall. This historical catastrophism has been a central theme of modern art, and the concomitant view of the present as a waste land, now that civilization is destroyed and human nature changed, becomes, with its wrenching sense of loss, the dominant myth. (33)

Chiari, for example, located the emergence of modernism in "the partial disintegration of Christianity and in the growth of a type of rationalism which has finally reached the stage of being an end in itself" (17). Howe argued that "the modernist sensibility posits a blockage, if not end of history:

an apocalyptic cul-de-sac in which both teleological ends and secular progress are called into question" (5). Hassan constructed a modernism that was a product of "radical crisis of art, language and culture." Citing Jerzy Peterkiewisc's account of the purpose of an aesthetics of silence—"to investigate the poets' desire to die with poetry and the desire to go beyond the words and whether this means the ultimate failure of poetry as a literary medium or whether, on the contrary, it suggests that poetry reaches the sublime when it ceases to be a medium" (22)—Hassan described a modernism profoundly alienated from both society and language. Vainly seeking refuge in transcendence, this modernism retreated more and more into silences that reflected back the horror of the metaphysical void it believed it had discovered. Conversely, "the postmodern spirit," he concluded, "participates in the renewal of shapes, straining the structures of human life. Thus the reign of terror, wonder, and burlesque in our age" (256).

It was this reading of modernism as preoccupied with personal and cultural failure, and straining for the transcendence which only silence could offer, which informed my survey of Canadian literature for *From There To Here*. It remains a useful reading, one of few able to account for the austerities of Imagism, the reductions of Dada, the metaphysical void beneath Hemingway's 'codes' of style and honour, Joyce's and Stein's replacement of metaphysics with language, the chosisme of Robbe-Grillet, the repetitions and silences of Beckett. This reading informed John Bentley Mays's responses to the poetries of Phyllis Webb and Daphne Marlatt in his *Open Letter* essays of 1973-74. It also appears frequently in the pages of one of the first journals to incorporate postmodern into its title:

Boundary 2: a journal of postmodern literature, founded by William Spanos and Robert Kroetsch in Binghampton, N.Y., in 1972 (in the first issue are not only poems by 'Frank Davey' but a review by Hassan, reviews of Louis Kampf's *On Modernism*, Poggioli's *The Theory of the Avant-Garde*, and Hassan's anthology *Liberation*, and an article by David Antin "Modernism and Postmodernism"). In a Canadian poetry issue of *Boundary 2* in 1974, almost concurrent with publication of *From There To Here*, Kroetsch would make his notorious pronouncement that Canadian literature had "evolved directly from Victorian into Postmodern" (1).

The insertion of postmodernism as a concept into American critical debate in the late 1960s and early 1970s seemed to me in 1973 a symptom of a general sense in the United States critical community that some sort of radical, potentially epistemic, change had occurred or was occurring in American culture. In a variety of spheres, cultural 'shocks' had occurred: the racial shocks of the 1965 Watts riots (parts of which I had witnessed, from an apartment within the 'curfew zone'), the rise of the Black Panthers, the emergence and assassination of Martin Luther King and Malcolm X, the generational shock of the counterculture and anti-war movements, the growth of the power of television, the increasing globalization of economics and culture. In literature there were perceived to have been 'landmark' events: Grove Press's successful publication of Miller's *Tropics*, the publication of Donald Allen's *The New American Poetry* (Antin constructs it as "a turning point," "an alternate view of the history of American modernism" [100]). In criticism, the existentialism of Sartre and Camus, structuralisms of Lévi-Strauss, Barthes, and Foucault, and the phenomenology of Husserl, Merleau-Ponty, and Poulet were unsettling established methodologies, as were indigenous texts like Hartman's *The Unmediated Vision*, Steiner's *Language and Silence*, and Brown's *Life Against Death*. Postmodernism was a word strategically and politically useful both in defining something new—a banner under which a new journal like *Boundary 2* could announce itself—and in closing off modernism and opening the way to alternate theoretical and cultural discourses. Together with "what was modernism," "postmodernism" became a new critical field in which theories could be elaborated and texts published. Simultaneously ways were 'opened' into cultural discourses at least covertly supportive of progressive politics. For Hassan, after modernism's "self-parody, self-subversion, and self-transcendence, after the pride and revulsion of anti-art will have gone their way, art may move toward a redeemed imagination, commensurate with the full mystery of human consciousness" (258). For Spanos, arguing from Heidegger and Merleau-Ponty, postmodernism is to reintegrate the individual subject into history and participatory politics:

> Our time calls for an existence-Art, one which, by refusing to resolve discords into the satisfying concordance of a *telos*, constitutes an assault against an *art*-ificialized Nature in behalf of the recovery of its primordial terrors. The most immediate task, therefore, in which the contemporary writer must engage himself...is that of undermining the detective-like expectations of the positivistic mind, of unhoming Western man, by evoking rather than purging pity and terror—anxiety. It must, that is, continue the *iconoclastic* revolution begun in earnest after World War II to dislodge or, to be absolutely accurate, to *de-occident*, the objectified modern Western man, the weighty, the solid citizen, to drive him out of the fictitious well-made world, not to be gathered into the "artifice of eternity," but to be exposed to the existential realm of history, where Nothing is certain. (167)

Although the cultural conditions in Canada were

somewhat different than they were in the United States, my use of postmodernism was—both in my memory and in its present appearance in *From There to Here*—similarly strategic. Canada, in fact, had been experiencing national affirmation rather than the national interrogation the United States had experienced through the civil rights movement and the Viet Nam war protests. Canada's nationally celebratory centennial year had coincided with a dramatic rise of civil protest in the United States and increased emigration of American citizens to Canada. While McLuhan's *Understanding Media* was often read in the United States in apocalyptic terms, in Canada both his message that a "global village" might subvert aggressive national ideologies such as the American and his own example of Canadian international influence tended to aggrandize nationalist sentiment. The intellectual influence of phenomenology and structuralism had had little unsettling impact in Canadian criticism, which continued to be founded on the humanism of Woodcock and Frye, and on centralist conceptions of humanity in Woodcock's case, and of both humanity and Canada in that of Frye. With Dudek and Gnarowski's *The Making of Modern Poetry in Canada* (1967) the task of conceptualizing and affirming Canadian modernism had barely begun—a sharp contrast to the United States effort to interrogate American and international modernism. Nevertheless, there had been changes in both Canadian culture and literary practice. The 1960s had seen not only national celebrations but also the increased cultural importance of regions, regional centres, and regional publishing. From 1961 onward there had been a proliferation of little magazines and small presses, the construction of numerous new universities in regional cities, the establishment and protection of regional television stations, and a steady increase in provincial power. It was on behalf of this kind of decentralized politics that I deployed "post-modernism" in *From There to Here*:

> The replacing of strong central direction with a network of interacting and conflicting forces on a world scale, recurs at each level of social organization. The city decentralizes to become a 'field' of strong individuals and groups; the province decentralizes to accommodate the interacting assertions of its cities and municipalities; the nation-state decentralizes to accommodate the yearnings of its provinces. Technology's 'global village' has no dominant centre—neither in itself nor in its parts. (16)

There is a considerable contrast between the political agendas of this deployment of postmodern and that of Spanos or Hassan. Their move from modernism to postmodernism is predominantly one from Sade, Hemingway and Beckett to Heidegger and Merleau-Ponty, from a modernism of disillusionment and the futility of all action to a postmodernism which will seek fullness through the individual's imbrication into history and the social/political order. It takes place on an ostensibly non-national stage of European and American writers (Hassan's major chapters are on Sade, Kafka, Hemingway, Genet, and Beckett; Spanos's principal quotations are from Beckett, Heidegger, Dostoevsky, Sartre, Kierkegaard, Yeats, and Joyce). My move from modernism to postmodernism is from a transcendence-seeking 'high' Anglo-American modernism, its reductions of the image, search for impersonality and 'pure poetry,' and rejection of a 'worldly' mass-culture. My postmodernism is deployed on a field of colonial-imperial relations, tracing modernism from Pound through Eliot, Joyce, Ford, and Dos Passos to the New Critics (an Anglo-American lineage more visible in Canada, at least in 1973, than European modernism), and posing their recurrent concern with cultural inheritance and fear of both cultural and artistic contamination against regional interests in the dissemination of power. My move from modernism to postmodernism is one from the centralization of power and authority to a "decentralized and retribalized culture" (23)—from Eliot to McLuhan as much as from Kafka to Merleau-Ponty. And while Spanos's constructions tend to place Heidegger's critique of metaphysics and Merleau-Ponty's refusal of systematic philosophy in the background, mine foregrounds these in repeated denials of universal truth and systematicity. These differences imply very different cultural imperatives, and different national, regional, and class contexts.

•◊

What has happened to postmodernism in Canada since 1974 has in many ways limited its theoretical usefulness. The political dimension of the term has remained problematical, being recurrently subverted by understandings from Europe and the United States that associate it with "free play" and arbitrary construction, and by characterizations by Fredric Jameson and others as a new aestheticism that seeks to divert readers from things political. It has been harmed (through Jameson in particular) by confusion with 'postmodernity,' the general late twentieth-century cultural condition of global capitalism and its international marketing of mass-culture against which my postmodernism directed its various social critiques. It has also been damaged by association with avant garde, and the various linear and progressivist associations that term carries. One major advantage of postmodernism as a concept lay in the way in which it could be distinguished from the historic avant garde through its designating of numerous alternative cultural possibilities without privileging any one of them. Postmodernism was 'post' modernism—i.e. it signalled where it had come *from*—but it was not arguing any one route toward the future. It opened into a field of possibilities, offering choice rather than direction. Association with avant garde has tended to contaminate postmodern with a baggage of military metaphors, as in Baudelaire's reactionary and sardonic portrayal:

> Littérature militante. Rester sur la brèche. Porter haut le drapeau. Tenir le drapeau haut et ferme. [...] Les poëtes de combat. Les littérateurs d'avant-garde. Ces habitudes de métaphores militaires dénote des esprits, non pas militants, mais faits pour la discipline, c'est-à-dire la conformité.... (634-35)

Whereas avant garde came into common use late in the nineteenth century with a blurring of the romantic socialism of the Paris Commune and the social Darwinism of Victorian discourses of progress, and led to beliefs in the sequential 'advance' of civilization, like an army on the march, and in the intuititive participation of artists in the 'vanguard' of such progress, postmodern had emerged among various 1960s discourses of alternativity and multiplicity.

Of particular damage to postmodernism have been associations with avant garde connotations of both industrial and scientific competition and of stylishness or fashionability. It was the progressive concept of art—as a competition that echoed industrial and armaments 'races'— that Wyndham Lewis rejected in 1954, labelling it "the demon of progress in the arts." Associations with fashion, in which avant garde became an entertainment page synonym for 'exciting' or 'trendy' had led Leslie Fiedler to pronounce the term unusable in 1964—a concept once dedicated to anti-fashion had become "widespread fashion" (9). Popular discussions of postmodernism have frequently displayed both associations, as in a Gaile McGregor review of Linda Hutcheon's *The Canadian Postmodern* in which she terms postmodernism a "stampede for the bandwagon" *(43)* "a *trendy* occasion," one of "the latest literary fashions" (44).

Myself, I have not found much use for the term since 1974 and its strategic function in *From There to Here*. Its lack of specificity limits its function in both theoretical and interpretive discourse, and tends to turn the focus of a text back on the term itself. It is only on occasions when debate is strategically directed at postmodernism—such as the 1983 "Our Post-modern Heritage" conference for which I wrote the paper "Some. (Canadian.) Postmodern. Texts." (*Reading Canadian Reading* 105-122)—that its use seems practical. Even then, as the syntax of that essay title reflects, postmodernism's confused and embattled history can move one to take extreme care to signal that the word is anything but an unproblematic, uncontradictory, and totalizable sign. Other, more strategically specific signs and discourses have been needed for arguments that would further open the Canadian discursive field to conflict, dissent, and dissemination of power.

Most of the further deployment of postmodern in Canada has been the work of Robert Kroetsch and Linda Hutcheon. There are a number of similarities between my early use of postmodern and the concurrent one of Kroetsch. His postmodern appears also to arise out of phenomenology, out of his association with William Spanos as co-editor of *Boundary 2*. It foregrounds phenomenology's mistrust of systematicity at least as much as its search for some Heideggerian indwelling: "as a Postmodernist I resist those overriding systems [Marxism, Thomism, Darwinism] just as much as I resist religious or political ones" (Neuman and Wilson 31). It implicitly defines the modernism it reacts against as the unity-seeking 'high' Anglo-American one of Eliot, Joyce, Pound and Woolf ("Modernists wanted things to be all of a piece again" [28]).[1] Moreover, like my own, it openly defines modernism as a centralist and imperialist enterprise.

> The Moderns had a strong sense of immediately being involved in history, an incredible sense that Europe was the centre of the world and they were the centre of Europe and they were writing it down. [...] It's funny that even yesterday I was rather gratuitously attacked by another professor in a class because of my notion of Postmodern; what it really came down to was that I had challenged the great story of Modernism.
> (Neuman and Wilson 198)

This definition has led Kroetsch to a similarly political postmodern—a postmodern that is postcolonial, specifically "Canadian," but can also serve to legitimate the Canadian west. Because there isn't, in Kroetsch's view, "much Modernism" in Canadian literature, Canada "came into contemporary writing with relative ease" (111).

> we came into contemporary writing easily. I think that has been because we had little contact with Modernism but also because we have a different sense of communication here. We have basically an open, discontinuous system of communication. A great deal of what happens in Canada, including our literature, has to do with our having always to deal with gaps and spaces. Our national discontinuities made us ripe for Postmodernism.
> (Neuman and Wilson 112)

The theory informing Kroetsch's postmodernism, however, has changed considerably since 1973 to accommodate the work of numerous poststructuralist theorists, notably Bakhtin, Derrida, Kristeva, and Foucault. Their suitability to Kroetsch's political project has lain in their challenge to systematicity, unitary truth, and the authority of metaphysics. The function of his appropriation of them is evident throughout Shirley Neuman and Robert Wilson's extended 1982 "conversations" with Kroetsch, *Labyrinths of Voice*, because of Kroetsch's insistent characterization of himself there as a "postmodernist."

> I think that is why I am attracted to deconstructionist critics like Derrida who talk about violence and free play. The writer asserts his writerliness by doing violence. (42)

> I have also been concerned with what we might call deconstructing the myth. I think that one of the ways one deconstructs myth is by resisting that further naming....One can try to move the other way, back to the specifics, the occasions of narrative. (92)

> I suppose one of the things the archaeological model allows us to do is keep those systems very tentative. Instead of a sense of failure at not being able to put it all together, what excites us is that very incompleteness. (28)

Postmodernist criticism has become in Kroetsch's practice a criticism that applies poststructuralist theory. In "Carnival and Violence" he uses Bakhtin's theory of the carnivalesque to re-read a passage from Moodie's *Roughing It In the Bush* as perceiving the New World as a carnival disruption of European order. In "The Exploding Porcupine" he takes deconstructive theories of violence to re-read various Canadian novels as implicitly and paradoxically destructive of their own forms; in "For Play and Entrance" he elaborately proposes the Derridean notion of deferral as a structural principle of the Canadian poem. Throughout, however, a nationalist, postcolonial political imperative flickers: it is Canadianness that, in some momentary but privileged Heideggerian unveiling, these various theories are directed to reveal.

In the contrasts between the postmodernisms and

critical practices of Kroetsch and myself can be found divergent applications of two of the 'power' discourses—Canadianism and literary theory—in Canadian criticism. Ironically, although postmodernism is an international discourse within which Canadian constitutes a particular variant (a configuration explored at length by Hutcheon), within Canada it is a term with little power unless theorized as either a subset of Canadian or as a correlative of poststructuralism. In Kroetsch's practice there is uncertainty about whether to deploy theory to legitimate postmodernism (arguably what the juxtaposition of quotations from Bakhtin, Barthes, Derrida, Foucault, Kristeva etc. with Kroetsch's recurrent mention of postmodernism accomplishes in *Labyrinths of Voice*) or to deploy simultaneously the power signs "Canadian" and "theory" to interlegitimate one another and 'reveal' Canada to have been the unsuspected subject of phenomenological, formalist, structuralist and poststructuralist theory (arguably the effect of many of the essays in *The Lovely Treachery of Words*). Running across his criticism is an aesthetic admiration of both postmodernist construction and poststructuralist figure, which often combine in phrases like "the *lovely* treachery of words." In my own practice since *From There to Here* (as far as I can conceptualize it from deep within), "Canadian" seems to be foregrounded as a taken-for-granted power term, and "theory" backgrounded, either as a framing or enabling discourse through which the foregrounded "Canadian" is to be theorized or interpreted, or as a discourse to be conducted within a Canadian context. Canada, rather than theory or postmodernism, is the pre-condition of the writing. The argument the writing undertakes is that Canada is distinguishable not because it is postmodernist or poststructuralist, but because it is a specific site of social contestation which theory can both articulate and facilitate.

Linda Hutcheon's association with postmodernism has seen her take the term itself as a power term and construct both structuralism/poststructuralism and "Canadian" within it. Although her thesis in both *The Poetics of Postmodernism* and *The Politics of Postmodernism* is that 'postmodernism' is "resolutely contradictory as well as unavoidably political" (*Politics* 1), her eclectic and combinatory methodology, together with her tendency to condense large subjects into small books, has operated to construct an impression of a postmodernism that is relatively homogenous, systematically paradoxical, and coherent. In her various studies, poststructuralism tends to become a postmodernist discourse, its deconstructions of older texts a postmodernist disruption of them; its theorizings of aporias, deferrals, self-unpresent subjects, the impossibility of mimesis, the double gesture of signifier and signified, become examples of postmodernist paradox and uncertainty.

> Umberto Eco has written that he considers postmodern "the orientation of anyone who has learned the lesson of Foucault, i.e. that power is not something unitary that exists outside us" (in Rosso 1983:4). He might well have added to this, as others have, the lessons learned from Derrida about textuality and deferral, or from Vattimo and Lyotard about intellectual mastery and its limits. In other words, it is difficult to separate the 'de-doxifying' impulse of postmodern art and culture from the deconstructing impulse of what we have labelled poststructuralist theory. (1989, 3-4)

It is not only, as she says, "difficult to separate" postmodern and poststructuralism, it is also difficult to conclude here that she tries.

Hutcheon's associating of her texts with 'postmodernism' as a powerful transnational term gives them a much different focus and agenda from those of myself and

Kroetsch. Her primary concern is not to facilitate a particular Canadian politics, nor to construct Canada as a postmodern country, or even to argue the existence of the 'postmodern,' but to re-construct and direct international understandings of the term itself. Her conceptions of both modernism and postmodernism are hence much larger and more diffuse. While Kroetsch's and my own are vulnerable to criticism for being excluding, hers are vulnerable for being so including that they lose specificity and meaning. She spends much less time than either of us in arguing either the nature of modernism or the existence of 'postmodernism'—by the simple expedient of basing her definitions on understandings of the less elaborately constructed field of architecture (architecture can self-reflexively cite itself but, unlike literature, cannot discursively construe itself) rather than on literature. Her understanding of modernist architecture, however, as austere, pure, formalistic, and dedicated to transcending the social and historical so as to acquire a greater sense of order, implies much the same high modernism that Kroetsch and I employ. Modernism, Hutcheon argues briefly, "rejects the historical city," it has an "ahistorical purism," "a faith that technical innovation and purity of form can assure social order" (1989, 11-12); it engaged in a "search for order in the face of moral and social chaos" (1988a, 2). Her tendency to take 'judicial notice' of both modernism and postmodernism, rather than seek to argue and interrelate them, is reflected in the nearly complete absence in her books of even the names the numerous exemplars of European modernism examined by Hassan, Spears, or Spanos, or the Anglo-American and Canadian modernists named by myself and Kroetsch.

Hutcheon's *The Canadian Postmodern* has some contrasting resemblances to both Kroetsch's conceptions and my own. Like me, Hutcheon here constructs Canadian postmodernism as a variant subset of international postmodernism, and as politicized discourse through which social conflicts are conducted. Her theorizing of postmodernism as a conflicted discourse, however, which is frequently complicit with the ideologies it acts to refuse, and as a parodic discourse that must maintain the discourses it parodies, leads her to construct a much larger Canadian postmodernism that I could construct, and to appropriate into it many texts other theorists have characterized as realist or modernist: Atwood's *The Edible Woman*, Munro's *Lives of Girls and Women*, Engel's *Bear*, Richler's *St. Urbain's Horseman*, Cohen's *Beautiful Losers*, Wiebe's *The Temptations of Big Bear*. Like Kroetsch, she moves to define Canada as *specially* postmodern, although—unlike him—firmly qualifies his concept "ripe for Postmodernism" with words such as "seem," "might," and "perhaps":

> Canada's own particular moment of cultural history does seem to make it ripe for the paradoxes of postmodernism, by which I mean those contradictory acts of establishing and then undercutting prevailing values and conventions in order to provoke a questioning, a challenging of 'what goes without saying' in our culture. [...] Since the periphery or the margin might...describe Canada's perceived position in international terms, perhaps the postmodern ex-centric is very much a part of the identity of the nation. (1988a, 3)

While there is contradiction implied here, between a Canada which may be intrinsically postmodern and one which has, within Western discursive history, participated in the development of a transnational discourse and charged this discourse with its own politics, Hutcheon is often able, by means of the figure of paradox, to recuperate this and numerous other contradictions as simple indications of the continuing operation of paradoxical postmodernism.

Reliance on this figure of paradox to recuperate conflicts between critique of capitalism and complicity with capitalism, between rejection of realism and incorporation of it, between some feminisms' appropriation of postmodern figures but rejection of postmodernism itself as masculinist, operates overall in Hutcheon to move her own critique outside of politics. The approval of postmodernism which she signals in her discourse—postmodernism has brought "a new vitality," "a new willingness to enter into...dialogue," a "perhaps healthy" move toward "acceptance of responsibility" (1988a, 23) tends, as the paradoxical tensions accumulate, to lose its political edge and become a generalized and specular celebration of ironic contrast. "The postmodern does not reject or exemplify, lament or celebrate, the results of our decentralized, post-industrial, communications-obsessed age," she suggests as she brings *The Canadian Postmodern* toward its close. "It does both—and neither" (183).

◆

Like any new cultural construct that promises to offer new criteria for the evaluation of cultural productions, new categories for publication, and new fields for academic research, postmodernism has been often vigorously or condescendingly disputed. It was precisely because it had such potential power that I deployed it *From There To Here*—to offer new criteria by which texts by writers like Godfrey, Bissett, Marlatt, Thomas, Gilbert, Bowering, Nichol, Kroetsch, and Wah could be read and valued in the place of criteria by which they appeared peculiar or unsuccessful, to suggest new models for configuring Canadian culture in place of centralist 'Laurentian' models, and to theorize alternative categories for political action. Similar goals can be inferred from Kroetsch's and Hutcheon's deployments—in

Kroetsch at very least a project to legitimize various fictional and critical discourses, in Hutcheon a project to open a new array of texts to interpretation and possible canonization.

In Canada, as elsewhere, disputants have most often addressed at some point the ambiguous relationship postmodernism bears to modernism—its claiming to be its successor (*post*modernism) and its seeming admission of dependency upon it (post*modernism*). Some critics have simply ignored the complication of postmodernism, like W.J. Keith who, in his *Canadian Literature in English*, repetitively extends his modernist criteria of directness and control to all authors whether they have been elsewhere claimed as modernists or postmodernists: he praises A.J.M. Smith for his "controlled vocabulary" (61), Ethel Wilson for "straightforwardness" and "exquisite control of tone" (145), Laurence's *The Stone Angel* for "control of voice" (161), and Kroetsch for his "verbal poise and control" (115). Others, like Warren Tallman in the essay "Wonder Merchants: Modernist Poetry in Vancouver during the 1960s" (175-207), have counter-theorized modernism itself as a heterogenous discourse, and the recent texts of postmodernism as neo-modernist extensions of less publicly successful aspects of modernism rather than postmodern departures. Adopting this strategy, but with more emphasis than Tallman on balance and inclusiveness, Shirley Neuman has asked "which modernisms" is postmodernism "talking about?" "Is postmodernism not continuous with modernism rather than opposed to it, and do we not find modernism's traces in postmodernist writing, particularly when that writing had its impetus in Canada from Black Mountain poetics, which had its impetus from Pound...?" (Neuman 55). Still others have characterized the texts claimed by 'postmodernism' as trivializations or degenerations of modernism, as in

Woodcock's remark "minor, inconsequential figures like bpNichol, Victor Coleman and Gerry Gilbert" (1987, 247). The political effects of these maneuvers can be to save the prestige of modernist texts and evaluative criteria, as in the cases of Woodcock and Keith, to enhance the prestige of specific modernists, like Stein or Zukofsky, whose texts can be theorized as having inspired 'neo-modernism,' to save texts that might fall 'between' modernism and postmodernism, as Neuman works to 'save' texts by Page, Jones, Birney, Livesay, and Wilfred Watson, or to enlarge the power of modernism generally by appropriating any newly acclaimed text to it. Among postmodern theorists, the effect of such criticism has been to encourage more careful nuancing of the relationship between modernism and postmodernism, as in Hutcheon's positing of postmodernism's "complex relationship to modernism: its retention of modernism's initial oppositional impulses, both ideological and aesthetic, and its equally strong rejection of its founding impulse of formalist autonomy" (1989, 26). As seen earlier, Stephen Scobie makes a similar negotiation in his 1991 essay "Leonard Cohen, Phyllis Webb, and the End(s) of Modernism" when he proposes that

> [t]he 'end' (purpose) of modernism may be to fulfil itself, its own aesthetic, or it may be to provide the opening out of its own mode into that of postmodernism. So modernism may or may not 'end' (finish): it may be seen as being superseded by a subsequent movement, or it may be seen to be living on (in) its own post-.(59)

and that this 'post' constitutes a "deconstruction" of modernism (69).

The most recent 'postmodern' books by Hutcheon and Kroetsch, her *The Canadian Postmodern*, and his *The Lovely Treachery of Words*, have received a number of reviews, however, that were not merely skeptical, nuanced, or disputatious but openly hostile to their critical projects. This is a new development, at least in Canada, in the reception of postmodernism. It suggests to me that the link both Hutcheon and Kroetsch have theorized between postmodernism and poststructuralism may have become perceived in some quarters as a large threat to specific theoretical/political projects. Gaile McGregor's "Postmodernism and its Discontents," a review of both *The Canadian Postmodern* and *A Poetics of Postmodernism*, appears at first glance to be a not unexpected by-product of the affiliation of a powerful new discourse with powerful established publishers—Oxford and Routledge: envy. The opening ad hominem sarcasm portrays Hutcheon as the beginner who has unmerited success, who has become a scholar through packaging rather than scholarship.

> Whatever else one may say about her, Linda Hutcheon has to be considered a success story. Content aside, the very shape of her career marks her as one of the best strategists to come down the pike in years. Talk about being in the right place—intellectually speaking—at the right time! In 1980 this then-novice is clearly self-identified as a formalist. A scant few years later—just in time to anticipate the stampede for the bandwagon—she had managed, by dint largely of relabelling, to transform herself into the guru of Canadian postmodernism. (43)

Through its colloquial style, it also inscribes its own writer as non-strategic, a populist rather than an academic, as being unwilling to "transform" herself into scholarly discourse in order to become "a success story." Repressed in this paragraph, and only hinted at in the editor's note that describes McGregor as "a Canada Research Fellow in the Sociology Department of York University and the author of a three-volume series of semio-ethnographic studies of post-frontier cultures, collectively entitled Voice in the Wilderness," is the contrast of McGregor's own academic career path to that of Hutcheon, and the so-far unequal contest between her "post-frontier" theory and postmodernism.

Power contests involve individual careers as well as discursive conflicts inside which individual careers occur. McGregor began her publishing career in 1985 with *The Wacousta Syndrome: Explorations in the Canadian Langscape*, a book which attempted to employ the discourse and methodologies of thematic criticism to construct a paradigmatic relationship between Canadian and United States cultures. It was much less well received than Hutcheon's first book. Characteristic of its reception were Tracy Ware's suggestion that, although derivative of the criticism of "Jones, Atwood, and Frye," it was "not up to the standards of these previous critics," and showed "little awareness that the moment of thematic criticism has passed" ("Notes" 573), and that its arguments that there is a particular paradigmatic Canadian 'view' rested on a naive assumption that there can be "neutral, innocent, or unmediated perception" (574). Rather than leading to further well-publicized publication and to senior academic appointments as had Hutcheon's first book, *The Wacousta Syndrome* had led McGregor, by the time of her review article on Hutcheon in 1990, to the virtual ignoring of her second book by Canadian reviewers and to the limited-term academic role of Canada Research Scholar. In a certain sense she had, to borrow her own figure, missed rather than anticipated a "bandwagon." Thematic criticism, with its simplified structuralism, weak epistemology, and ignorance of the critique of metaphysics that had been ongoing in Western philosophy since Hegel, had been no match for the arguments poststructuralism had directed against it in the 1970s and early 80s. 'Thematics,' as a power contestant, had largely retreated by 1985 into the vague humanism of Woodcock and Keith, in which "our" writers could be seen to pass balanced judgements in humane texts which were not only 'Canadian' but reflected the values of a larger 'civilized' world.

Beneath the rhetoric of envy in McGregor's article lie numerous signs of this discursive history. The "Canadian lit crit establishment" which skeptically received *The Wacousta Factor*'s thematics is characterized by her as having "a general old-fangledness" (44), as being impressed with Hutcheon "because it came late to postmodern modes of critique" (43). This establishment's judgment is momentarily impaired by an infatuation with theoretical discourse: "[m]ore and more now in Canadian journals and conferences and colloquia we see name-studded, jargonized, Hutcheon-style 'think' pieces being privileged above all other modes of critique" (45). Intermittently and obliquely, McGregor's article defends her own paradigmatic "mode of critique." For McGregor, the textual features Hutcheon finds to be postmodern are long-standing and defining aspects of Canadian culture. "Canadian literature was recursive, historical, evasive, subversive, ironic, collective, parodic, poetic, and feminist long before such features became fashionable." Hutcheon's particular definition of postmodernism as political, McGregor suggests, is itself paradigmatically Canadian rather than consistent with international writing or international theories of the postmodern (regarding the latter, McGregor cites McHale,

Jameson and Eagleton); it "'fits' Canadian literature much better than it does the international oeuvre from which it was ostensibly derived" (45). The historically close relationship between Canadian thematics and Canadian humanist criticism is evident in many of the specific criticisms McGregor levels against Hutcheon. McGregor's working values are austerity (Hutcheon is a "wordy guru"), originality ("Hutcheon's work is derivative in the most profound and far-reaching sense"), decorum (her work has been "taken up most enthusiastically" [43]), civilization (Hutcheon practises "intellectual cannibalism" [43-44]), and consistency (despite Hutcheon's focus on postmodernism "she's still very much a closet modern" [44]). Often lost within these criticisms, but giving the essay nevertheless its own inconsistent inconsistency, are a number of fairly trenchant, somewhat exaggerated, covertly marxist observations. McGregor notes that Hutcheon's four books on aspects of postmodernism appear to be aspects of capitalist "packaging" that re-pack and market once-successful products: "a recasting rather than a broadening of her vision" (43). She argues that Hutcheon's writing erases differences between 'postmodern' practices, "normalizing what is ostensibly ambivalent (her text is dotted with phrases like '*typically* postmodern,' '*distinctively* postmodern,') totalising what is ostensibly diffuse ('postmodernism is...,' 'postmodernism always,' 'postmodernism *never*...), and personalizing what is ostensibly decentered ('postmodernism attempts to be...'" (44). These are important criticisms, which will soon be taken up with greater effect by Lorraine Weir, but within McGregor's overall agenda of discrediting a competitive discourse, they appear tactical and opportunistic rather than programmatic.

In "Back to the Future: Plus or Minus Canadian?," a review of *The Canadian Postmodern* by Sylvia Söderlind, a very different constituency's view of postmodernism occurs. Söderlind begins by questioning Hutcheon's "assumption that the post-colonial and 'ex-centric' status of Canadian writers is analogous to that of women and ethnic minorities" (631). In postmodernism as it has developed in Canada, at least in my *From There to Here*, in Kroetsch's essays, and in Hutcheon, there has been a continuing assumption that the decentralization of culture and authority theorized by all of us as postmodern (i.e. Lyotard's demise of "master-narratives") both facilitated and was evidenced by the growing empowerment of those formerly with minimal power: smaller nations, regions within nations, women, non-white races, minority ethnicities, gays and lesbians. Similarly there has been an assumption that cultural decentralization operated to empower transgressive discourses: those of the various constituencies noted above, those of 'postmodern' artists, *and* those of literary and cultural theory. These were all, in effect, aspects of 'postmodernist' discourse. In the final chapter of *The Politics of Postmodernism*, "Postmodernism and Feminisms," Hutcheon goes to considerable length to distinguish international postmodernism, with its "doubly coded" complicity "with and contesting of the cultural dominants within which it operates," from feminisms which "have distinct, unambiguous agendas of resistance" (142). This is not an entirely successful distinction, since it contrasts a deconstructed postmodernism against an intentional "feminisms" which, if subjected to the same analysis as Hutcheon has directed against postmodernism, would likely disclose a similar double coding of complicity and contestation. Hutcheon goes on not to argue that postmodern interrogations of authority and representation opened a way for any disempowered constituency to assert its own cultural readings, but to argue that various feminisms redirected postmodernism itself—"radicalized the postmodern sense of difference" (142) and "*made* postmodernism think...about the female body...both as socially and historically constructed through representation" (143). She makes particular note of the different and more specifically political agendas of feminisms, and concludes with a list of distinctions in which the *intentional* aspects of feminisms repeatedly separate them from a postmodernism that is paradoxically both 'intended' and without theories of agency and subjectivity. Hutcheon offers a briefer version of this argument in *The Canadian Postmodern*.

Söderlind, however, discounting these distinctions and analyses—perhaps because Hutcheon's discussions of Canadian feminisms in *The Canadian Postmodern* are firmly contained within her book's governing term—focuses her critique on what she suggests is for Hutcheon "the presumed synonymity of all oppression," a synonymity which "tends to reduce ethnicity, race, and gender to metaphors of eccentricity" (635). Söderlind's argument here rests in part on her subtle conversion of Hutcheon's term *ex-centric* (things away or apart from the centre) to *eccentric* (things odd or peculiar). This is potentially an enormous move, for it acts to depoliticize Hutcheon's postmodernism from an affirmation of the non-empowered to an aesthetic affirmation of the unusual. Noting that Hutcheon's study ends with a naming of Robert Kroetsch as "Mr. Canadian Postmodern," Söderlind comments that "[i]f women's writing becomes a new paradigm for the writing of eccentricity and is epitomized by a male white member of his country's ethnic majority, it loses its difference" (635). Both 'Canadian' and 'female' risk "getting absorbed or reduced into a kind of universal marginality typical of (or should we say central to?) the post-modern condition" (636). Here Söderlind makes another conversion of Hutcheon's terms, conflating her *postmodernism* (a cultural and political response to the end of master narratives and the globalization of capitalism) with *postmodernity* (a socio-economic, "social and philosophical period or 'condition'" [1989, 23]). The effect again is to depoliticize postmodernism from a stance which enables contending politics to a homogenizing "condition," "a kind of universal marginality."

The politics of Söderlind's reading of Hutcheon are to extricate feminisms from postmodernism by constructing the latter as homogenizing and patriarchal, putting "more emphasis on the *Mr* [of 'Mr. Canadian Postmodern'] than Hutcheon does" (635). In a sense, Söderlind's is a strong postmodern gesture. It insists on feminisms being themselves "ex-centric," even to postmodernism; it constructs the 'other' as homogeneity, and itself as difference; it refuses the authority of Hutcheon's book on the grounds that unlike much women's writing Hutcheon's criticism is un-selfconsciously complicitous with a male-dominated "traditional way of looking" (636), and asserts this despite Söderlind's own very likely unavoidable situation of 'complicitously' writing of her commentary on Hutcheon within the traditions of book review and university academic quarterly. There is apparently power to be had here in "ex-centricity"; it is a contested position for which feminisms, ethnicities, racial groups may avidly compete, just as they will do in 1990 in the anthology *Language in Her Eye*, in its collision of essays by Janice Kulyk Keefer, Dionne Brand, Margaret Atwood, Marlene Nourbese Philip, Paulette Jiles,

Phyllis Webb, Sharon Thesen, and others.

⁕

Lorraine Weir's "Normalizing the Subject: Linda Hutcheon and the English Canadian Postmodern" appears in Robert Lecker's anthology *Canadian Canons: Essays in Literary Value* in 1990, an anthology explicitly framed by its editor as an interrogation of canon formation in Canada and the powers that present canons confer. Weir writes not from the "women's writing" (636) position taken by Söderlind, or from the anti-academic, exiled-from-establishment position imagined by McGregor, but from a much more complex position both within the criticism community ("We are, of course, still being told that theory—a mere fashion, a disease—is in bad taste," she begins) and within a general context of postmodern writers (a Bowering epigraph heads the essay). The complexity of this position is increased when Weir problematizes her opening "We" by making a recurrent attack on theories of "community, shared values" which she argues have become "canonic" in English-Canadian literary criticism (180).

Although Weir's title could be read as contesting a normalizing of postmodernism, it becomes evident by the second page of her essay that it is Hutcheon's distinguishing of postmodernism from modernism that she is going to challenge.

> Subjecting Canadian as well as international modernism to a normalizing influence, domesticating deviance and inscribing it within her postmodern paradigm, Hutcheon converts danger into safety, the marginalized into the mainstream, the non-referential into the referential. Presenting a classically "anti-modern, pro-postmodern" [Jameson, 106] position, Hutcheon undertakes what Robert Kroetsch has called a 'righting of the culture' ["Present Tense": 244] which returns it to its long-held values,

its code of civility, and privileging of clarity, good taste, and 'standard English.'

Weir's 'modernism' here is one not necessarily understood by most Canadian literary users of the term; characterized by "deviance," "danger," marginality, and non-referentiality, it recalls John Bentley Mays's controversy-stirring modernism of "dangerous, uncontrolled presences" (1973, 10); similarly, Weir's accusation that Hutcheon "domesticates" deviance echoes Mays's charge that John Hulcoop's essays on Webb "rehabilitated" her extravagances and rendered them "harmless" (9). Weir's understanding of modernism could only in a diluting, metaphoric usage include the anglicanism of Eliot, the political engagements of Yeats, or the "civility" of A.J.M. Smith. Two pages later she provides "us" with a "sketch-map of modernism," taken from Andreas Huyssen's *After The Great Divide*. This "map" includes artistic autonomy, rejection of mass-culture, self-referentiality, irony, rigorous experimentality, affirmation of individuality over mass consciousness, persistent exploration of language, rejection of realism, "content," and personal expression. The map undergoes a mutation through dada, surrealism, and constructivism in which the claim to autonomy and rigid "separation from mass culture disappear." It leads to what Weir calls the "Joycean" tradition in modern writing "from Stein, Beckett, and Borges to Zukofsky, Neidecker, Calvino, Eco, Jane Bowles, Lyn Hejinian, and so on into the 1990s" (184).The later stages of this map, particularly its "so on into the 1990s," is—to say the least—a supplement to Huyssen's argument, much the same as Hutcheon's representation of Huyssen in *The Politics of Postmodernism* as supporting her proposal that "the historical avant-garde...prepares the way for postmodernism's renegotiation of the different possible relations...between high and popular forms of culture" (27-28) is also a supplement.

Weir follows this with a second "history of modernism." This is a history of theory, beginning with the Russian Formalists Jakobson, Tynjanov, and Eichenbaum, with Bakhtin and Saussure, and moving through the Prague school and French structuralism to contemporary poststructuralisms. She accuses Hutcheon of deriving much of her practice from these theorists, while simultaneously constructing them, in the equation "structuralist/modernist/formalism" (Weir 185, Hutcheon 1988b 52) as a repression of process and history which 'postmodernism' with its reader-response understandings of language and its "hermeneutic process of reading" (Weir 189, Hutcheon 1988b 156) will end.

> Hutcheon thus derives from Kristeva and Benveniste an understanding of novelistic discourse in general which she then grafts onto postmodernist discourse in specific, characterizing postmodernism in terms which are provided by dynamic models of the reading process developed by such theorists as Bakhtin, Eichenbaum, Tynjanov...and by speech emphatic/performative models of language and novelistic processing from Benveniste, Kristeva, and many others.... (188)

She further suggests that in theorizing her implicitly phenomenological understandings of reading and process, Hutcheon telescopes them with terminology from the incompatible marxist textual production theories of Macherey, giving to her text the appearance of materialist analysis while actually working in a contrary direction—reconstructing a metaphysics:

> Borrowing Pierre Macherey's Marxist lexicon of writing as production, text as product [Macherey: 66-68], Hutcheon attempts to empty these terms of their ideological significance

> and to expropriate them for reinscription in a canonic
> postmodernism which, grounded in 'life' as process, returns to
> Presence, to a normative theory of the utility value of 'art'—a
> product rendered processual via the theory of the performative—
> in the service of 'life.' (191)

Rather than attempting to contest "modernism/formalism/structuralism" and its resolute resistance to cultural dominants, Hutcheon's new socially and ethically engaged postmodernism, Weir concludes, passes itself off as both consistent with it and an 'improvement' upon it. "[M]odernism/formalist/structuralism," she argues, are conflated by Hutcheon into a single non-political and aestheticizing paradigm which, through phenomenology and paradox, "postmodernism" can eventually endow with the appearance of social readability and political engagement.

> Hutcheon's argument is, then, fundamentally concerned not to
> defeat modernism/formalism/structuralism but, via the equation
> of postmodernism/realism/hermeneutics, to reinscribe the
> conditions of communal understanding, the *boundaries* of the
> interpretive community, in the face of deconstruction's assault
> on the liberal-humanist subject. (194)

Weir's argument is a complex one, painstakingly constructed out of fragmentary quotations, inferences from passages cited by Hutcheon, and analysis of the many disjunctions in Hutcheon's synthesizing discourse. It rests particularly on the claim that Hutcheon conceals the political engagement of Russian Formalism beneath the ambiguous term "formalism," and that she merges the Formalist's communication models with Fish's reader-response theories to humanize Formalist semiosis into the shared knowledge of a "communitarian" postmodern "interpretive community." It rests also on the intriguing assumption that Saussure, Jakobson, Tynjanov, Bakhtin, Benveniste, Macherey and

Kristeva must be considered as contributors to modernism, and that any postmodernism which both claims to be different from modernism but founds this difference on these (modernist) theorists, has assumed a contradiction that is beyond the power of paradox to dissolve.

To mount this challenge to Hutcheon and postmodernism Weir must, that is, theorize a modernism that was not directly experienced by Canadian literature or by much of Anglo-American literature before the 1960s—a modernism that was marginal to the projects of Pound, Eliot, Yeats, Auden, Joyce, Woolf, Williams, Faulkner, Hemingway, Richards, Empson, and the New Critics through which modernism became defined in Britain and North America. The politics of this move are not difficult to discern. The received high modernism of Britain and North America has become a "normalized" one, one whose politics have been thematized and figures aestheticized into socially nondisturbing textuality. Weir is moving here to reinscribe as a canonic modernism the texts of the historical avant garde, including the transgressive "blasting and bombardiering" modernisms of Vorticism, Constructivism, Futurism, Dada, and Surrealism, and the socially interrogative modernisms of the Russian Formalists, the Prague School, and French structuralism. She refuses to have Russian Formalism aestheticized by covert conflation with New Criticism's formalism, and thereby opens the way for it and other explicitly socially engaged modernisms to become standards by which postmodernism itself must be evaluated. Her ultimate charge against Hutcheon is that by aestheticizing radical modernist cultural and artistic theory, and associating postmodernist textuality with a "community of readers whose competence meshes with the semantic and ideological demands of the text," she reintroduces "the liberal humanist ideology of the transparency of reality" (194). That is, Weir claims that Hutcheon tangentially affirms liberal humanist values while at the same time arguing that postmodernism opposes them, that she reinstates liberal humanism under the guise of refusing it.

Weir's literary history would reclaim modernism—its enormous cultural credibility and power within educational institutions—for the "subversive, anti-humanist drive" (190) of radical politics. Implicit within her arguments is a dismissing of much of Anglo-American high modernism as bourgeois corruptions—'normalizations'—of a modernism that was historically, as she quotes Huyssens, an adversary of the normal: "adversary to the bourgeois culture of everyday life as well as adversary to mass culture and entertainment which are seen as the primary forms of bourgeois cultural articulation" (184). This politics leads her to deplore Hutcheon's optimism that postmodernism might lead to changed "living habits" and a "perhaps healthy" turning away from "single meaning" (Weir 234n, Hutcheon 1988a 35 and 23). Such goals, for Weir, reflect a Polyanna vision of social process. In terms of Canadian literary politics, Weir's position arrays her in opposition to the recent feminist attempts, such as Mallinson's or Wachtel's, to reclaim 'Phyllis Webb' for 'health' and good judgment. But her insistence on social engagement keeps her arguments distinct also from John Bentley Mays's romanticized vision of radical modernism and the refusal of bourgeois "health." In Weir's view, "Canadian modernism, like the dissenting tradition in Canadian social and political thought with which it is strongly aligned, has still not been considered in Canadian theory" (194-5). Whether one is to conclude from this argument that Canadian modernist texts have had their "social and political" engagement "normalized" by Canadian criticism, or that Canadian modernism itself has been "normalized" by the critical suppression of its radical texts, Weir does not specify.

A second element in Weir's political agenda is to reclaim many of the texts of Hutcheon's postmodernism for a vigorously continuing, subversive, anti-humanist modernism. This move would apparently re-write the histories of much of both Western and Canadian literature as long-evolving, subversive critiques of bourgeois humanism, monopoly capitalism, and the liberal self-present subject. The move resembles elements in Hutcheon's declared agenda, and her characterization of the agenda of postmodernism, but declines her concept of "complicity," and deplores the concealments of entertainment and "good taste" (195) that it suggests both Hutcheon and many of her postmodern authors employ to make their texts "accessible" to otherwise resistant readers. Weir's modernism would both include and erase postmodernism; it would be confrontational, in 'bad taste,' uncivil (Weir links this essay with her earlier essay on Canadian criticism as "The Discourse of 'Civility'"). Its acceptance would entail not only a revision of the twentieth-century canon, but also an overthrowing of the liberal humanism that presently runs through Canadian literary institutions, the teaching of Canadian literature as entertaining and personally enriching, the packaging of Canadian books as aspects of community enterprise, the concern of some feminists with "health" and psychological adjustment, and the assumption of nationalists that the texts build Canadian nationhood.

In two long review articles that appear in 1990 and 1991 in issues of *Canadian Poetry*, "Disfiguring the Post-modern" and "Forget Heidegger, or Why I am Such a Clever Postmodernist," David L. Clark shows neither of Lorraine Weir's concerns for modernism and radical politics. Clark's concern is with the relationship between postmodernism and philosophy and critical theory, and with saving at least some poststructuralist theory from what he calls "the postmodernization of the critical gesture" (1990, 76).

In most discussions and debates of postmodernism in Canada, there tends to be an assumption that poststructuralist discourse, if not at least one of the adopted discourses of postmodernism, is one of the characterizing discourses of postmodernity. Kroetsch writes as if postmodernism and poststructuralism shared common projects; Hutcheon constructs the relationship between the two as "inseparability" (1989, 4). Neuman offers a list of "postmodern attributes" that includes most of the concerns of poststructuralism: "self-reflexivity; playfulness; open-endedness; an acknowledgement of the impossibilities of origin; strategies of deferral and discontinuity; metonymy; formal, rhetorical and generic eclecticism; intertextuality; a conception of language as inescapably mediating our knowledge or perception of the real; and a repudiation of holistic notions of the self" (Neuman 66). Clark attempts to depart decisively from this practice by proposing the new category, "postmodernist criticism." This category, to which he assigns both Kroetsch's *The Lovely Treachery of Words* and my *Reading Canadian Reading*, enables him both to appraise the books in terms of their consistency to "postmodernist fashion" ("In a most *un*postmodernist fashion, Kroetsch's collection is a powerfully thesis-driven book" (1991, 59) and to detach them from "poststructuralism," the category he will attempt to protect.

The novelty of Clark's strategy contrasts bluntly with

earlier constructions. Texts about postmodernism, such as those of Bertens, Lyotard, Foster, or Hutcheon, have not become known as postmodernist criticism, nor have non-monological theoretical texts like Derrida's *Glas*, Godard's "Becoming My Hero, Becoming Myself" (Scheier, et al. 112-122) or Sarah Murphy's "How the Cunt Lost its Tongue" (Neuman and Kamboureli 1-16). What seems to have moved Clark to this strategy is that several of Kroetsch's essays, and one of mine, both employ non-monological discourses *and* consider postmodernism. The difficulty with his strategy lies in its circularity: it defines "postmodernist criticism" through the operations of *The Lovely Treachery of Words* and *Reading Canadian Reading* at the same time as it defines the two books' limitations both by reference to what postmodernist criticism 'should' do and by reference to a variety of poststructuralist criteria: avoidance of totalization, resistance to aesthetic representation, denial of the possibility of an autonomous self, denial of a possibility of external perspective, refusal of idealisms, etc. In the review of the Kroetsch book this strategy requires a recurrent blurring of the terms "postmodernist" and "poststructuralist," as when, after outlining a number of poststructuralist theories which Clark believes Kroetsch's criticism fails to enact, he terms these "Kroetsch's postmodernist assertions" (62). In the review of my book, however, he argues a "need for Canadian theorists to desynonymize post-modernism and post-structuralism" (84).

Even without the invoking of meaning-production theory, one can argue that it is Clark who appears most involved in this synonymization. Despite its recurrent interest in postmodernism, Kroetsch's book does not explicitly name itself as postmodernist; only by pointing to the book's "poststructuralist" figures—archaeology, dialogism, the decentered self, radical indeterminancy, skepticism toward meta-narrative, and postulating these as signs of "postmodernism," is Clark able to construct the book as such. My book directs only one of its sixteen essays to postmodernism; Clark attempts to construct it as "post-modern" (he drops the hyphen for the review of Kroetsch) by both surmising intent and pointing to the figure of "self-reflexiveness"—the poststructuralist self-positioning gesture such as the one that begins this chapter: "Davey's self-reflexivity rather exhibits his intent to write a specifically *post-modernist* literary criticism..." (76).

The clues about why Clark may need to construct these two books as "postmodernist"/"post-modernist" are relatively few in his Kroetsch review. But when the reviews are placed together, some recurrences emerge. In reading *The Lovely Treachery of Words*, he is skeptical of the political claims Kroetsch makes of the postmodern texts of which he writes—of their ability to "'uninvent the world' through 'the radical process of demythologizing the systems that threaten to define them'" (59). In an argument similar to Weir's that Hutcheon's criticism "normalizes" disruptions, he suggests that Kroetsch's "tendency to celebrate notions of difference and discontinuity in Canadian writing without examining the consequences of this disruptiveness is...the sign of Kroetsch's commitment to an aesthetic ideology" (65). In the earlier review of *Reading Canadian Reading* he expresses much greater skepticism about political action, and does so on poststructuralist grounds:

> It is by no means apparent how or what kind of political action is possible or even desirable once it is demonstrated that the self will never know itself and thus be in a position to 'ground' action in such knowledge. (82)

Here two pages later he repeats this point about the non-self-knowing self in order to argue, citing Paul de Man, the impossibility of self-insight or self-criticism:

> what is claimed or argued is always just that a positing, an intent, and therefore an expression of hermeneutical desire or belief rather than a statement of simple fact. Even the most fervently argued interpretation is permanently in the subjunctive mood, unsaying itself at the moment that it speaks. As de Man argued more than thirty years ago, a critical text "states its own truth in the mode of error" [*Blindness and Insight* 18]. (84)

Taken together, these points about "aesthetic ideology," critical self-blindness, and the difficulty of theorizing political action once metaphysics and the autonomous subject have been denied, comprise an extremely condensed version of the salient contributions of de Man to poststructuralist theory. Clark's title "Dis-figuring Postmodernism" gestures to a chapter in de Man's *The Rhetoric of Romanticism*, "Shelley Disfigured." Clark's only essay to date on a Canadian literary text is titled "Monstrous Reading: *The Martyrology* after de Man."[2]

Although Clark constructs himself in these two reviews as a friend of an homogenous poststructuralism (recurrently understood as represented only by deconstruction), defending it against what he characterizes as contradiction and aestheticization in *The Lovely Treachery of Words*, and ingenuous political and critical expectation in *Reading Canadian Reading*, the position he enacts is much narrower than this—as it would have to be, given the fissures he neglects to speak about within poststructuralism. It is Paul de Man's position, and displays not only its powerful critique of aesthetic ideology, and its methodological focus on rhetoric and figuration, but also its paralyzing hypothesis that without metaphysics and self-knowing subjectivity political action may be untheorizable and meaningless. As Clark remarks in his review of my book, on noting what he suggests is a "swerve out of post-modernism and back into 'metaphysics,'" metaphysics is "the only field in which notions of human freedom and responsibility can have any meaning." He continues,

> The disturbing possibility arises that post-modernism describes the abstention of criticism from politics as naive, when it is, in fact, itself the very abstention to which it refers. Under these conditions, political action is more complexly the horizon that post-modernism projects but which recedes even as it is approached. (82)

This is an ideological position to which none of myself, Hutcheon, Kroetsch, Keith, McGregor, Söderlind, or Weir would subscribe. The politics of Clark's embracing of it are not directly visible, but connect, whatever the motives he might claim, with the larger politics of North American critical theory: with the various struggles for possession of 'theory' and 'poststructuralism' as power terms, and the particular struggle to defend deconstruction from postcolonial and feminist appropriations, from marxist critique, and from the discrediting impact of the discovery and re-publishing of Paul de Man's Second World War publications. Despite the demystifying effects throughout the 1970s and 80s of deconstruction's analyses of metaphysical figuration, the current political struggle over the social meaning of deconstruction and of Paul de Man's contribution to it is defensive and revanchist. Clark's reviews, with their insistence of reading synchronically essays informed by various sociological contexts, with their discounting of the Derridean performative (1990: 77), with their implicit refusal to consider that a 'deconstructed' subject continues to exist as a position in language and in politics, and with their assumptions that deconstruction refutes metaphysical concepts rather than relineating them within society as contingencies of language that continue *en jeu*, appear to enact ideological moves within American deconstruction, to work covertly and allegorically against Derridean understandings of deconstruction as a political, time-bound project, as well as against marxist and feminist critiques. Despite Clark's claim to be critical of Kroetsch for his aestheticizing of potentially progressive political elements in postmodern texts, the *effect* of his two reviews is regressive in the sense that they advocate extreme skepticism toward politics and political process. Where Weir claimed that Hutcheon's postmodernism normalizes dissenting texts, and argued for a politically activist criticism, Clark— reintroducing with de Man the skepticism of empiricism— proposes that dissent of any kind, including self-dissent, may be an hallucination, an "uncomplicated naivëte" (1990, 84): "it is (to cite de Man) 'without an objective correlative that can be unambiguously be pointed to in empirical reality'" (85).

> To represent Canadian poetry as having leaped from the pinnacle of a nature-and-nationalism verse, across the abyss of modernism, to land surefooted on an opposite plateau of postmodernism is at least in part a narrative of postcolonial resistance to colonial debates and tropes that dominated discussion of Canadian literature from the 1930s through the 1970s.
>
> (Neuman 56)

If there is such a figure as postmodernist paradox, one major example of it must be the strategy of attempting to marginalize writers or movements by constructing them as central, and to legitimize oneself by claiming marginality. This has been the strategy of theorists of postmodernism against Anglo-American high modernism and Canadian modernism, and has become in recent years the strategy of many contesters of postmodernism, whether these 'splinter' from the postmodernism which once believed itself to be in part constituted by them, or represent earlier positions. A feminist critic like Söderlind may construct postmodernism as implicated in patriarchy; postcolonial theorists construct it along with poststructuralism and structuralism as a discourse which operates "to appropriate and control the Other" (Ashcroft et al. 162); marxist critics like Jameson construct it as implicated in "the cultural logic of late capitalism." In the 1990s in Canada, the margins get increasingly crowded, as numerous groups vie for the legitimacy marginality can bestow. Latvian-Canadian writer Karl Jirgens prefaced a reading at the 1990 small press book fair with remarks about the connection between his fictions and the struggle of Latvians against what was then the USSR, and was met by sharp rebuffs from two lesbians of colour who read after him and announced that he and Latvia had little understanding of what actual oppression comprised. At the concluding panel at the 1991 University of Calgary conference, "Interventing the Text," a conference which had addressed small press publishing, literary criticism, magazine publishing, textual silence, First Nation writing, Japanese-Canadian redress, discontinuous textuality, performance art, and the interview, as implicitly parallel forms of dissent, a number of panelists announced that they saw themselves as tokenized and objectified by being included in the panel. Inclusion (in the panel, or the conference) was here strategically translated as exclusion. Foremost among those claiming having been excluded by being included was the widely published and once postmodernist Daphne Marlatt, who suggested she was on the panel only because she was a lesbian feminist. The other panelists, an assortment of gender, age and race—First-Nation Canadians, Indo-Canadians, a Japanese-Canadian, inscrutably white Canadians—were left scrambling by her intervention to either protest the panel's ecumenicity or proclaim their own marginality. Visually, the panel, with more than a dozen panelists on chairs across a small stage, was a sign of how coveted marginality had become, how crowded the margins. Fred Wah, ex-*Tish* editor, Governor-General's Award winner, conference co-organizer, third-generation Canadian, one-quarter Chinese descendant of one of the CPR's builders, was at far stage-right barely able to make himself room.

The parable that panel implies is the parable of the history of the sign 'postmodernism' in Canada. It is not a sign of power eagerly embraced by writers. There are no major institutions affiliated with it, no publishing houses constructed as publishers of postmodernism, no journals of 'Canadian postmodernism.' The only recent institutional conference on postmodernism, the University of Toronto's "Our Post-modern Heritage," was obliged by its host, University College, to be intrinsically skeptical toward the postmodern, and to twice encode that skepticism in its title. Postmodernism's struggle against hegemonies have been taken up within Canadian literature by various constituencies under specialized banners—postcolonialism, gay rights, Canadian regionalism, feminism, aboriginal rights, south Asian culture, poststructuralist theory—almost all of which have developed their own institutions and publishers, and have represented themselves more effectively, both in literary and general politics, than they ever did under a postmodernist umbrella.

The cumulative effect of this process is the depoliticizing

of postmodernism as a sign. No longer a banner waved by holders of a 'postmodernist' ideology, it becomes increasingly—like modernism—an academic term denoting a complex of textual convictions and practices: Neuman's "postmodern attributes." It takes a place in parallel with the similarly academic term 'postmodernity.'

The political task that this depoliticizing of postmodernism creates is the finding of new common ground among those with continuing interest in opposing hegemony. Too often, as at the concluding panel of "Interventing the Text," the marginalized are left competing with each other for space on the dissident stage, matching off their disadvantages and victimizations in bizarre, carnivalesque contestations. Worse, they are left, like David L. Clark, cynical about a general political process but struggling anyway for power within a specific discourse community. Yet the success of all their projects depends most of all on an effort to valorize *politics*, to enrich and open political process so that contestation and negotiation within it are available to as many groups within one's culture and literature as possible. It is politics that hegemonies within one's culture would take from less powerful groups, controlling with their multinational corporations the space in print and electronic media, controlling publishing houses and magazines, controlling through their accumulations of money and donations to political parties and candidates even the possibility of running for national, political, or urban municipal office. In the 1988 Canadian federal election only the corporate business community, with its multinational affiliations, possessed—through loopholes in the Electoral Expenses Act and through its own disproportionate wealth—effectively unlimited media representation of its views.

Politics are among humanity's most valuable constructions. They enable us to live together despite differences, dislikes, disagreements, and intolerances. When politics fail utterly, we have Nazi Germany, or Lebanon of the 1970s, or Yugosalvia and Somalia of 1992-4. Literary power itself can be deployed to construct more openings in society, to organize institutions and structures that facilitate diversities and communication among diversities, to interrogate and disempower hegemonies and oligarchies; it can make the political gesture of claiming to dissent from politics; it can be deployed in self-serving ways that construct solitudes and abet hegemonies by slowing social dialogue.

❧

"What is an indigenous theory," Gayatri Spivak asks in response to three New Delhi interviewers who ask her to comment on what they characterize as "a certain uneasiness here about the ideological contaminations of [First World elite] theory by the specific historical origins which produce it and therefore about the implications of employing it in our own context" (69). For Spivak this appears to be one of the most uncomfortable moments in the set of interviews published in 1990 under the title *The Post-Colonial Critic*. Rather than engaging the issue the interviewers have proposed, she begins her response by defending her own practice—"I don't use only First World theory" (69)—as if the question had been directed to her practice, as if she did her own work not in the United States but in a Third World "context," or as if indeed something called "First World Theory" were easily distinguishable from the theory of 'other worlds.'

For a Canadian this is a poignant and troubling moment—not merely the "uneasiness" of Spivak and her interviewers but the latter's unanswered concern that the "post-colonial intellectual's dependence on Western models" might be a "historical necessity" (69). This concern evokes not only recent complaints such as McGregor's about the "importation" of critical models but longer-standing fears about Canadian participation in multinational culture or about literary 'influences' from other countries (usually the United States, but often France or Britain)—fears that these 'influences' will come to 'contaminate' Canadian writing and culture. In their most general form, these are fears that transnational theory will damage or disable Canadian cultural constructions. Here is Robin Mathews in 1978, commenting on post-war Canadian writing:

> Since...the establishment of the undeniable presence of the United States as the major imperial power in the lives of Canadians, its ideology has affected and infected more and more Canadian writers. As power in the world shifts, many Canadian writers shift with it, accepting big power aesthetics as ideas are developed abroad and handed to them at home. (316)

Mathews figures United States "aesthetics" as monologically both political ("imperial," "big power") and diseasing ("affected and infected") and Canadians as apolitically passive ("handed to them"). He locates the development of aesthetics "abroad" and posits only passive acceptance "at home." The overall effect of his figures is to characterize politics as occuring only outside Canada. In 1985 he comments similarly on the critical assumptions of William Toye's recently published *The Oxford Companion to Canadian Literature*:

> the *Companion* gives off all the signs of a frightened colonialism: fear of the real Canadian culture, fixation on so-called cosmopolitan ideas, embarrassment at unique Canadian consciousness; and an attempt to prove by means of internationally approved ideas that Canada 'can hold its head up.' (81)

What was in the question of Spivak's Delhi interviewers only a latent opposition between "First World theory" and "our own context" is in Mathews an overdetermined dichotomy between two equally idealized terms—"real Canadian culture" and "big power aesthetics." Although there is a hint of political process in "big power," there is none at all in the monolithic constructions of Canada as 'real culture' and 'unique consciousness.' Canadian political 'realities' seem to Mathews beyond disputation.

Similar politics-disabling constructions have appeared repeatedly in recent Canadian nationalist criticism. In one example, T.D. MacLulich's study *Between Europe and America: the Canadian Tradition in Fiction* (1988), Europe and America are eventually conflated with some of the very terms of this chapter: "experimental, avant garde, or postmodern" (249). Canadian "postmodernist writers and their critical accomplices" (244) are said to advocate a Canadian literature "that is determined by the example of the literary avant garde in other countries" (229); they "introduce students to works that satisfy the latest dictates of literary fashion" (249); they "create a small group of enthusiasts whose tastes are narrowly avant garde"; they encourage a literature...increasingly written in conformity with an intricate set of conventions that are of interest to a small group of specially trained readers...the assimilation of our literature to the style of the international avant garde" (251). To Robin Mathews' idealizations of an homogenous international style and a "real" Canadian tradition, and to his metaphors of imperial power, MacLulich adds other ideologically charged figures. The international style is a dubious, perhaps even inauthentic or fascist cultural manifestation—an arbitrarily dictating "literary fashion." Those who associate themselves with it are "accomplices"—

participants not in community political process but in illegal activity. They also form an undemocratic elite class, a "small group of [the] specially trained": "postmodernist writing does not rest on a broad cultural consensus. Instead, it is the private preserve of a trained literary elite" (244).

In a second instance, Laurence Mathews, reviewing John Moss's collection *Future Indicative: Literary Theory and Canadian Literature*, adds a further figure to the construction of oppressive "internationally approved" critical ideas. "The works of Bakhtin (or Lacan, or whatever guru of the postmodern is favored by the individual critic)," he writes, "are regarded as Holy Writ, to be interpreted and applied, but never questioned." "A certain religiosity...permeates this volume." Like MacLulich and McGregor, Laurence Mathews perceives critics who engage with non-Canadian theory as a quasi-religious elite—"the community of the elect" (190). This theory for them constitutes not only a new colonizing force but a new potential structure of domination—a new intellectual elite with cult-like power. It configures the political force of such criticism as religious, thus disqualifying it from political legitimacy. While such nationalist commentaries claim to defend "Canada," they are at base anti-political. The oppressive structures they invent—elitist and homogenous international theory, "big power" aesthetics—duplicate the monological constructions of a "real Canada" they propose for consensual approbation. This "real Canada" too is enacted as a religion, transcendent and beyond debate, rather than as a politics.

In the current political dynamics of both Canada and its global context, there can be no easy transportability of theory from one cultural moment to another—whether this theory be romantic nationalist, marxist, deconstructionist, feminist, or 'postmodern.' There are no homogenous first, second, or third 'worlds,' no easy and indisputable 'Canadas' to defend from the *sang impur* of alien influence. Particularly visible in Canada because of its numerous contesting minorities, its disparate regions, and its clashing provincial priorities, is the condition of contemporary nationhood, in which a multiply-focused political process loosely contained by a national boundary interacts with globally circulating constructions and processes. National and provincial boundaries, as porous as they may be to 'cross-border shopping' or literary theory, remain determinative today because they continue to enclose and legitimize specially and locally produced institutions, discourses, contestations and practices—such as the ones this book has considered—and to enable their modification and supplementation. The appropriation of a globally circulating construction is most appropriately theorized as an internal political act, an act meaningful only within the contestations of the national politics. This is why, as Godard has pointed out in "Structuralism / Poststructuralism: Language, Reality and Canadian Literature," such cultural appropriations become modified in the process of being put into local use—the exigencies of particular politics de-form, trans-form, or in-form the construction borrowed to serve it. Despite their attempts at paralyzing idealization of Canadian reality (with their echoes of German idealism, and nineteenth-century European nationalism), McGregor, MacLulich, and the two Mathews are not defenders of a "real" Canada but participants—with Hutcheon, Söderlind, Weir, Clark, and Kroetsch, with the various contestants for "Phyllis Webb," *As for Me and My House*, and "Daphne Marlatt," and with, one hopes, countless others—in anglophone-Canadian political contestation. While some of these contestants may act from time to time as if to foreclose debate, it is in all our interests—whatever the particular discursive fate of a term like postmodernism—that such debate not be foreclosed, that it remain 'political,' and that 'Canada' remain a site of dialogue and argument.

NOTES

[1] See Shirley Neuman's interrogation of him on this point in *Labyrinths of Voice*, p. 195.

[2] In the same year as "Monstrous Reading" and "Disfiguring the Postmodern" Clark also published, in *Recherches Sémoitiques*, a review of Hermann, Humbeeck, and Lernout, ed., *(Dis)continuities: Essays on Paul de Man*.

Bibliography

Airhart, Sharon. "Political action and the march of time." *The Globe and Mail.* 7 July 1992: A16.

Altieri, Charles. "An Idea and Ideal of a Literary Canon." In Robert von Hallberg, ed., *Canons* (Chicago, U of Chicago P, 1984): 41-64.

Antin, David. "Modernism and Postmodernism: Approaching the Present in American Poetry." *Boundary 2*, I, 1 (Fall, 1972), 98-132.

Ashcroft, Bill, Gareth Griffiths, and Helen Tiffin, ed. *The Empire Writes Back.* London, Routledge, 1989.

Atwood, Margaret. *The Animals in that Country.* Toronto, Oxford, 1968.

———. *The Circle Game.* Toronto, Anansi, 1966.

———. Letter to the editor. *Books in Canada* 19, 1 (January-February 1990): 10-13.

———. *Procedures for Underground.* Toronto, Oxford, 1970.

———. *True Stories.* Toronto, Oxford, 1981.

———. *You Are Happy.* Toronto, Oxford, 1974.

Atwood, Margaret, ed. *The New Oxford Book of Canadian Verse in English.* Toronto, Oxford UP, 1982.

Barbour, Douglas. "Late Work at the Kitchen Table: Phyllis Webb's *Water and Light.*" *West Coast Line* 6 (Winter 1991-2): 103-117.

Baudelaire, Charles. *Oeuvres complet*. Paris, Editions du Seuil, 1968.

Bennett, Donna, and Russell Brown. *An Anthology of Canadian Literature in English*. 2 vols. Toronto, Oxford UP, 1982.

Blodgett, E.D. "Ethnic Writing in Canadian Literature as Paratext." *Signature* 3 (Summer 1990): 13-27.

Bloom, Harold. "Criticism, Canon-formation, and Prophecy." *Raritan* 3 (Winter 1984): 1-20.

Bowering, George, ed. *The Contemporary Canadian Poem Anthology*. Toronto, Coach House Press, 1983.

———, ed. *Fiction of Contemporary Canada*. Toronto, Coach House Press, 1980.

———. "A Great Northward Darkness: The Attack on History in Recent Canadian Fiction." *Imaginary Hand* (Edmonton, NeWest Press, 1988): 1-21 [1986].

———. "A Poem for High School Anthologies." In Douglas Barbour and Stephen Scobie, ed., *The Maple Laugh Forever*. Edmonton, Hurtig, 1981: 38-9.

Brand, Dionne. *No Language Is Neutral*. Toronto, Coach House Press, 1990.

Burnham, Clint. *Allegories of Publishing: The Toronto Small Press Scene*. Toronto, Streetcar Editions, 1991.

Butling, Pauline. "'Hall of Fame Blocks Women': Re/Righting Literary History." *Open Letter* VIII, 8 (Summer 1990): 60-76.

———. "Preface." *'You Devise. We Devise': A Festschrift for Phyllis Webb*. *West Coast Line* 6 (Winter 1991-92): 14-17.

Cameron, Anne. "The Operative Principle Is Trust." In Libby Scheier, et al., ed., *Language in Her Eye*. Toronto, Coach House Press, 1990: 63-71.

Cameron, Donald. "Robert Kroetsch: The American Experience and the Canadian Voice." *Journal of Canadian Fiction* 1, 3 (Summer 1972): 48-52.

Canada. *Multiculturalism Act*. 21 July 1988.

Canada. White Paper on the Implementation of a Policy of Multiculturalism within a Bilingual Framework. Hansard, Friday, October 8, 1971: 8545-8546.

The Canada Council. *Block Grant Program Book Publishing Statistics for 1982 and 1983 Titles*. Ottawa, The Canada Council, 1986.

———. *Block Grant Program Book Publishing Statistics, 1985 Titles*. Ottawa: The Canada Council, 1988.

———. *Block Grant Program Book Publishing Statistics, 1986 Titles*. Ottawa: The Canada Council, 1990.

———. Block Grant Program book publishing statistics available from the Council in photocopied manuscript for 1987-1992.

Carr, Brenda. "Genre Theory and the Impasse of Lyric?: Reframing the Questions in Phyllis Webb's Lyric Sequences." *West Coast Line* 6 (Winter 1991-92): 67-79.

Chiari, Joseph. *The Aesthetics of Modernism*. London, Vision Press, 1970.

Clark, David L. "Dis-Figuring the Post-Modern" *Canadian Poetry* 26 (1990): 75-86.

———. "Forget Heidegger, or Why I Am Such a Clever Postmodernist," *Canadian Poetry* 29 (Fall/Winter 1991): 59-70.

_____. "Monstrous Reading: *The Martyrology* after De Man." *Studies in Canadian Literature* 15:2 (1990): 1-32.

_____. Rev. of Luc Hermann, Humbeeck, and Lernout, ed. *(Dis)continuities: Essays on Paul de Man*, *Recherches Sémoitique* 10, 1-2-3 (1990): 175-180.

Connolly, Cyril. *The Modern Movement*. London, Deutsch, 1965.

Cooley, Dennis. "Recursions and Incursions: Daphne Marlatt Wrestles with the Angel Language." *Line* 13 (Spring 1989), 66-82.

_____. *The Vernacular Muse*. Winnipeg: Turnstone Press, 1987.

Cruickshank, John. "Canada's poets need no apology," *The Globe and Mail*, 2 Jan. 1991, C1.

Cude, Wilfred. "Beyond Mrs Bentley" and "Getting Philip Straight," in *A Due Sense of Difference: an Evaluative Approach to Canadian Literature*. Boston, University Press of America, 1980: 31-49, 50-68.

Daniells, Roy. "Introduction," to Sinclair Ross, *As For me and My House*, Toronto, New Canadian Library, 1957.

Davey, Frank. "Atwood Walking Backwards." *Open Letter* II, 5 (Summer 1973): 74-84.

_____. "Canadian Canons," *Critical Inquiry* XVI, 3 (Spring 1990): 672-681.

_____. *From There to Here: a Guide to English-Canadian Literature Since 1960*. Erin, Ont., Porcepic, 1974.

_____. *Reading Canadian Reading*. Winnipeg: Turnstone, 1988.

_____. "Surviving the Paraphrase: Thematic Criticism and

its Alternatives." *Canadian Literature* 70 (Autumn 1976): 5-13.

———. "Words and Stones in *How Hug a Stone.*" *Line* 13 (Spring 1989): 40-46.

David, Jack, and Robert Lecker, ed. *Canadian Poetry.* 2 vols. Toronto, General Publishing, and Downsview, ECW Press, 1982.

David, Jack, and Robert Lecker, ed. *The New Canadian Anthology.* Scarborough, Ont., Nelson Canada, 1988.

Daymond, Douglas, and Leslie Monkman, ed. *Literature in Canada.* 2 vols. Toronto, Gage, 1978.

Defoe, John. "Equal senate looks innocuous but symbolism is potent." *The Globe and Mail*, 19 July 1992: D2.

de Man, Paul. *Blindness and Insight.* Minneapolis, U of Minnesota P, 1983 [1971].

Denham, Paul. "Narrative Technique in Sinclair Ross's *As For Me and My House.*" *Studies in Canadian Literature* V (Spring 1980), 116-126.

Di Michele, Mary, ed. *Anything Is Possible.* Oshawa, Mosaic, 1984.

Dooley, D.J. "*As for Me and my House*: the Hypocrite and the Parasite." In *Moral Vision in the Canadian Novel.* Toronto, Clarke Irwin, 1979; 38-47.

Drainie, Bronwyn. "Making a case for the reinvention of the Canada Council." *The Globe and Mail*, 16 Feb. 1991, C3.

Edwards, Brian. "Deconstructing Canadian Literature." *West Coast Line* 3 (Winter 1990): 150-57.

Fagan, Cary. "Aversion to Verse," *Books in Canada*, October 1990, 9-10.

Fiedler, Leslie. *Waiting for the End*. New York, Stein and Day, 1964.

Fitzgerald, Judith. "Poetry Is Dead," *Canadian Author and Bookman*, 64:1 (Fall 1988): 14.

_____, ed. *Sp/elles: Poetry by Canadian Women*. Windsor, Black Moss Press, 1986.

Francis, Wynne. "Literary magazines in English 3." In William Toye, ed., *The Oxford Companion to Canadian Literature*. Toronto, Oxford, 1983, 458-61.

Fraser, Marian Botsford. "Devolution of cultural policy symbolizes demolition of the country." *The Globe and Mail*. 26 August 1991: C1.

Frey, Cecelia. "The Left Hand of Webb." *Prairie Fire* 7 (August 1986): 37-48.

Frye, Northrop. *Anatomy of Criticism*. Princeton, Princeton UP, 1957.

Geddes, Gary, and Phyllis Bruce, ed. *15 Canadian Poets*. Toronto, Oxford UP, 1970.

Geddes, Gary, and Phyllis Bruce, ed. *15 Canadian Poets Plus 5*. Toronto, Oxford UP, 1978.

Geddes, Gary, ed. *15 Canadian Poets X 2*. Toronto, Oxford UP, 1988.

Godard, Barbara. "'Body I': Daphne Marlatt's Feminist Poetics." *American Review of Canadian Studies*, XV, 4 (1985): 481-496.

_____. "El Greco in Canada: Sinclair Ross's *As For Me and My House*." *Mosaic* XIV, 2 (Winter 1981), 55-76.

_____. "Mapmaking: A Survey of Feminist Criticism." In Godard, ed., *Gynocritics/La Gynocritique*. Downsview,

ECW Press, 1981: 1-30.

―――. "Structuralism / Poststructuralism: Language, Reality, and Canadian Literature." In Moss, ed., *Future Indicative*: 25-52.

Godfrey, Dave. "The Canadian Publishers." *Canadian Literature* 57 (Summer 1973): 65-82.

Godfrey, Stephen. "Minority writers to raise their voices." *The Globe and Mail,* 23 May 1992: C9.

―――. "Canada Council asks whose voice is it anyway?" *The Globe and Mail*, 21 March 1992: C1,C15.

Goldie, Terry. "Fresh Canons: The Native Canadian Example." *English Studies in Canada*. XVII, 4 (December 1991): 373-384.

Gunnars, Kristjana. "The Search for our Passion," *The Globe and Mail*, 18 August 1990, p. C15.

Gustafson, Ralph, ed. *The Penguin Book of Canadian Verse*. Revised Edition. Markham, Ont., Penguin, 1984.

Halpin, Marjorie. "First Words." *Canadian Literature* 124-125 (Spring-Summer 1990): 313-16.

Hassan, Ihab. *The Dismemberment of Orpheus: Toward a Postmodern Literature*. New York, Oxford, 1971.

Howe, Irving. *Decline of the New*. New York, Harcourt Brace, 1963.

Hulcoop, John. "Introduction." In Phyllis Webb, *Selected Poems* (Vancouver, Talonbooks, 1971): 9-41.

―――. "Phyllis Webb and the Priestess of Motion." *Canadian Literature* 32 (Spring 1967): 29-39.

―――. "Webb's 'Water and Light'." *Canadian Literature* 109

(Summer 1986): 151-59.

Hutcheon, Linda. *The Canadian Postmodern*. Toronto, Oxford UP, 1988.

_____. *A Poetics of Postmodernism*. New York, Routledge, 1988.

_____. *The Politics of Postmodernism*. London, Routledge, 1989.

Huyssen, Andreas. *After the Great Divide: Modernism, Mass Culture, Postmodernism*. Bloomington, Indiana UP, 1986.

Ioannou, Susan. "The Future of Poetry," *Cross-Canada Writers Quarterly*, 10, 1 (1988): 9, 32.

Jameson, Fredric. *The Ideologies of Theory*. 2 vols. Minneapolis, U. of Minnesota P, 1988.

_____. *Postmodernism, or, The Cultural Logic of Late Capitalism*. Durham, Duke UP, 1991.

Jones, D.G. *Butterfly on Rock*. Toronto, U of Toronto P, 1970.

Jones, Wayne. "Leave Language Alone!" *Books in Canada* 21: 4 (May 1992): 27.

Kallen, Evelyn. "Multiculturalism: Ideology, Policy and Reality." *Journal of Canadian Studies* XVII,1 (Spring 1982): 51-63.

Keeshig-Tobias, Lenore. "The Magic of Others." In Libby Scheier, et al., ed., *Language in Her Eye*. Toronto, Coach House Press, 1990: 173-177.

Keith, W.J. *Canadian Literature in English*. London, Longmans, 1985.

_____. "Struggles with Silence." Rev. of *Wilson's Bowl* by

Phyllis Webb. *Canadian Literature* 91 (Winter 1981): 99-102.

Klinck, Carl F., and Reginald E. Watters, ed. *Canadian Anthology* [1966]. Third edition. Toronto, Gage, 1974.

Knight, Alan R. "Growing Hegemonies: Preparing the Ground for Official Anthologies of Canadian Poetry," in E.D. Blodgett and A.G. Purdy, ed., *Prefaces and Literary Manifestoes*. Edmonton, Research Institute for Comparative Literature, 1990: 1946-57.

Kroetsch, Robert. "A Canadian Issue." *Boundary 2*, III, 1 (Fall 1974): 1-2.

_____. *The Ledger*. London, Ont., Applegarth Follies, 1975.

_____. *The Lovely Treachery of Words*. Toronto, Oxford, 1989.

_____. *Seed Catalogue*. Winnipeg, Turnstone, 1977.

_____. *The Stone Hammer Poems*. Nanaimo, Oolichan, 1975.

_____. "Unhiding the Hidden: Recent Canadian Fiction." *Journal of Canadian Fiction* 3, 3 (1974): 43-45.

Kroetsch, Robert, et al. "Present Tense, the Closing Panel," in John Moss, ed., *Future Indicative: Literary Theory and Canadian Literature*. Ottawa, U of Ottawa P, 1987: 239-245.

Lalonde, Michèle. *Speak White*. Montreal, L'Hexagone, 1974.

Lane, Patrick. "The Fabled Poets' Market," *Cross-Canada Writers Quarterly* 12, 1 (1990): 3-4.

Lecker, Robert. "The Canonization of Canadian Literature: an Inquiry into Value," *Critical Inquiry* XVI, 3 (Spring 1990): 656-671.

———. "A Country without a Canon?: Canadian Literature and the Esthetics of Idealism." *Mosaic* 26, 3 (Summer 1993): 1-19.

———. "Introduction," *Canadian Canons*, ed. Robert Lecker. Toronto, U of Toronto P, 1991: 3-16.

———. "Response to Frank Davey,' *Critical Inquiry* XVI, 3 (Spring 1990): 682-689.

Lee, Dennis, ed. *The New Canadian Poets, 1970-1985*. Toronto, McClelland and Stewart, 1985.

Leith, Linda. "Quebec Fiction in English during the 1980s: A Case Study in Marginality." *Studies in Canadian Literature*. XV, 5 (1990): 1-20.

Lewis, Wyndham. *The Demon of Progress in the Arts*. London, Methuen, 1954.

Loriggio, Francesco. "The Question of the Corpus: Ethnicity and Canadian Literature." In Moss, ed. *Future Indicative*: (1987) 53-70.

Lyotard, Jean-François. *The Postmodern Condition: a Report on Knowledge*. Tr. Geoff Bennington and Brian Massumi. Minneapolis, U of Minnesota P, 1984 [1979].

Macherey, Pierre. *A Theory of Literary Production*. Tr. Geoffrey Wall. London, Routledge, 1978.

MacLulich, T.D. *Between Europe and America: The Canadian Tradition in Fiction*. Toronto, ECW Press, 1988.

MacMurchy, Archibald. *Handbook of Canadian Literature*. Toronto, William Briggs, 1906.

Mallinson, Jean. "Ideology and Poetry: an Examination of some Recent Trends in Canadian Criticism." *Studies in Canadian Literature* 3, 1 (Winter 1978): 93-7.

———. "A Reply to John Bentley Mays." *Studies in Canadian Literature* 3, 2 (Summer 1978): 284-5.

Malone, Caroline. *Avebury*. London, English Heritage, 1989.

Mandel, Eli, ed. *Contexts of Canadian Criticism*. Chicago, U of Chicago P, 1972

———, ed. *Poets of Contemporary Canada*. Toronto, McClelland and Stewart, 1972.

Marlatt, Daphne. "Changing the Focus." In Betsy Warland, ed., *Inversions: Writing by Dykes, Queers and Lesbians*. Vancouver, Press Gang, 1991: 127-134.

———. *How Hug a Stone*. Winnipeg, Turnstone, 1983.

———. "In the Month of the Hungry Ghosts." *Capilano Review* 16/17 (1979): 45-95.

Mathews, Laurence. "Calgary, Canonization, and Class: Deciphering List B." In Robert Lecker, ed., *Canadian Canons*. Toronto, U of Toronto P, 1991: 150-166.

———. "Future Imperfect." Rev. of John Moss, ed., *Future Indicative*. *Essays on Canadian Writing* 40 (Spring 1990): 163-65.

Mathews, Robin. Rev. of *Oxford Companion to Canadian Literature*. *Canadian Poetry* 16 (Spring/Summer 1985): 74-82.

———. "Survival and Struggle in Canadian Literature." *This Magazine IS About Schools*, VI, 4 (Winter 1972-73): 109-24.

———. "The Wacousta Factor." In Diane Bessai and David Jackel, ed., *Figures in a Ground*. Saskatoon, Western Producer, 1978: 295-316.

Mays, John Bentley. "Ariadne: Prolegomenon to the Poetry of

Daphne Marlatt." *Open Letter*, III, 3 (Fall 1975): 5-33.

_____. "Notes on Critical Practice: a Reply to Jean Mallinson." *Studies in Canadian Literature* 3:2 (Summer 1978): 282-3.

_____. "Phyllis Webb." *Open Letter*, II, 6 (Fall 1973): 8-33.

McGregor, Gaile. "Postmodernism and its discontents." *Border/Lines* 18 (Spring 1990): 43-45.

McMullen, Lorraine. *Sinclair Ross*. Boston, Twayne, 1979.

Metcalf, John, ed. *The Bumper Book*. Toronto, ECW Press, 1986.

_____, ed. *Carry On Bumping*. Toronto, ECW Press, 1988.

_____. *What is A Canadian Literature?* Guelph, On., Red Kite Press, 1988.

Miki, Roy. "Notes on Contributors." *West Coast Line* 10 (Spring 1993): 5-8.

Mitchell, Barbara. "Paul: the Answer to the Riddle of *As for Me and My House*." *Studies in Canadian Literature* XIII, 1 (1988): 47- 63.

Moss, John, ed. *Future Indicative: Literary Theory and Canadian Literature*. Ottawa, U of Ottawa P, 1987.

_____. *Patterns of Isolation*. Toronto, McClelland and Stewart, 1974.

Murray, Heather. "Reading for Contradiction in the Literature of Colonial Space." In Moss, ed., *Future Indicative*: 71-84.

Moyes, Lianne. "Writing, the Uncanniest of Guests: Daphne Marlatt's *How Hug a Stone*." *West Coast Line* 1 (1991): 203-221.

Mukherjee, Arun P. *Towards an Aesthetic of Opposition: Essays on Literature, Criticism, and Cultural Imperialism*. Toronto, Williams-Wallace, 1988.

Neuman, Shirley. "After Modernism: English-Canadian Poetry Since 1960." In Arnold E. Davidson, ed., *Studies on Canadian Literature*. New York, MLA, 1990: 54-73.

Neuman, Shirley, and Smaro Kamboureli, ed. *A Mazing Space: Writing Canadian Women Writing*. Edmonton, Longspoon Press / NeWest Press, 1986.

Neuman, Shirley, and Robert Wilson. *Labyrinths of Voice: Conversations with Robert Kroetsch*. Edmonton, NeWest Press, 1982.

Newlove, John, ed. *Canadian Poetry: The Modern Era*. Toronto, McClelland and Stewart, 1977.

Philip, Marlene Nourbese. "Expletive Deleted." *Fuse* 13, 3 (Winter 1990): 17-22.

_____. *Frontiers*. Stratford: Mercury Press, 1992.

Powe, Bruce. *A Climate Charged*. Oakville, Mosaic Press, 1984.

Rooke, Constance. "Getting Into Heaven: An Interview with Diana Hartog, Paulette Jiles, and Sharon Thesen." *The Malahat Review* 83, (June 1988): 24-42.

Ross, Morton L. "The Canonization of *As For Me and My House*: a Case Study," in Diane Bessai and David Jackel, ed., *Figures in a Ground*. Saskatoon, Western Producer, 1978: 189-205.

Ross, Sinclair. *As For Me and My House*. Toronto, McClelland and Stewart, 1957 [1941].

Ross, Val. "Contradictory by nature." *The Globe and Mail*, 16

September 1993: E1, E2.

Rudy Dorscht, Susan. "poems dressed in a dress and naked: sweet lines from phyllis." *West Coast Line* 6 (Winter 1991-2): 54-63.

Sanger, Richard. "Poetry could use a bit more Beauty, a bit less Truth," *The Globe and Mail*, 12 December 1990: C1.

Scheier, Libby, S. Sheard, and E. Wachtel, ed. *Language in Her Eye*. Toronto, Coach House Press, 1990.

Scobie, Stephen. *bpNichol: What History Teaches*. Vancouver, Talonbooks, 1984.

_____. "I and I: Phyllis Webb's 'I, Daniel'." *Open Letter* VI, 2-3 (Summer-Fall 1985): 61-8.

_____. "Leonard Cohen, Phyllis Webb, and the End(s) of Modernism." In Lecker, ed., *Canadian Canons*: 57-70.

_____. *Signature Event Cantext*. Edmonton, NeWest Press, 1989.

Scott, Gail. *Heroine*. Toronto, Coach House Press, 1987.

Simpson, Jeffrey. "Rights are rights and equality is equality? Not in Canada." *The Globe and Mail*, 21 May 1992: A16.

Söderland, Sylvia. "Back to the Future: Plus or Minus Canadian." *Queen's Quarterly* 96, 3 (Autumn 1989): 631-638.

Solway, David. "The End of Poetry," *Canadian Literature* 115 (Winter 1987): 127-34.

Spanos, William V. "The Detective and the Boundary: Some Notes on the Postmodern Literary Imagination." *Boundary 2*, I, 1 (Fall 1972): 147-168.

Spears, Monroe K. *Dionysus and the City: Modernism in*

Twentieth-Century Poetry. New York, Oxford UP, 1970.

Spivak, Gayatri Chakravorty. *The Postcolonial Critic*. Ed. Sarah Harasym. New York, Routledge, 1990.

Steele, Charles, ed. *Taking Stock: The Calgary Conference on the Canadian Novel*. Downsview, ECW Press, 1982.

Steward, Gillian. "Too much tolerance a risk to basic rights." *London Free Press*, 21 May 1992: B9.

Stouck, David. *Major Canadian Authors: an Introduction*. Lincoln, University of Nebraska Press. 1984.

Tallman, Warren. "Wonder Merchants: Modernist Poetry in Vancouver during the 1960s." *Boundary 2* III, 1 (Fall 1974): 57-89. Rpt. in *Godawful Streets of Man. Open Letter* 3, 6 (Winter 1976-77): 175-207.

Terdiman, Richard. *Discourse / Counter-Discourse*. Ithaca, Cornell UP, 1995.

Thesen, Sharon. "Introduction." In Phyllis Webb, *The Vision Tree: Selected Poems*. Vancouver, Talonbooks, 1982: 9-19.

_____. "Why Women Won't Write: Literary Theory's Dark Shadow." *The Vancouver Review* 5 (Summer 1991): 14-16.

_____, ed. *The New Long Poem Anthology*. Toronto, Coach House Press, 1991.

Tostevin, Lola Lemire. "Daphne Marlatt: Writing in the Space that is her Mother's Face." *Line* 13 (Spring 1989): 32-39.

Tregebov, Rhea, ed. *Sudden Miracles*. Toronto, Second Story, 1991.

Twigg, Alan. "Books." *The Magazine*, 15 January 1984: 6.

Wachtel, Eleanor. "Intimations of Mortality." *Books in Canada* 12 (November 1983): 8-13.

Ware, Tracy. "A Little Self-Consciousness is a Dangerous Thing: a Response to Robert Lecker," *English Studies in Canada*, XVII, 4 (December 1991): 481-493.

_____. "Notes on the Literary Histories of Canada." *Dalhousie Review* 65 (Winter 1985-86): 566-576.

Webb, Phyllis. *Selected Poems 1954-1965*. Ed. with an introduction by John Hulcoop. Vancouver, Talonbooks, 1971.

_____. *The Vision Tree: Selected Poems*. Ed. with an introduction by Sharon Thesen. Vancouver, Talonbooks, 1982.

_____. *Wilson's Bowl*. Toronto, Coach House Press, 1980.

Weir, Lorraine. "Daphne Marlatt's 'Ecology of Language.'" *Line* 13 (1989): 58-65.

_____. "Maps and Tales: the Progress of *Canadian Literature*, 1959-87." In I.S. MacLaren and C. Potvin, ed., *Questions of Funding, Publishing and Distribution*. Edmonton, Research Institute for Comparative Literature, 1989: 141-160.

_____. "Normalizing the Subject: Linda Hutcheon and the English-Canadian Postmodern." In Lecker, ed., *Canadian Canons*: 180-195.

Wiebe, Rudy. "Proud Cree Nation deserves much more than 'funny' stories." *The Globe and Mail*, 17 Feb. 1990: C3.

Williamson, Janice. "The Feminine Suicide Narratives of Phyllis Webb." *West Coast Line* 6 (Winter 1991-92): 155-174.

———. *Sounding Differences: Conversations with Seventeen Canadian Women Writers*. Toronto, U of Toronto P, 1993.

Woodcock, George. "Introduction." In Woodcock, ed., *The Canadian Novel in the Twentieth Century*. Toronto, McClelland and Stewart, 1975: vii-ix.

———. *Northern Spring: The Flowering of Canadian Literature*. Vancouver, Douglas and McIntyre, 1987.

Index

Acorn, Milton 12, 13, 14, 192
Airhart, Sharon 10, 12-13
Alive 9, 13
Allen Lillian 96
Altieri, Charles 57, 68-9
Antin, David 248
Appelbaum-Hebert Commission 81
Ariel 104
Armstrong, Jeannette 30
Arnason, David 98
Art Gallery of Ontario (AGO) 43n
Association of Canadian Publishers (ACP) 11, 12, 27, 62
Association of National Non-Profit Artist Centres (ANNPAC) 11
Association of Canadian University Teachers of English (ACUTE) 48, 49, 62, 65,
Atwood, Margaret 9, 13, 22-3m 33, 41, 43n, 47, 53, 71, 72, 84, 89, 90, 97, 99, 108, 111, 112, 113, 114, 116, 129, 151-65, 192, 224, 227, 260, 270
Avison, Margaret 113
Barbour, Douglas 98, 228, 242n, 240
Barth, John 246
Barthes, Roland 243n
Baudelaire, Charles 253
Beddoes, Julia 119
Bennett, Donna 91
Bentley, D.M.R. 74, 104-5, 110
Bernstein, Charles 243n
Birney, Earle 7, 94, 97

bissett, bill 9, 13, 15, 18, 89, 90, 94
Blaise, Clark 47
Blew Ointment 9
Blodgett, E.D. 43n, 58, 119
Bloom, Harold 56, 58, 60
Body Politic 16
Books in Canada 38, 121
Borealis Press 73
Boundary 2 247, 248, 249, 254
Bowering, George 7, 9, 13, 14, 47, 50, 83, 90, 105, 106, 108, 227, 240, 242n, 271
Brand, Dionne 44n, 96, 98, 270
Breakwater Books 86
Brick 104, 121
Bringhurst, Robert 91
Brossard, Nicole 119
Brown, Russell 91
Brown, E.K. 126
Bruce, Phyllis 89-90
Butling, Pauline 42n228, 231-33, 234, 240, 241
Callaghan, Morley 105
Callwood, June 22
Cameron, Elspeth 57
Cameron, Donald 97
Cameron, Anne 29
Canada Council 11, 22-23, 24, 27, 34, 46, 55, 62, 105 120-22, 165; Block Grant Programme 82-3, 85-6, 101n
Canadian Authors Association 7
Canadian Civil Liberties Association 43n

Canadian Forum 9
Canadian Literature 9, 71, 103, 104, 105, 108-12, 113, 114, 115, 117, 118, 119, 121, 123, 203
Canadian Poetry 103, 104, 105, 108-9, 113-4, 115, 120, 121
Canadian Booksellers Association 62
Canadian Magazine Publishers Association 11, 12, 62
Canadian Federation for the Humanities 55, 62
Canadian Poetry Magazine 94
Canadian Women's Studies 16
Carman, Bliss 66
Carr, Brenda 228-29
Catapult 11
Cataract 11
Charlottetown Accord 12, 26, 44n
Chiari, Joseph 246
Chodorow, Nancy 185
Christakos, Margaret 78n
Cisecki, Robert 35
Cixous, Hélène 183, 195n
Clark, David L. 278-283, 286, 291, 293n
Coach House Press 1, 38, 73, 83, 85
Cohen, Leonard 6, 17, 41, 260
Cohen, Matt 9
Coleman, Victor 89, 90, 202
Common Agenda Alliance for the Arts 27-8
Connolly, Cyril 246
Cooley, Dennis 47, 50, 58, 94, 96, 98, 187
Coteau Books 86
Crawford, Isabella Valancy 47, 108
Critical Inquiry 48, 49, 50, 51, 54, 55, 57, 62, 65, 66
Crozier, Lorna 96

Cruickshank, John 80
Cude, Wilfred 49, 53, 54, 58, 127
CVII 16, 21
d'Alfonso, Antonio 96
Daly, Mary 170
Daniells, Roy 126, 130
Daurio, Bev 101n
David, Jack 55, 90, 104
Davies, Robertson 47, 108, 112, 113
Day, Sheilagh 22
Daymond, Douglas 91
de Man, Paul 32, 281-3
de Mille, James 119
de la Roche, Mazo 66
Defoe, John 42n
Denham, Paul 127
Derksen, Jeff 96
Derrida, Jacques 188, 243n, 279
Descant 12
Dewart, Edward Hartley 45, 99
Dewdney, Christopher 83, 91, 94, 98
di Cicco, Pier Giorgio 96
di Michele, Mary 94, 96 102n
Dooley, D.G. 49, 53, 54, 58, 127
Douglas and McIntyre 73
Downing, Christine 182, 196n
Dudek, Louis 7, 66, 98, 250
Duncan, Mark 96
Dutton, Paul 101n
Eagleton, Terry 118
ECW Press 55, 61, 62-4, 65, 70
Edwards, Carolyn 182
Edwards, Brian 101n
Elliott, George P. 246
Ellmann, Mary 170, 181
Emberley, Julia 78n
Engel, Marian 260
English Studies in Canada 104
Essays on Canadian Writing 103, 104, 108-9, 112, 113, 114, 115, 118, 121, 123

INDEX

Fagan, Cary 80
Farkas, Andre 96
Farrar, Janet 182
Fawcett, Brian 42n
Fiedler, Leslie 253
Finch, Robert 8
Finch, Robert 94
Findley, Timothy 34, 39, 40, 108, 227
Fireweed 16
First Statement 7, 94
Fitzgerald, Judith 79, 84, 94, 96, 98, 102n
Francis, Wynne 7-10
Fraser, Marian Botsford 26
French, D.G. 45
Frey, Cecelia 221-22, 225, 238
Friesen, Patrick 84, 94, 98
Frye 53
Frye, Northrop 49, 53, 72, 95, 98, 148, 224, 250
Fuse 104, 105
Fuss, Diana 193, 229
Gallant, Mavis 47, 66, 108, 113
Geddes, Gary 71, 89-91, 92-94, 227
General Publishing 85
Georgia Straight 9
Gilbert, Gerry 13
Gill, M. Lakshmi 83
Gimboutas, Marija 196n
Globe and Mail 23
Gnarowski, Michael 250
Godard, Barbara 53, 57, 74, 75, 98, 104, 105, 119, 127, 170, 183-5, 186, 187, 192, 193, 195n, 279, 291
Godfrey, Dave 9, 13, 83
Goldie, Terry 74, 75
Goldsmith, Oliver 113
Goldstein, Philip 57
Governor-General's Award 14
Grace, Sherrill 57

Graff, Gerald 57
Grant, George 47
Greenblatt, Stephen 56-7, 58
Grove, F.P. 105
Guillory, John 56, 65
Gunnars, Kristjana 33, 40, 43n, 47, 80, 94, 96, 98
Gustafson, Ralph 91-2, 93
Halpin, Marjorie 43n
Harbour Press 86
Haslam, Karen 43n
Hassan, Ihab 246-7, 248, 249, 251, 259
Henderson, Jennifer 44n, 78n
Herrnstein Smith, Barbara 56
Hodgins, Jack 13, 108,
Hood, Hugh 9, 47
Hospital, Janice Turner 47
House of Anansi 20, 38, 85
Howe, Irving 246
Hulcoop 197-201, 202-03, 206, 213, 215234, 235, 238, 241, 272
Hurtig, Mel 47
Hurtig Publishers 20
Hutcheon, Linda 51, 58, 71, 74, 119, 239, 245, 253, 254, 257-61, 263, 264-77, 282, 291
Huyssen, Andreas 272
Idler, The 38
Ioannou, Susan 79, 81
Irigaray, Luce 187
Israel, Charles 8
Jacoby, Joy Ann 34
Jameson, Fredric 252, 284
Jiles, Paulette 33, 40, 43n, 270
Jirgens, Karl 284
Jones, D.G. 49, 53, 72, 90, 224, 102n
Jones, Wayne 43n
Journal of Canadian Poetry 104
Kallen, Evelyn 43n
Kamboureli, Smaro 71, 98, 105, 228, 240

Kearns, Lionel 9
Keefer, Janice Kulyk 33, 39, 40, 43n, 58, 71, 270
Keeshig-Tobias, Lenore 28, 30, 36-7, 42n, 44n
Keith, W.J. 47, 49, 53, 54, 58, 59, 74, 105, 126, 215-16, 219, 222, 223, 225, 235, 238, 240, 241, 262-3, 266, 282
Kermode, Frank 56, 58, 60, 68
Kernan, Alvin 57
Kinsella, W.P. 29, 47
Kiyooka, Roy 227, 240
Kizuk, R. Alex 110
Klein, A.M. 93, 108, 109, 113
Klinck, Carl F. 52, 53, 59, 89-90
Knight, Alan R. 99
Knutson, Susan 119
Kogawa, Joy 108, 111
Kolodny, Annette 56, 58, 68
Kristeva, Julia 118, 183
Kroetsch, Robert 9, 47, 57, 74, 78n, 84, 93, 97, 108, 111, 112,139, 141, 143, 148, 224, 238, 242n, 247, 248, 254-7, 258, 259, 261, 264, 268, 269, 278-83, 291
Lane, Patrick 79, 81, 92, 95
Laurence, Margaret 47, 108, 109, 113
Layton, Irving 8, 41, 192
Lecker, Robert 45-77, 90, 105, 271
Lee, Dennis 5, 13, 41, 47, 92, 94-6, 192
Leith, Linda 26
Lester & Orpen Dennys 20
Levin, Harry 246
Levine, Norman 47
Lewis, Marian 202
Lewis, Wyndham 253
Line 103, 116-7,
Livesay, Dorothy 8, 47, 90, 92-3, 108, 113
Logan, J.D. 45
Loriggio, Francesco 51
Lorimer, James 47
Lowry, Malcolm 108, 109, 111
Lowther, Pat 93
Lush, Richard 94
Lyotard, Jean-François 88
MacEwen, Gwendolyn 8, 9, 13, 14, 89, 90
Maclean's 38
MacLennan, Hugh 108, 192
MacLeod, Alistair 47
MacLulich, T.D. 115
MacLulich 289-90, 291
Macmillan Company of Canada 7, 9, 10, 85
MacMurchy, Archibald 45
Mahoney, Kathleen 25
Malahat Review, 105
Mallinson, Jean 71, 78n, 210-14, 219, 220, 230-31, 232-33, 234, 235, 236,238, 241, 276
Malone, Carolyn 195n
Mandel, Eli 47, 89
Manguel, Alberto 35, 40, 41, 47
Marlatt, Daphne 6, 13, 71, 77, 83, 90, 94, 98, 105, 116, 129, 167-195, 209, 227, 229, 243n, 247, 284
Mathews, Laurence 125-8, 290, 291
Mathews, Robin 47, 71, 95, 105, 288-9, 291
Mays, John Bentley 201-209, 211-14, 215, 219, 220, 222, 225, 229-31, 233, 234, 236, 240, 241, 242n, 243n, 272, 247, 276
McCaffery, Steve 84, 94, 96, 98, 116, 120, 243n
McCallum, Pamela 119
McClelland and Stewart 7, 9, 59, 83, 85

INDEX

315

McClelland, Jack 47
McCourt, Edward 126
McFadden, David 9, 83
McGee, Thomas D'Arcy 45
McGill Group 7, 94
McGill-Queen's University Press 73
McGregor, Gaile 253, 264-67, 271, 282, 288, 291
McLaren, Ian 115
McLuhan 250
McLuhan, Marshall 12
McMechan, Archibald 45
Meech Lake Agreement 44n
Meigs, Mary 164
Mercury Press 101n
Metcalf, John 47, 51, 52
Mezei, Kathy 110
Miki, Roy 105, 240-41
Millett, Kate 170
Mitchell, W.O. 108
Mitchell, Barbara 145
Moi, Toril 118
Moment 11,
Monkman, Leslie 91
Montrose, Louis 56
Moodie, Susanna 4
Mosaic 104
Moss, John 49, 53, 102n
Mountain 11
Mouré, Erin 94, 227
Moyes, Lianne 187-89, 191, 192, 193, 196n
Mukherjee, Arun 51
Multiculturalism Act 26
Munro, Alice 66, 108, 113, 260
Munton, Ann 228
Murphy, Sarah 279
Murray, Heather 53
National Action Committee on the Status of Women 22, 42n, 43n
NC Press 85
Neuman, Shirley 57, 74, 98, 262-3, 283, 293n
New, W.H. 57, 74, 104, 105
New Yorker, The, 66
NeWest Press 38, 86
Newlove, John 9, 89, 90, 101n,
Nichol, bp 1, 30, 84, 89, 90, 94, 224, 226, 242n
Norris, Ken 92
Nowlan, Alden 13
Oberon Press 85
Ondaatje, Michael 13, 47, 83, 90, 98, 108, 111
Ontario Indian 16
Ontario Association of Art Galleries 27
Ontario 44n
Ontario Arts Council (OAC) 55, 62, 105, 120-22
Ontario Royal Commission on Book Publishing 81
Open Letter 103, 104, 105, 116, 119-20, 121
Orwell, George 31-2
Ostenso, Martha 66
Outram, Richard 35
Oxford University Press 10, 73, 85, 161
Pacey, Desmond 234, 235
Page, P.K. 90, 93, 97
Pemmican Publications 16, 86
PEN International 21, 22, 164
Persky, Stan 13, 47
Peterkiewisc, Jerzy 247
Philip, Marlene Nourbese 22-23, 43n, 44n, 96, 270
Pierce, Lorne 45
Pink Triangle Press 16
Pivato, Joseph 96
Platt, Gordon 82
Pound, Ezra 66
Powe, Bruce 51
Prairie Fire 104
Prairie Bookworld 105

Pratt, E.J. 8, 47, 93, 97, 108, 109
Press Gang 38, 86
Press Porcepic 85
Preview 7, 94
Prycz, Heather 227
Pulp Press 86
Purdy, Al 5, 84, 102n, 108, 113
Québec 25-6, 27, 44n, 70, 88-9
Quill and Quire 105
Racial Minority Writers Committee 28, 240
Ragweed Press 38, 86
Rampike 104
Rebick, Judy 42n
Reid, Jamie 13
Rhodenizer, V.B. 45
Richler, Mordecai 47, 51, 108, 260
Ricou, Laurence 78n, 234
Roberts, Charles G.D. 66, 108, 113
Rooke, Leon 108
Rooke, Constance 42n
Room of One's Own 16
Rooney, Francis 96
Rosenblatt, Joe 18, 89
Ross, Sinclair 125-149
Ross, Malcolm 107
Ross, Morton 125-8, 130
Rudy Dorscht, Susan 228, 243n
Ruebsaat's Magazine 38, 105
Ryerson Press 7, 9, 10
Ryga, George 108, 111
Safarik, Alan 96
Salutin, Rick 47
Sanger, Richard 80, 81, 98
Sarah, Robin 93, 94
Saturday Night 19, 39
Scheier, Libby 227
Scobie, Stephen 94, 98, 105, 197, 221, 222-7, 237, 238, 240, 241, 242n, 245, 263
Scott, F.R. 8, 93
Scott, Gail 6, 14-5, 98, 101n
Second Story Press 44n

Shields, E.F. 110
Shikatani, Gerry 96
Siegler, Karl 101n
Signature 103, 104, 105, 118-9, 121-2, 123
Silliman, Ron 243n
Sister Vision Press 12, 38, 86
Smith, A.J.M. 8, 47, 95, 98, 105, 112
Smith, Barbara Herrnstein 61, 68
Social Sciences and Humanities Research Council of Canada (SSHRCC) 46, 55, 62, 105, 120-2,
Söderlind, Sylvia 268-71, 282, 282, 291
Solway, David 79, 81, 95, 98
Souster, Raymond 7, 108
Spanos, William 247, 249, 251-2, 254, 259
Spears, Monroe 246, 259
Spivak, Gayatri 287-9
Srivastava, Aruna 74
Steele, Charles 54
Steward, Gillian 24-5
Stouck, David 49, 53, 54, 58
Stratford, Philip 58
Studies in Canadian Literature 103, 105, 108-9, 112-3, 115, 123
Stuewe, Paul 105
Suknaski, Andrew 94, 96, 98
Sullivan, Rosemary 96
Sutherland, John 8, 94, 105
Swan, Susan 47
Sweet Grass 16
Symons, Scott 13
Szumigalski, Anne 93
Tallman, Warren 262
Talonbooks 38, 101n, 197
Tamarack Review 9
Terdiman, Richard 88
Tessera 16, 103, 104, 105, 116,

117-8, 121, 123
Thesen, Sharon 31-2, 39, 40, 41, 42n, 43n, 102n, 164, 217-8, 219, 222, 223, 227, 270
Theytus Books 16, 38, 86
Thistledown Press 86
Thomas, Audrey 47, 110
Tish 1, 11, 13, 95, 118, 217
Tod, Joanne 118
Toronto South Asian Review 12, 121
Tostevin, Lola Lemire 94, 185-7, 189-90, 193, 240
Tregebov, Rhea 102n
Trickster 16
Trilling, Lionel 66
Turnstone Press 38, 86
Twayne World Author Series 73
Twigg, Alan 164
Underwhich Editions 101n
University of Waterloo Press 73
van Herk, Aritha 47, 227, 240
Vancouver Review 38
Vanderhaegh, Guy 112
Vassangi, M.G. 47
Wachtel, Eleanor 219-21, 222, 235, 236-7, 241, 276
Waddington, Miriam 93
Wah, Fred 13, 47, 227, 240, 243n, 285
Wallace, Bronwen 6, 96, 91, 93, 94, 98, 116, 120
Ware, Tracy 53, 58, 60, 64, 68-9, 73, 76-7, 265
Warland, Betsy 96, 98
Watters, Reginald 90
Wayman, Tom 8, 9, 98
Webb, Phyllis 13, 42n, 47, 84, 90, 125, 197-244, 247, 270
Weir, Lorraine 71, 78n, 114, 192, 242, 267, 271-7, 282, 291
West Coast Line 103, 240-41
What 104

White, Howard 98
Wiebe, Rudy 9, 29, 47, 108, 260
Williams, W.C. 77
Williams-Wallace Publishers 12, 86
Williamson, Janice 71, 78n, 228-31, 232, 235, 243n, 241
Wilson, Ethel 8, 47
Windspeaker 16
Women's Press 16, 21, 37, 38, 43n, 73, 164, 86
Woodcock, George 58, 63, 71, 95, 103, 221, 222-3, 225, 235, 238, 240, 250, 262-3, 266
Woolger, Jennifer 196n
Writers Union of Canada 11, 21, 27, 28, 44n, 62
Zemans, Joyce 22-3, 34-6